GERMANTOWN CAMPUS LIBRARY

**Great Britain
Great Empire**

THE UNIVERSITY OF QUEENSLAND PRESS
SCHOLAR'S LIBRARY

Great Britain Great Empire

An Evaluation of the British Imperial Experience

W. Ross Johnston

University of Queensland Press
St Lucia • London • New York

© University of Queensland Press, St Lucia, Queensland 1981

This book is copyright. Apart from any fair dealing for the purposes of private study, research, criticism, or review, as permitted under the Copyright Act, no part may be reproduced by any process without written permission. Enquiries should be made to the publishers.

Typeset by University of Queensland Press
Printed and bound by Silex Enterprise & Printing Co.,
Hong Kong

Distributed in the United Kingdom, Europe, the Middle East, Africa, and the Caribbean by Prentice-Hall International, International Book Distributors Ltd, 66 Wood Lane End, Hemel Hempstead, Herts., England.

National Library of Australia
Cataloguing-in-Publication data

Johnston, W. Ross (William Ross), 1939-
   Great Britain, great empire.

   ISBN 0 7022 1576 7

   1. Imperialism. 2. Great Britain — Foreign relations.
I. Title.

325'.341

Contents

Publisher's Note *vi*
List of Tables *vii*
Introduction *ix*
Introductory General Sources *xiv*

PART I THE MERCANTILIST FOUNDATIONS OF POWER *1*
1. The desire to be strong *3*
2. And the desire to be rich *12*
3. It's a white man's world *18*
4. Government for the whites and by the whites *25*
5. Developing an empire for England? *31*

PART II RIDING TO A CREST ON FREE TRADE *43*
6. Comfortable power *45*
7. Free trade and settlement colonies *56*
8. Problems in the tropics *69*
9. The soul of empire civilization *78*

PART III CLINGING TO THE PEAK *95*
10. Power in check *97*
11. Economic challenge *107*
12. A commonwealth of dominions *120*
13. The sentiment of imperial glory *128*
14. Tropical trusts *133*
15. Economic growth *140*

PART IV FALLING AWAY *157*
16. Little Britain *159*
17. Preparing an independent new commonwealth *170*
18. Developing economic independence *183*
19. Imperial conscience and culture *191*
20. An evaluation *200*

Index *205*

Publisher's Note

As the costs of labor-intensive book production have risen astronomically over the past few years, it has become increasingly difficult to produce short print run scholarly books at a reasonable price. This book is in a series designed by the University of Queensland Press to make available such reference and specialist works.

Books in the series will be set on an IBM Electronic Composer and of necessity certain technical refinements will be replaced by cheaper substitutes. Ordinarily they will not be stocked by booksellers and may be obtained by writing directly to the publisher.

The University of Queensland Press hopes that its Scholars' Library will be recognized by the scholarly and specialist community as a genuine effort to preserve the important role of the specialist book.

Tables

1. English World Trade, 1701-1800   *15*
2. British Overseas Investment, 1870 — by Place and Type   *61*
3. British Overseas Investment, 1870s — Average Yield   *62*
4. British — Empire Trade, 1890-1938   *109*
5. Trade of Empire Countries, 1913-37   *110*
6. Amount of British Overseas Investment, 1885, 1913-14, 1938   *114*
7. Type of British Overseas Investment, 1913, 1938   *115*
8. Rate of Return on British Overseas Investment, 1907-8, 1930, 1934   *116*
9. United Kingdom World Trade, 1948, 1963, 1972   *162*
10. Destination of Trade of Commonwealth Countries, 1948, 1963   *163*
11. Destination of Trade of Commonwealth Countries, 1972   *164*
12. Destination of Overseas Investment of United Kingdom, 1948, 1973   *167*

Introduction

During the 1970s the vilification of imperialism has been the automatic password of the student and the handy slogan of the protestor. This denunciation has flowed on from the condemnation of the European empires made during the 1940s by two different groups of critics. On the one hand, socialist inspired propaganda emanating from the USSR pointed to the exploitativeness and repression of the colonial systems. Rising nationalist elites in third world countries readily responded. On the other hand, Americans fighting for liberty and democracy in the 1939—45 war could see no justification for the continuance of colonial rule, which they themselves had rejected almost two centuries earlier.

Yet both groups of critics had made some fundamental miscalculations, at least as to the nature and operation of British imperialism. For Britain's empire has not easily fitted into the Marxist model, trying to explain expansion as a phenomenon induced primarily by economic factors. Nor has it readily confirmed Lenin's dicta as to imperialism being the final outgrowth of the power of banks and finance capitalism. This, of course, does not mean to say that the economic agents of imperialism, the traders and financiers, did not play an important role in the history of British expansion; indeed, in some places and at certain times they were the prime movers and throughout the whole scope of the history they have been an indispensable cog.

This study shows that the traders and financiers were an ever-present factor, always seeking opportunities, often bringing some kind of pressure, but not necessarily wanting the creation of a formal colonial system and not necessarily having the ear of the government. Although they were always interested in informal or economic British influence, the political ramifications of British control and power did not necessarily concern them. So neither the traders nor the banker-investors played the role of prime determinants in the operation of British power in the imperial setting (whether in the formal colonial situation or informally).

The politicians-administrators-military men were the ultimate fashioners of the British empire. These were the people who made the assessment of how, where and when British imperial power should be used — of whether economic interests should be protected or ignored, of when territory should be annexed, of where British security interests lay. The build-up and the maintenance of that imperial power was their essential concern. Certainly in their assessment of British power they gave earnest consideration to economic factors, and sometimes such factors were crucial. But the might of Britain was also called into action because the life rather than the economic well-being of a British subject on the frontier was threatened.

By and large it seems that the major determinant was security — the need to protect or extend the existing British power base (including the economic aspects of that base), the breakdown of authority on the frontier creating a threat to existing British power, the need to have strategic linkages between the existing sources of power. Economic factors were inextricably woven into the whole web of British power, as were the lives of British subjects. The importance of each aspect of power varied according to time and the place involved.

So, British imperial power is a total concept — it is not just the economic base although this is certainly a most important factor (and often the most important). British power was also measured in terms of lives — the survival of settlers and missionaries — and perhaps more importantly, of prestige, a way of life, a culture. British politicians and officials in London, as well as administrators overseas, had to make their decisions on the extension, maintenance or retraction of British imperial power upon the basis of a total assessment of all the British way stood for: so that a British trader could operate freely in China, or a British investor in the Argentine would not be unfairly treated, so that a settler in South Africa need not fear for his life from attack by the indigenous inhabitants, while a missionary carried out his humanitarian task of ending slavery, and an administrator collected taxes, built roads and stopped "pagan barbarities". In making this assessment the responsible person had to weigh up the cost of action (or inaction) and decide whether it added to, maintained or detracted from the total.

In the early centuries (through to the mid-nineteenth century) the decision-makers were most affected by thoughts of expanding the power-base. The mercantilist world-view was very much influenced by the concept of total power — colonies, trade, people, military force, bases, prestige. The first part of the nineteenth century, however, was viewed more in terms of a flourishing, expanding economic base.

Twentieth century American critics miscalculated British imperialism because they conceived it in terms of American operations. Steeped in a philosophy of efficiency and good management, the Americans of the 1940s thought the British had operated their empire in the same manner. This was at the very time when American capitalists were so skilfully spreading neo-colonial tentacles around the world, to reap the greatest possible profits through the most efficient management. Little did they realize how bumbling, haphazard, accidental and inefficient was so much of the British creation. For one could never hold up British imperialism as a model of efficient exploitation of the colonies or ruthless suppression of subject peoples. Admittedly there were exceptional cases but the general situation was one of moderation — moderate profits for traders (even for most slave-traders) and investors (except a few lucky ones); moderation in political matters — such as West African newspaper editors having the liberty to criticize their colonial masters. At the same time such casualness, sometimes bordering on inactivity, meant that little development was promoted in many colonial areas. So, for example, education and health changes were sluggish. Yet this could bring certain advantages in that it meant that the cultural implant of British civilization tended to be rather light — especially, for example, in comparison with the case of French rule in Africa.

This does not deny the destructive influences that accompanied British imperialism. The traditional life of non-European peoples was disrupted in varying ways. Traditional polities were undermined; old established trading patterns and industries were often largely eliminated. In their place British attempts to modernize and to bring these areas into the western international order have had only chequered results. Most success was achieved in areas where British migration occurred on a large scale; but even their economies showed weaknesses, attributable partly to the colonial experience. At the same time, traditions were able to survive to some extent the British transplant, perhaps most marked in the political arena where many nationalist leaders today can still draw upon traditional bases. So, there has been destruction, but not total destruction.

Of course Britain could have paid more attention to the social, educational and health needs of colonial peoples: she could have done the same at home. Of course she nearly always put her own needs first: like any selfish being. At the same time, the colonial yoke was not placed too tightly and the exploitation was not too rapacious. Although there was slowness and delay in giving full political autonomy, imperial rule was generally not too heavy-handed or arbitrary; scope was given for the development of a political consciousness and the grasping of political initiatives by colonials. Probably the most distressing aspect of British imperialism was the sense of British racial and cultural superiority shown to coloured peoples, a matter which has only recently suffered any real abatement.

By the closing decades of the nineteenth century the decision-makers began to think increasingly in terms of simply maintaining and protecting the huge power base that had already been established, in colonies, trade, investment, population, bases, prestige. Often it seemed to the decision-makers that such maintenance of power could best be achieved by extending the base further, so that the heartland could be protected by a peripheral ring of more diffuse British power. As a result British imperial power kept increasing through to the 1920s, but it was becoming over-extended and holding together by rather tenuous, even fragile links. By the early twentieth century the appearance of power and imperial prestige had become more important to the British than the more tangible aspects. This growing hollowness in Britain's position came in for increasing testing, so that after the second world war a new stage of thinking emerged.

Now, the imperial decision-makers had to contemplate the retraction of British imperial power, and, especially after the mid-1950s, they showed themselves ready to untie quickly the links of the vast, overgrown empire. No longer did colonies, population and military bases seem so important; now, the prestige of empire had been pricked. Britain began rather to look in upon herself, and towards Europe, and to worry primarily about her economic links with the rest of the world. So the great imperial power of the 1890s — the extensive colonies, economic links around the world, naval and strategic influences far and wide, a cultural and racial arrogance that lauded Britain's greatness and insisted upon her standards of civilization — was whittled away, into a loose, diffuse grouping of independent nations who had a common, colonial heritage.

A balance-sheet of empire cannot yet be fully drawn up. For every advance or advantage a regression or disadvantage can be found. Yet the current vilification has gone too far and some correction is needed. For example, attention should be given to the positive aspects of the theme of neglect. For the first two centuries the main approach of Britain was benign colonial neglect while imperial power was being accumulated. In the nineteenth century scope was allowed to white settlers to do virtually what they wanted, at a time when British power was riding to a peak. So white colonies developed fairly much on their own, following (with adaptations) the basic British pattern. The tropics were largely neglected until the twentieth century when the imperial trust for coloured people began to receive belated content. The result has been that, except for the West Indies, the British influence in the tropics has been somewhat limited and in many ways reversible.

It was probably fortunate that the British government was so frequently unenthusiastic about the empire, that British traders and investors generally thought more of home and foreign countries than of the colonies, and that the British public, except for the emigrants, were not usually interested in those lands across the seas. Perhaps colonials should offer special tribute to that parsimonious Treasury which decried the costly burden it thought colonies to be. In the long run these attitudes allowed the colonies enough local initiative so that, once British power was called into question, the weaning away could proceed fairly effortlessly, both in white settlement areas and in the tropics. So passed a moderate, haphazard imperialism. The sacred trust was not fulfilled, the people were not lifted up on high — but also they were not stamped deep down into the mire.

This study is basically Brito-centric, explaining how Britain came to acquire her empire and illustrating the nature of British rule. This necessarily involves a study of the interaction between the rulers and the colonial subjects; so themes of racism, of political, economic and especially social development in the colonies have been linked to the theme of the rise and fall of British imperial power. At the same time no attempt has been made to explain the domestic history of the different colonies. Nevertheless, the contrast in progress between the white settlement colonies and the non-white tropical areas becomes a constant theme when dealing with the various kinds of development in the area.

Obviously I have used illustrative examples from select colonies to explain the various points being made; no comprehensive listing of such examples could be attempted. Furthermore, in the selection I have tried to emphasize developments outside India. The so-called "jewel of the empire" has always received full treatment, to the neglect of other areas. Here, more attention is given in examples to the vast expanse of empire beyond India, to those territories administered by the Colonial Office. In particular, I have chosen the populous colonies of Africa and, by way of contrast, the small, scattered dependencies in the Pacific. The white settlement areas have received least treatment, since they were for so long in former years the centre of attention.

Problems arose in footnoting. It is clearly not possible to give comprehensive acknowledgement, otherwise, the book would be nearly all footnotes. Again, I have had to be selective, choosing the most useful, general sources as a guide for further reading. Generally this has meant referring to the whole of the work, rather than to specific pages.

Introductory General Sources

British Imperialism Generally

Established standards, such as *The Cambridge History of the British Empire*, 8 vols., (Cambridge: University Press, 1929–59); Charles E. Carrington, *The British Overseas: Exploits of a Nation of Shopkeepers* (Cambridge: University Press, 1950).

Recent Popular Accounts

Edward Grierson, *The Death of the Imperial Dream: The British Commonwealth and Empire, 1775–1969* (London: Collins, 1972); Geoffrey C. Bolton, *Britain's Legacy Overseas* (London: Oxford University Press, 1973); Bernard Porter, *The Lion's Share: A Short History of British Imperialism* (London: Longman, 1976); John Bowle, *The Imperial Achievement* (Harmondsworth: Penguin, 1977).

Comparative European Imperialism

D. K. Fieldhouse, *The Colonial Empires* (London: Weidenfeld & Nicolson, 1966).

Bibliography

Robin E. Winks, ed., *The Historiography of the British Empire and Commonwealth: Trends, Interpretations and Resources* (Durham, N.C.: Duke University Press, 1968); H. J. Hanham, comp., *The Zenith of Empire 1851–1914* (Oxford: Clarendon Press, 1974).

Documents

Arthur B. Keith, ed., *Speeches and Documents on British Colonial Policy 1763–1917* (London: Oxford University Press, 1961) (1918).

Statistics

The annual *Colonial Office List* (1862–), an invaluable collection of material on the individual colonies; Brian R. Mitchell and Phyllis Deane, *Abstract of British Historical Statistics* (Cambridge: University Press, 1962) and *Second Abstract of British Historical Statistics* (Cambridge: University Press, 1971); Werner Schlote, *British Overseas Trade from 1700 to the 1930s*, trans. W. O. Henderson and W. H. Chaloner (Oxford: Blackwell, 1952).

Political/Economic Trends

George Bennett, ed., *The Concept of Empire: Burke to Attlee, 1774–1947*, 2nd ed. (London: Black, 1962); Ernest Baker, *The Ideas and Ideals of the British Empire*, 2nd ed. (Cambridge: University Press, 1951); Martin Wight, *Development of the Legislative Council 1606–1945* (London: Faber, 1946; Lilian C. A. and C. M. Knowles, *The Economic Development of the British Overseas Empire*, 3 vols. (London: Routledge, 1924–36).

General Area Studies

Canada

Edgar W. McInnis, *Canada: A Political and Social History*, rev. ed. (New York: Holt, Rinehart and Winston, 1959); Donald G. Creighton, *Dominion of the North: A History of Canada* (Toronto: Macmillan, 1957); William T. Easterbrook and H. G. J. Aitken, *Canadian Economic History* (Toronto: Macmillan, 1956); Craufurd D. W. Goodwin, *Canadian Economic Thought: The Political Economy of a Developing Nation 1814–1914* (Durham, N.C.: Duke University Press, 1961).

Australia

Francis K. Crowley, *A New History of Australia* (Melbourne: Heinemann, 1974); Charles M. H. Clark, *A Short History of Australia* (Sydney: Mentor, 1963) and *A History of Australia*, 4 vols. (Melbourne: Melbourne University Press, 1962–); Brian C. Fitzpatrick, *The British Empire in Australia: An Economic History, 1834–1939* (Melbourne: Melbourne University Press, 1941).

New Zealand

Keith Sinclair, *A History of New Zealand* (Harmondsworth: Penguin,

1959); Colin G. F. Simkin, *The Instability of a Dependent Economy: Economic Fluctuations in New Zealand 1840–1914* (London: Oxford University Press, 1951).

South Africa

Monica Wilson and L. Thompson, eds., *The Oxford History of South Africa*, 2 vols. (Oxford: Clarendon Press, 1969–70); Donald Denoon, *Southern Africa since 1800* (New York: Praeger, 1973).

India

Vincent A. Smith, *The Oxford History of India*, 3rd ed. (Oxford: Clarendon, 1958); R. C. Majumdar et al., *An Advanced History of India*, 3rd ed. (London: Macmillan, 1967); Percival Spear, *India* (Ann Arbor: University of Michigan Press, 1972).

West Indies

Alan C. Burns, *History of the British West Indies* (London: Allen & Unwin, 1954); Eric Williams, *From Columbus to Castro: The History of the Caribbean 1492–1969* (London: Deutsch, 1972); John H. Parry and P. Sherlock, *A Short History of the West Indies* (London: Macmillan, 1956).

West Africa

J. F. A. Ajayi and M. Crowder, eds., *The History of West Africa*, 2 vols. (London: Longman, 1972–74); J. D. Fage, *An Introduction to the History of West Africa*, 4th ed. (Cambridge: University Press, 1969); William E. F. Ward, *A History of Ghana*, rev. 2nd ed. (London: Allen & Unwin, 1958); George E. Metcalfe, ed., *Great Britain and Ghana: Documents on Ghana History 1807–1957* (London: Nelson, 1965); Michael Crowder, *Short History of Nigeria* (New York: Praeger, 1962); Christopher Fyfe, *A History of Sierra Leone* (London: Oxford University Press, 1962); Harry A. Gailey, *A History of the Gambia* (London: Routledge & Kegan Paul, 1964); A. G. Hopkins, *An Economic History of West Africa* (London: Longman, 1973); Elizabeth Isichei, *History of West Africa since 1800* (London: Macmillan, 1977).

East Africa

History of East Africa, 3 vols. (Oxford: Clarendon Press, 1963–74); Kenneth Ingham, *A History of East Africa* (London: Longman, 1962); George Bennett, *Kenya: A Political History* (London: Oxford University Press, 1963); Kenneth Ingham, *Making of Modern Uganda* (London: Allen

& Unwin, 1958); I. N. Kimambo and A. J. Temu, eds., *A History of Tanzania* (Nairobi: East African Publishing House, 1969); August Toussaint, *History of Mauritius* (London: Macmillan, 1977).

Central Africa

Alfred J. Wills, *An Introduction to the History of Central Africa* (London: Oxford University Press, 1973); Lewis H. Gann, *A History of Northern Rhodesia* (London: Chatto & Windus, 1964) and *A History of Southern Rhodesia, Early Days to 1934* (London: Chatto & Windus, 1965).

High Commission Territories

Richard P. Stevens, *Lesotho, Botswana and Swaziland* (London: Pall Mall, 1967).

Malaysia

Nicholas Tarling, *Imperial Britain in South-East Asia* (London: Oxford University Press, 1975); Richard O. Winstedt, *Malaya and its History*, 7th ed. (London: Hutchinson, 1964); Wang Gungwu, ed., *Malaysia: A Survey* (Melbourne: Cheshire, 1964).

Ceylon

Lennox A. Mills, *Ceylon under British Rule 1795–1932* (London: Cass, 1964); Sydney D. Bailey, *Ceylon* (New York: Hutchinson, 1952); E. F. C. Ludowyk, *The Modern History of Ceylon* (London: Weidenfeld & Nicolson, 1966).

Hong Kong

George B. Endacott, *A History of Hong Kong* (London: Oxford University Press, 1964).

Pacific

Douglas L. Oliver, *The Pacific Islands* (Cambridge, Mass.: Harvard University Press, 1962).

PART ONE

The Mercantilist Foundations of Power

Sixteenth to Early Nineteenth Century

1
The Desire to be Strong

In 1920 Britain ruled over the largest empire the world had ever known, largest in area and in population. Yet the British were late-comers in the phenomenon of European expansion that had characterized the previous four centuries of world history. When the first colony was successfully established at Virginia in 1607 the English trailed the Portuguese and the Spaniards in colonial expansion by about one hundred years. In later decades, however, the British not only subdued local leaders in America, Asia, Africa and the Pacific but also vanquished their European rivals, the Spanish, Portuguese, Dutch and French, and held at bay other imperialist competitors such as the Germans, Russians and Americans.

How were these achievements realized? One basic impetus, operating in the fifteenth century and continuing through to the twentieth, was the consideration of power. Initially the English felt themselves so threatened that they had to make stronger than usual efforts to circumvent or thwart the stronger powers that stood in their way. Starting as an inferior in the power stakes the English had to struggle to establish their identity and self-respect; the alternative was to be crushed by the power of continental Spain, and later France. Prior to the seventeenth century, little England, perched precariously on the edge of the great landmass of Europe, had never been very noteworthy, except as the subject of occasional toing and froing by Teutonic and Gallic peoples. England was a centre neither of civilization, of military power nor of economic importance. But during the sixteenth century there were signs of impatience with such a status and of some anxiety to flex whatever military or economic muscle she might be able to develop. Spain had grown magnificently strong through the acquisition of a great empire in America, yielding up fabulous treasures of silver and gold, while Portugal waxed rich on the spices and jewels of the east. What was left for poor, little England, the world having already been divided between the two Catholic powers, Spain and Portugal, by the papal bull of 1493. The leftovers were the less fortunate temperate zones of the north, areas seeming to offer no prospects to the Spaniards although they were entitled to them. Apart from those areas the English could see virtue, and value, in trade, a pursuit that did not fire the valour and zeal of the Iberians.

Elizabethan England was dominated by the awesome power of Spain, with its Hapsburg dominions, its vast American empire and a political power that joined with the religious power of the catholic church. Philip II of Spain was determined to champion the catholic cause around the world and in particular to advance the counter-reformation in Europe. This was at a time when Elizabeth was fashioning, or being pushed into, a somewhat uncertain and personal protestant alignment. The might of Spain was ready to strike down Elizabeth, portrayed as a sinful and blasphemous heretic. But the seemingly weak and defenceless Elizabeth would not be cowed by the bullying of Spain, and although Philip sent a great armada against the English in 1588 it failed. This was the first significant check to the imperial and religious might of Spain.

By the end of the sixteenth century the English were set upon a course of imperial expansion that was not to be brooked until the 1930s. During Elizabethan times the groundwork was being laid upon which English imperial might was to grow. Most importantly an ideological base was being prepared and commercial foundations were being set. An imperial creation was being conceived upon the notions that the English (later the British) needed to secure their independence and identity by the dispersal of their influence, not to continental Europe, but to the new worlds across the seas, so that England would always have access to raw materials and markets, so that wealth could be accumulated through expanding trade outlets, so that colonies could be established wherein the English example would be established as a counter to rival powers and ideologies, always with the ultimate aim of contributing to the greater power of England.

Early the English saw the significance of expansion through trade rather than through gold and silver which had been the hallmark of Spanish power; but of equal importance was their belief in themselves as a people offering a superior way of life. The religious passions of the sixteenth and seventeenth centuries took on an intensity and drive that is hard to appreciate today. But to Englishmen then, the spread of catholicism to new, pagan countries was an evil, cancerous growth that had to be eradicated and stifled. Nevertheless, underpinning both these commercial and ideological concerns in overseas endeavour was the realization and belief that English security could only be assured by the accumulation of power. It was ridiculous to think of assaulting Spain on its home-ground (except with petty, piratical forays); the solution seemed to be to circumvent Spain, by planting colonies where Spain was not interested, building up trade wherever possible, even with the Iberian peninsula, allowing privateers and pirates to chip away at Spanish Imperial might on the periphery. This was the pattern of events that occurred during Elizabeth's reign, sometimes as matters of conscious state policy, often not; these were the foundations upon which the British empire was to develop.

Essential to the job of imperial expansion were the propagandists, preparing the public mind for involvement in the imperial scramble. A glorious tradition of English exploration and colonization was uncovered, dating from 1170 when the Welsh prince Madoc was supposed to have sailed to the vicinity of Florida and the West Indies. The discoveries of John Cabot, in Nova Scotia, Newfoundland and Baffin Island in 1497 and 1498 added more substance to English claims across the seas.[1] In 1517 John Rastell planned a settlement in Newfoundland but a mutiny off the Irish coast ended these hopes of establishing England's first colony in America. In the 1540s English colonization in south America was considered. Later, the example of the French Huguenots who had tried, albeit unsuccessfully, to challenge Spanish power by setting up settlements in Florida sparked off a strong sense of opposition to Spain among Englishmen. Even Elizabeth herself was affected and she engaged Thomas Stukeley to lead an expedition; but that also failed.[2] The distrust, fear and hatred of Spain continued to grow, yet the many English challenges to Spanish might usually ended in disaster, largely because of inadequate planning. Sir Humphrey Gilbert, a keen advocate of the idea of finding a north-west passage to China, urged the importance of England establishing a colony in north America as a half-way stop. The queen in 1578 granted him a royal patent to plant such a colony, empowering him

> to search, find out and view such remote, heathen and barbarous lands, countries and territories not actually possessed of any Christian prince or people . . . and the same to have, hold, occupy and enjoy to him, his heirs and assigns for ever.[3]

Gilbert planted an expedition of settlers in Newfoundland; but driven on by the desire to spread English influence further and to annoy the king of Spain, he impetuously moved southwards along the American coast, until disaster struck. Sir Walter Raleigh continued in Gilbert's footsteps, but his two efforts at colonization, further south on the North Carolina coast, in 1585 and 1587 also failed. Again the planning and support were inadequate.

While such attempts at colonization were unproductive the propagandists of the sixteenth century were having more success in arousing some degree of community interest in favour of exploration and colonization.[4] They aimed at converting both government officials and the general public, or at least the more affluent members of the latter — nobility, gentry and merchants — so that money would be made available to sponsor such expeditions. The propagandists realized they should present a wide range of reasons for such activity: for trade and profits, for demographic and social reasons, for moral and religious purposes, but especially so that England would come to acquire an empire and be more able to compete with Spain. Spain was the antagonist who had to be beaten at its own game; England backed up by an empire would be able to catch up in the time-lag that had put her at a disadvantage in the power stakes. Sir

George Peckham, a close friend of Gilbert and a financial backer for the latter's Newfoundland scheme, published in 1583 a strong case for English colonization in America. Anxious to humble Philip and Spain he argued that Elizabeth held lawful title to the lands of north America, through the discoveries of English explorers, from Madoc to Cabot. Consequently the English should without delay make good their claims to the northern areas not yet occupied by the Spaniards. Realizing the government would not be anxious to spend money on colonization schemes he argued that no financial claims would have to be made on the public purse: transportation to the colony would be provided on empty fishing vessels going to the rich grounds near Newfoundland; while the abundance of the American soil in natural products meant that only minimal supplies would have to be sent to help colonists starting off.

The most effective propagandist was Richard Hakluyt, the younger. Through his *The principal navigations* . . . he acquired, both then and subsequently, a preeminence above all the other advocates of imperialism.[5] In his *The discourse of western planting*, written in 1584 at the request of his friend Raleigh for the furtherance of the latter's cause in North Carolina, he propounded a doctrine which although not accepted as offical policy embodied a full account of reasons for English colonization. Again, it was the threat of Spanish power that weighed most heavily in his considerations. So he pointed out the strategic advantages England would gain through establishing plantations in north America, protected by two or three strong forts between Florida and Cape Breton. From these bases attacks could be made on the West Indies, so that Philip would be put "in hazarde in loosinge some parte of Nova Hispania". From these bases too, the Spanish fleet returning to Spain laden with gold could be harassed. An English fort in the Newfoundland area could seize the numerous Spanish and Portuguese fishing vessels that worked there every year. Furthermore, these bases could give succour to the various Indian tribes and "savages" who were continually fighting against the Spaniards. In all, English bases would be "such an advantage" to England and "such a bridle" to Philip that his position might be seriously weakened. The way 'to bring kinge Philippe from his highe Throne and make him equall to the Princes his neighboures" was to encourage disruption in his American possessions.[6] Hakluyt also urged that the English strike through the West Indies, "there to laye a chefe foundation for his overthrowe". The slaves in the Spanish colonies were assumed to be ripe for revolt. Wishfully Hakluyt wrote "and the people revolte in every forrein territorie of his, and cutt the throates of the proude hatefull Spaniardes their governours".

The English were already asserting their sense of cultural superiority. In contrast to the Spaniards Hakluyt saw the English as humane and courteous in their attitude towards the original inhabitants of America. The English went out as bearers of freedom — and protestantism — so

THE DESIRE TO BE STRONG

counteracting the evil, tyrannical hold that Spain was establishing over the native inhabitants. For this reason he urged that English people be planted on a large scale, preferably with state aid, in those parts of north America discovered by English explorers. Apart from such humanitarian and moral concerns Hakluyt was also pleased to recommend colonies because of their military value to England, and not only as bases from which to attack Spain's colonial power. The need to protect her colonies would force England to maximize her naval power. Also the existence of colonial trade would lead to a build-up of the merchant marine; and in times of international crisis such marines could be drafted into the fighting service. So the possession of colonies would lead to the strengthening of England's fighting power.

In mentioning trade and a merchant marine Hakluyt was only too mindful of another important motive for English expansion, the build-up of power through gaining wealth from trade. America was described as a fertile source of a wide range of raw materials, and possibly of minerals, which would boost English treasuries. Furthermore ample naval stores, timber, flax, pitch, could be obtained there to supply English naval requirements.

Although the advantages to be gained from increased trade, the moral duty of spreading English civilization and the social pressures in favour of disbursing population were all considered, the overriding factor influencing Hakluyt, and the other propagandists, was the strategic consideration of how to strike at the power of Spain. But it was not until the failure of Philip's armada that the English took more heart in furthering the grand imperial design. With colonization being more carefully planned, and with the propagandists continuing their preparation of a wider base of popular interest, success had to come at last. In 1607 the first permanent settlement was established in Virginia, and after the first tentative years began to flourish. In 1612 an off-shoot colony was established on the island of Bermuda, and in 1623 the English broached the West Indies, with a permanent settlement on St Christopher; earlier (1605) there had been a temporary settlement on St Lucia. Thereafter the imperial scramble was under way, with twelve English colonies springing up along the north American seabord, as well as British penetration into Arcadia, Newfoundland and Hudson Bay. And from one small island in the Caribbean a whole web of English interests was established — Barbados, Antigua, Montserrat, Honduras, the Bahamas, Nevis, Anguilla, Jamaica, the Virgin Islands, the Turks and Caicos group.

Throughout the seventeenth and eighteenth centuries official interest in English expansion was continually dominated by the problem of rival powers. Spanish power, although checked, had still to be reckoned with, and it gave Cromwell immense pleasure, out of both pride and religious conviction, to be able to wrest Jamaica from Spain in 1655. In the current rash of imperial expansion this was England's first significant, permanent capture from another imperial power, the other colonies becoming established by way of English settlement. In the seventeenth century, however, Spain was not the only rival and England found herself engaged in a running battle on the frontier with the Dutch and the French.[7] English fortunes swayed to and fro, especially in the Caribbean; for example, the Dutch replaced the English in Tobago in 1632; the British ousted the Dutch from St Croix in 1645, only to find themselves expelled soon after by the Spaniards who were themselves replaced by the French in 1650; the English and the French haggled over the destiny of a number of islands, such as St Lucia and St Vincent. In all this flux and flow, however, the English were able during the seventeenth century to show their military mastery over the Dutch, symbolized most clearly by the acquisition of New York in 1664.

While the Dutch threat was declining the French menace was rising, and the continual bickering and sniping of the seventeenth century gave way in the next century to an all-out battle between Britain and France for dominance and power. Firstly the French were overcome in Arcadia (later to become Nova Scotia and New Brunswick). The culminating coup came in the seven years' war (1756—63) when the French were vanquished, not only in India but also in the Americas. As a result the French yielded up Tobago, Dominica, St Vincent and Grenada in the West Indies and the whole province of Canada and the eastern Mississippi basin in north America. Spain also handed over Florida to England. In this age of mercantilism, with the emphasis on monopoly of power, Britain had come out on top.[8] Although the French tried to recover some of these losses at the turn of the century the final defeat of Napoleon spelled an end to the French empire and France's rivalry to Britain. By 1815 British power was unchallenged and unchallengeable, as much in its imperial manifestations as in its economic. During the previous twenty years of war colonies were acquired from a range of sources: Trinidad from Spain; Ceylon from the Dutch, the Cape of Good Hope and Guyana also from the Dutch, but at a cost of £5 million; Mauritius and St Lucia from the French; Malta from the Knights of St John; Heligoland from the Danes; Ascension and Tristan da Cunha were occupied; and a protectorate was taken over the Ionian Islands. This list included some economic gems such as Ceylon and Mauritius but it was more notable for its emphasis upon strategic bases, such as the Cape and Malta; earlier, in 1713, another vital base, Gibraltar, had been obtained from Spain. Britain, the epitome of mercantilist power, intended to ensure that her total position was adequately protected by a cluster of bases from which the navy could easily radiate and from which the merchant marine could obtain succour in the pursuit of Britain's trading interests.

While the political leaders in England through the sixteenth, seventeenth and eighteenth centuries were consumed with worries and fears about security and power, such considerations did not always bear so strongly on the reasoning of the many English subjects who went out to establish the various colonies around the globe. For some, religious, political or social dissatisfaction with conditions in England sent them out to start a fresh life in a new land. Throughout the seventeenth century religious grievances prompted much emigration, starting with the Plymouth fathers who sought in 1620 to escape the religious restrictions and harassment of England by setting up a colony in north America.[9] Between 1620 and 1640 it is estimated that about twenty thousand Englishmen fled to America because they could not agree with the state's religious policy insisting on conformity to the beliefs and practices of the Church of England. James I made the position clear: " . . . make them conform themselves or I will harry them out of the land". And so puritans fled to New England, quakers to Pennsylvania, catholics to Maryland — the religious rejects of England.

Other rejects also found their way to the colonies, although frequently not of their own free will. From the beginning colonies were seen as useful receptacles for felons and criminals and the transportation of such people from British gaols became a regular avenue for building up the population and workforce of certain colonies — in the West Indies, some of the north American colonies, and especially in the early settlement of Australia. Between 1788 and 1868 over 160,000 new Australians arrived "in chains" to help start settlement in New South Wales, Tasmania, Victoria, Queensland, Western Australia and Norfolk Island; previously, during the earlier part of the eighteenth century about thirty-thousand convicts had been transported to the American colonies. A different kind of transportation was involved in the founding of another colony, Sierra Leone. In 1788 a few British humanitarians started a settlement for freed African slaves who were struggling to survive as waifs in London. They were joined by freed slaves from Jamaica and Nova Scotia and later, after the slave trade was suppressed, by Africans rescued from slave-ships. In Sierra Leone they began to develop a distinctive culture of their own.[10]

Counsel was divided about the nature and effect of the flow of migrants from Britain. Criticism was raised about the kind of person that went out to settle. Some seemed quite unsuited to the conditions of privation and hardship that greeted these pioneers. Whether they were founding Jamestown in Virginia or the Swan River settlement in Western Australia many of the settlers were "idle much of the time", unwilling to turn their hands to hard work, often just reckless and irrational gamblers. Some critics condemned the policy of sending out the "refuse" and "incorrigible" of British society. From the earliest days Francis Bacon was sounding the warning

> It is a shameful and unblessed thing to take the scum of people and wicked condemned men to be the people with whom you plant . . . for they will ever live like rogues, and not fall to work, but be lazy, and do mischief, and spend victuals, and be quickly weary . . . The people

wherewith you plant ought to be gardeners, ploughmen, labourers, smiths, carpenters, joiners, fishermen, fowlers, with some few apothecaries, surgeons, cooks, and bakers.[11]

Yet the kind of person that settled the new colonies was not easy to typify. Certainly some were "scum"; some were petty-minded, insecure individuals, failures at home, who escaped to the colonies where they might put on a false front of bravado and intimidate the "inferior natives" into a position of subservience. But there were also settlers who resembled the model pioneering type, thrifty, hardworking, willing to make sacrifices, enterprising, resourceful, determined to overcome a difficult past and prosper in a new future.

At the official level doubts about the wisdom of emigration centred on the question of the weakening of England's power.[12] Some people argued that the loss of those people, even though to possessions across the seas, meant that England's power and military potential were being weakened in the face of her continental rivals. They argued that it was better to concentrate population-strength at home. But the prevalent view saw such emigration to colonies owned by England as adding to England's total power and as increasing her competitive ability against continental rivals. Indeed, if England did not possess colonies across the seas to which Englishmen could emigrate, they would nevertheless leave England, for foreign countries, to the perpetual loss of English power. Underlying this argument was the fear, frequently expressed both then and now, that the country was suffering a population-crisis.[13] Josiah Child reasoned that the surplus population — the religiously unhappy, the political refugees, the ruffians, vagabonds and unemployed, the criminals — could all be gainfully engaged in spreading English influence to other parts of the world. At home they were weakening England, in colonies abroad they were adding to her greater glory and power. Colonization and the export of population were put up as hallmarks of mercantilist power.

Operating as a basic motivating factor for expansion, by Englishmen and Europeans alike, was a spirit of enquiry and a certain restlessness, described later by historians as the phenomenon of Renaissance man. It might be argued that amongst Englishmen it took a more heightened form than on the continent, in the sense that they started from a greater base of insecurity and inferiority, when compared with the culture and power of the Mediterranean cities or of Portugal and Spain. By Tudor times the Renaissance Englishman was emerging, becoming more critical, assuming a greater confidence and assertiveness. He was more determined than previously to meet his rivals with the aim of overcoming his position of inferiority; he was not so prepared meekly to assume an assured position somewhere down the hierarchy of power. Armed with a more aggressive and domineering personality the Renaissance Englishman embarked on voyages of discovery, planted settlements across the seas, and challenged the Spanish and others who stood in his way, in a fierce determination to break down the old order and establish a new in his own image. This spirit was not possessed by all Englishmen, nor solely by the English; but among them emerged a group who expressed it ardently. It was these fervent nationalists and patriots who set England's destiny along the course of imperial greatness. Determined to overcome England's late start and inferior position they were prepared to make a greater effort and take more risks.

NOTES

1. On early British exploration in North America, see J. A. Williamson, *The Voyage of the Cabots and the English Discovery of North America under Henry VII and Henry VIII* (London: Argonaut Press, 1929), and David B. Quinn, *England and the Discovery of America, 1481—1620* (London: Allen & Unwin, 1974).
2. A. L. Rowse, *The Expansion of Elizabethan England* (London: Macmillan, 1955), and *The Elizabethans and America* (New York: Harper, 1959).
3. David B. Quinn (ed.), *The Voyages and Colonising Enterprises of Sir Humphrey Gilbert* (London: Hakluyt Society, 1940), I, 35.
4. John Parker, *Books to Build an Empire: A Bibliographical History of English Overseas Interests to 1620* (Amsterdam: N. Israel, 1965).
5. Richard Hakluyt (comp.), *The Principal Navigations, Voyages, Traffiques and Discoveries of the English Nation . . .* (London: Dent, 1907) (1589); Eva G. R. Taylor (ed.), *The Original Writings and Correspondence of the Two Richard Hakluyts* (London: Cambridge University Press, 1935). Re Ralegh and colonization attempts, David B. Quinn, *The Roanoke Voyages, 1584—90* (London: Cambridge University Press, 1955).
6. Taylor (ed.), *The Original Writings . . .* , II, 211—49.
7. Richard Pares, *War and Trade in the West Indies* (London: Cass, 1972)(1936); J. H. Parry, *Trade and Dominion: The European Overseas Empires in the Eighteenth Century* (London: Weidenfeld & Nicolson, 1971); Carl and R. Bridenbaugh, *No Peace Beyond the Line: The English in the Caribbean, 1624—90* (New York: Oxford University Press, 1972).
8. John H. Rose, *William Pitt and the Great War* (London: Bell, 1911).
9. Arthur P. Newton, *The Colonizing Activities of the English Puritans* (New Haven: Yale University Press, 1914).
10. John Peterson, *Province of Freedom: History of Sierra Leone, 1787—1870* (London, Faber and Faber, 1969).
11. Francis Bacon, "Of plantations", *Essays* (London; Dent, 1906)(1598), pp. 108—9.
12. For arguments about the growth of mercantilist power, see Eli F. Heckscher, *Mercantilism* (London: Allen & Unwin, 1935); Richard Koebner, *Empire* (Cambridge: Cambridge University Press, 1961) looks at the changing meaning of the word, see especially chapter III.
13. Klaus Knorr, *British Colonial Theories, 1570—1850* (Toronto: University Press, 1963) provides a full analysis of the various arguments for and against empire, including the factor of population. The writers of the time offered a wide range of arguments on the value (and cost) of empire, for example Josiah Child, *A New Discourse on Trade* (London, 1693), especially pp. 165—69, 183; Charles Davenant, *Discourses on the Publick Revenues and on the Trade of England* (London, 1698).

2
And the Desire to be Rich

Government fears about English security, social pressures for emigration and colonization, individual psyches betraying both insecurity and derring-do were not the whole formula for imperial expansion. The greed of merchants was also essential in the success of England spreading her influence to all parts of the globe and in gaining possessions in all continents. The merchants themselves developed as one category of Renaissance man, challenging the old establishment with a new emphasis upon the acquisition of wealth. Through their willingness to risk surplus wealth in ventures for gain, sometimes with a high factor of chance, the momentum of English overseas expansion gathered strength. It has been estimated that between 1570 and 1630 English speculators spent over £500,000 on ventures that had no foreseeable prospect of paying dividends.[1] The Renaissance capitalist could be shrewd and thrifty, but he might also be extravagant and wasteful. Yet without such boldness England would not have made the imperialist gains that she did make.

Starting in the 1550s with the Muscovy company, as it plunged into the icy wastes of north Russia in the search for profit, English merchants and investors soon spread their tentacles in all directions — into the Baltic, the Levant, Africa, India, the East Indies and America. Over thirty-five joint-stock companies had been formed by the 1630s, some concerned mainly with trade in eastern Europe and the orient, others looking to the establishment of settlements in America for the long-term production of goods for the European market.

The greatest, in terms of wealth, area and manpower, came to be the East India Company, chartered by Queen Elizabeth I in 1600 for "trading into the East Indies". Activities on the Indian subcontinent began after the Company resisted Portuguese attacks at Surat in 1612. Then, after 1640, using Madras as a base the pursuits of these merchants began to spread to to Bombay (1661–68) and Calcutta (1690). Through various trading and taxing rights Company wealth and influence kept spreading, and running into conflict with other European trading companies. As already noticed the mid-eighteenth century was marked by bitter fighting with French interests, resulting in English victory at Plassey and Wandiwash (1757–61). Meanwhile the various Indian rulers also found they could not resist the growing power of the Company, with the result that the East India Company by the early nineteenth century appeared as virtual ruler of many parts of the Indian subcontinent.

Other English chartered companies did not grow so powerful, yet they also played a similar role in helping to spread ultimate English power. For example, the Hudson Bay Company (chartered 1670), through its fur and other trading activities in the northern parts of Canada, was ever spreading an English influence which in laters years would allow the establishment of official British control. But this is jumping ahead. The companies were formed with economic intents; the accretion of political power was to follow as an indirect aspect of economic power. In the seventeenth century the joint-stock company operated as the main avenue of English economic expansion, enticing the adventurous speculator to sink his surplus wealth into commercial expeditions and plantation schemes which were too expensive or risky for a single person to undertake. Sometimes a quick profit was made, sometimes a loss. To those founding plantations Francis Bacon warned that there would be no speedy returns. "Planting of countries is like planting of woods; for you must make account to lose twenty years' profit, and expect your recompense at the end".[2] Mostly merchants participated, but a minority were gentry and some were politicians. In a period of expanded commercial prosperity new monied families were emerging, willing to go outside the more established avenues of economic activity; at the same time the profits and successes that some overseas ventures were making were snaring sections of the more traditional families.[3]

The significance of the merchants became symbolized in the system later called mercantilism. By the mid-seventeenth century English merchants were pressuring the parliament for protection and help against Dutch competition; it was another test of strength in an age of heightened rivalry. For example, the Dutch had a virtual monopoly of West Indian shipping to Europe, and they even supplied slaves, credit and advice to English planters growing sugar and tobacco in the Caribbean. Parliament responded with various pieces of legislation — starting with the Plantation Ordinance of 1650 and the Navigation Act of 1651 and built upon in later years — the aim of which was to eliminate foreign competition and create a monopoly for English ships in colonial trade. Englishmen were coming to realize that although they lacked gold and silver such as Spain had they could accumulate wealth and power through gaining control of trade and shipping and regulating it to afford a favourable balance of trade. The London merchant, Thomas Mun, wrote thus in the mid-seventeenth century

> The ordinary means therefore to encrease our wealth and treasure is by *Forraign Trade*, wherein wee must ever observe this rule; to sell more to strangers yearly than wee consume of theirs in value. For suppose that when this kingdom is plentifully served with the Cloth,

Lead, Tinn, Iron, Fish and other native commodities, we doe yearly export the overplus to forraign Countries to the value of twenty two hundred thousand pounds; by which means we are enabled beyond the Seas to buy and bring in forraign wares for our use and Consumptions, to the value of twenty hundred thousand pounds; By this order duly kept in our trading, we may rest assured that the Kingdom shall be enriched yearly two hundred thousand pounds, which must be brought to us in so much Treasure.[4]

To reduce dependence on foreign countries, colonies became an essential acquisition, acting both as a source of supply of those materials which England did not possess and as an outlet for English goods. Later writers, such as Charles Davenant and William Wood, sought to stress this idea of the empire as a self-contained, self-sufficient economic unit — mercantilism carried to the highest degree — although in practical terms this was not possible.

Control of shipping was an inevitable aspect of the trade factor. Legislation was passed specifying that goods from Africa, Asia or America could not be imported into England except in ships from England or her possessions;[5] certain enumerated goods such as sugar or tobacco grown in English colonies could not be exported, unless first to England or some English possession; goods from Europe could be imported only in English ships or those belonging to the exporting country. Such legislation illustrated the power of the merchants to arrange an economic order suiting their own interests, and pockets. But it also highlighted the basic concern of the day, that English power be increased to the disadvantage of her rivals, through the build-up of trade and shipping and the acquisition of an empire. Prime concern was for the development of England's wealth and power, although there was no objection to the colonies riding along on England's coat-tails.

The result was a strong increase in trade. Between 1663 and 1668 the amount of English shipping cleared outwards doubled from 95,000 tons; by 1699 it has almost quadrupled again, to 736,000 tons.[6] Until the mid-seventeenth century trade beyond Europe and Turkey was minimal; but by 1700 America and Asia provided about one-third of England's imports while about one-third of her exports were American and Asian goods re-exported. Sugar from the West Indies rapidly overtook European sources of supply, and sugar was England's second biggest import. Furthermore one-half of the sugar imports were re-exported to Europe, as were two-thirds of the tobacco. At the same time, by 1700 America and Asia had become England's third biggest export outlet, after northern Europe and southern Europe. Mercantilism seemed to be working well; Englishmen in the second half of the seventeenth century were pleased to watch the share of their exports increase faster than the share for imports, and the colonial share of total trade increase faster than the foreign share.

By the eighteenth century the primacy of the West Indies, north America and the East Indies as areas of supply became well-established, as indicated in table 1. As to markets for English goods, Europe kept its hold, though it was loosened a little by empire outlets.

Table 1. English World Trade, 1701-1800 (%).

	Imports into England (average annual values)			Exports from England (average annual values)		
	1701-5	1751-55	1796-1800	1701-5	1751-55	1796-1800
W. Indies	13	20	26	5	5	13
E. Indies	12	14	21	2	6	7
Contl. America	6	12	–	5	9	–
Rest empire	1	1	1	–	–	–
Ireland	6	7	11	–	9	9
Germany	14	8	9	16	11	30
Holland	12	–	–	36	22	4
Turkey	6	–	–	5	–	–
USA	–	–	8	–	–	18
Africa	–	–	–	2	2	3
Portugal	–	–	–	11	9	–
Spain	–	–	–	–	8	–
Canada	–	–	–	–	–	3

Source: Adapted from E. Schumpeter, *English Overseas Trade, Statistics, 1697 - 1808* (Oxford: Clarendon, 1960), especially pp. 11, 17-18; also see Werner Schlote, *British Overseas Trade from 1700 to the 1930s,* trans. W.O. Henderson and W.H. Chaloner (Oxford: Blackwell, 1952).

Through the seventeenth and eighteenth centuries the economic sponsors of English expansion, whether colonial or informal, were concerned mainly with what could be obtained from overseas, rather than with the export of manufactured goods from England — the latter were yet of secondary importance. The ideal structure was that, wherever possible, imports of food and raw materials needed in England should come from colonies, while English exports should consist of re-exports of colonial imports to foreign countries and the export of British manufactures to the colonies and foreign countries. If properly organized and controlled England should thereby be able to chalk up a very healthy trade balance, ultimately adding to her own strength and weakening her enemies.[7]

The goods which England most needed were tropical products and so the West Indies, the East Indies and the southern American colonies (Virginia and the Carolinas) seemed most attractive, with their sugar, tobacoo, rum, molasses, dye-woods, rice, indigo, chocolate, lime juice, salt, ginger, pepper. Some quite northerly areas also held potential, with timber, naval stores, furs, skins and fish. Colonies were needed which could supply England's deficiencies, but some in north America found themselves out of economic favour because they supplied competing goods to England.[8]

Complementariness, not competitiveness, was the key to mercantile success, at least from an English point of view. For their part, the New England colonies were not so interested in tying themselves into an economic structure centred on England; rather they looked more widely afield, to the West Indies and Europe. Around 1770 those northern colonies sent only eighteen per cent of their exports to Britain and obtained only sixty-six per cent of their imports from her; by contrast the figures for the southern colonies were eighty-four per cent and eighty per cent respectively.[9]

So England was pleased to obtain colonies which would boost her economic strength, and thus her total power. But this "grand plan" was of little interest to the selfish desires of the economic agents of empire. The merchants were out primarily for profits from opening up new trading outlets in the new worlds; and investors were interested because of the financial rewards that flowed from backing a trading or planting venture where skilful management and good luck managed to coincide. To the thinking of both economically involved groups the actual possession of colonies was not essential; profits were being made from the Levant without any British empire being created. From an official point of view, however, colonies performed two useful functions, as manifestations of great power, and as harbours of security for English settlers and traders against the incursions and restrictions of foreign competitors. And in an age of great power rivalry threats to security were never far afield, so that English merchants and investors themselves were usually not averse to the establishment of colonial protection even though they might not actively press for it.

NOTES

1. The best starting point on English overseas investment (and the chartered companies) is Theodore Rabb, *Enterprise and empire; merchant and gentry investment in the expansion of England, 1575–1630* (Cambridge, Mass.: Harvard University Press, 1967), especially pp. 2, 3, 99 and "The Expansion of Europe and the Spirit of Capitalism", *Historical Journal* 17 (1972): 75–89.
2. Francis Bacon, "Of Plantations", *Essays* (London: Dent, 1906)(1958), pp. 108–9.
3. R. Brenner, "The Social Basis of English Commercial Expansion" 1550–1650", *Journal of Economic History* 32 (1972): 361–84; also, B. E. Supple, *Commercial Crisis and Change in England, 1600–42* (Cambridge: Cambridge University Press, 1964), for the beginnings of the mercantilist system. William Cunningham, *The Growth of English Industry and Commerce* (Cambridge: Cambridge University Press, 1910) 2, provides a general background on the economic conditions in England allowing for imperial expansion.
4. Thomas Mun, *England's Treasure by Foreign Trade* (Oxford: Blackwell), 1949), p. 28.
5. Navigation Act of 1660.
6. George L. Beer, *The Origins of the British Colonial System, 1578–1660* and *The Old Colonial System, 1660–1754* (Gloucester, Mass.: Peter Smith, 1958)(1908)(1912) – for trade figures, see latter, 1, pp. 14–15, 42–44.

7. Re general trade, Ralph Davis, *English Overseas Trade, 1500–1700* (London: Macmillan, 1973).
8. James F. Shepherd and Gary M. Walton, *Shipping, Maritime Trade and the Economic Development of Colonial North America* (Cambridge, Cambridge University Press, 1972); also, slight revision, Jacob Price, "A Note on the Value of Colonial Exports of Shipping", *Journal of Economic History* 36 (1976): 704–24; Charles M. Andrews, *The Colonial Period of American History* 4, *England's Commercial and Colonial Policy* (New Haven, Yale University Press, 1938).
9. James F. Shepherd and Gary M. Walton, "Trade, Distribution, and Economic Growth in Colonial America", *Journal of Economic History* 32 (1972): 128–45.

3
It's a White Man's World

Expansion overseas immediately brought the English into contact with peoples of another race and culture, thereby posing the question of the whole nature of civilization. From the beginning the English blithely assumed that they held a certain superiority; this in itself gave them a kind of impetus to assert themselves and their way of life over the different peoples that they encountered. In theory, however, English officialdom found itself confronted by ambiguous statements on how to treat these other people. One line of thought wanted to regard them as equals, meaning that the full niceties of a yet fledgling and imprecise international law should be applied. In particular the rights of original inhabitants to their land should be observed and transfers obtained only by cession or conquest. And in keeping with this approach English officials at various stages propagated humanitarian policies, aimed at protecting other races from the greedy maraudings of white settlers.

In practice, a second line of argument held most sway, certainly for settlers but even among a number of officials. This stated that only if lands were cultivated should the above rules be observed and only if Englishmen were dealing with civilized people should proper regard be paid to equality in negotiations. It was easy for the English to find that most of these new lands were not cultivated but rather were waste and free for the taking while, apart from a few religious groups and humanitarian officials, little respect was paid to the culture of the American Indians and other such races. The result was that only exceptionally did a band of Englishmen negotiate and arrange fair land transfers with people of a different race; usually the English claimed whatever they wanted by right of first discovery (meaning first white, christian discovery), occupation, cheap sales or conquest. This pattern of land acquisition was repeated around the world, an example being in the case of the Maoris at the beginning of the nineteenth century. The prime consideration of the new settlers was always the violence of the response that the original inhabitants might make to the white incursion. For a while the exchange of a few cheap western goods for land could be arranged and relations between the two races proceeded reasonably smoothly. But these peaceful waters soon became disturbed, as whites kept demanding more land, as the indigenes came to realize that in transferring land to whites they were giving up all rights of usage, as the indigenes came to realize that land had a greater value to whites than a few cheap trinkets, a few lengths of cloth and a few tools and weapons. The increasing reluctance of the indigenes to make more land concessions almost inevitably led to a white response of more forceful and violent acquisition. So race relations soon became muddied by land-wars, and armed with a superior technology western man necessarily won, although not easily or spontaneously.

The theoretical ambiguity over the rights (especially land-rights) of indigenes was repeated in the question of regard for their welfare. No matter how fair or humanitarian a statement might be voiced by officials or religious bodies, the settler mentality of white dominance and self-interest generally prevailed in the long run. Initially official concern was expressed for the spiritual welfare of these other peoples. The king's instructions to the Cabots in the 1490s as they set out on their exploration of the American wastes listed the conversion of natives as a duty flowing on from territorial acquisition. The letters patent to the Virginia Company of 1606 expressed the hope that the christian gospel should be propagated among the Indian tribes. From the beginning the English, like their fellow European "conquistadors", had taken upon themselves the mission of civilization. These "backward, pagan, primitive, heathen" people had to be lifted out of their baseness and brought into the christian and civilized world. The English offered themselves up as the example of supreme civilization; the Indians and other less "fortunate ' races should be pleased to follow in their footsteps.

Early contact between English settlers and the American Indians proved not too disastrous; for both groups there was a period of waiting, of uncertainty about relative strengths. At first the Indians seemed pleasant, they even supplied food to the struggling settlements. But by 1622 attitudes of distrust and hatred were developing, with quarrels arising over food and land, over disrespect and ill-treatment, ending in violence and massacre.[1] Thereafter the whites held a worsening image of the Indian; thereafter most settlers gave little thought to trying to save, convert or civilize him. He became not a person worthy of respect or conversion but an object fit only for extermination. Throughout the rest of the seventeenth and eighteenth centuries the mainstream of English religion largely ignored the welfare and position of the Indian; only a few token gestures were made, as in the education of some Indians at places such as Dartmouth College. Whatever little concern was shown for other races was largely the work of smaller, individual protestant sects.

The racial situation was worsened by contact with black Africans.[2] But it should be noted that the English did not show a sense of racial superiority in all settings that concerned the black man. For example, in the seventeenth and eighteenth centuries there seems to have existed a situation of racial equality between the few English traders resident on the African coast and the local African population. Of course, in real power terms, the English could hardly afford to show a sense of racial superiority in that setting. Rather local circumstances dictated that the English be ready to work on a basis of coexistence, establishing friendly relations with African chiefs, sometimes even acting subserviently, and taking African concubines. But this apparent easiness in racial relations was dramatically altered in other settings. For example, back home in England Englishmen could afford to take a rather paternalistic view towards black people. In the eighteenth century it was fashionable for the well-to-do to have a black domestic servant, and by 1770 about ten thousand Africans were held in England as chattel-slaves, generally fairly well treated but held to be inferior.[3] Such slave-holding obviously connoted racist sentiments, and even the freeing of English slaves in the later eighteenth century could not eradicate the heritage of this kind of feeling. But it was in the Caribbean and the southern American colonies that the most virulent form of racism was festering. By the eighteenth century South Carolina and the West Indies were operating a most rigorous and inhumane slave system.

There were ideological foundations for such feelings, as revealed in both the Bible and Tudor literature.[4] Sometimes blackness was linked to evil and violence, sometimes fears arose because of the blackman's supposed sexual prowess, at other times he was related to the apes or seen only as a child. Such negative attributes were reinforced by the economic necessities of the developing colonies where a large supply of cheap labour was needed. Slaves seemed to provide the answer but the successful operation of such a system required that the blackman be degraded and institutionalized as a mere chattel. Psychologically, also, the white settlers found it necessary to relegate all slaves (and Africans, free as well as unfree) to a position of inferiority. The settlers, somewhat isolated, felt insecure in the face of possible, and real, slave insurrection. To overcome such feelings the settlers compensated by putting on a stronger air of superiority and intolerance, with the aim of cowing the slaves into submission.

The first slaves were carried on an English ship in the 1560s, by Jack Hawkins from Guinea to Hispaniola. The first slaves were taken to an English colony in 1619, to Jamestown, Virginia. Thereafter the English slave trade grew apace. English interest in Africa became consolidated through the growth of this trade. Since 1553 a number of attempts had been made by English companies to develop a trade in the Gambia and Gold Coast regions, in ivory, hides, and gold.[5] Some success was achieved; up to 1800 gold to the value of £600 million was taken from the Gold Coast although it was falling off markedly in the eighteenth century. After the 1660s permanent forts were established in both areas, to be used in the following decades by the Royal African Company as bases for the slave trade. Its success was later interrupted by the intrusion of a number of private carriers, riding on the crest of the slave trade boom. By the eighteenth century British slavers had far outstripped the activities of their French, Dutch and other European rivals. With the average rate of return of about ten per cent some large profits were made, and also losses. Liverpool and west coast ports developed rapidly.[6]

With slave-trading at a peak in the eighteenth century it was not surprising that attitudes towards the blacks became further hardened. Edward Long, a judge of the vice-admiralty court and a member of the legislative assembly in Jamaica, wrote in 1774 that the Negro was "void of genius", being "almost incapable of making any progress . . . They have no moral sensations . . . no wish but to idle".[7] In short, since they were dissimilar "to the rest of mankind, must we not conclude that they are a different species of the same genus?" Justification for the slave trade was offered along the lines that the slave was being saved from a life of barbarity and violence in Africa by being brought into contact with the civilized life of the planter in America.

The emergence of a class of planters — a planter aristocracy — in the West Indies and the southern American colonies involved the transfer o of English notions of social and political hierarchy.[8] This meant that a labouring class was needed to undertake the clearing of land and the growing of produce. In the early seventeenth century it was found that the local inhabitants, Caribs and Indians, were next to useless. Then white indentured labourers were brought in, mainly from Ireland. Between 1654 and 1686 over ten thousand were taken across the Atlantic.[9] But this source soon dried up and, in any case, much greater numbers of labourers were needed as the colonies entered a sustained development phase. This was associated with the running-down of the small-scale farming of tobacco, cotton and indigo in the mid-seventeenth century in favour of the growing of sugar on a large-scale. So the planter class emerged with huge land holdings acquiring large gangs of slaves from west Africa. Barbados became the model colony of the West Indies. In 1680 it had 175 big planters (holding sixty or more slaves) and although only seven per cent of the total number of land owners they owned over fifty per cent of the land. Apart from gaining an economic hold over the island they also took political power, by restricting the franchise. To control the gangs of labourers a comprehensive law code was worked out treating the slaves as private property and perpetual bondsmen. Indeed slaves in neighbouring Spanish colonies received more rights in law and greater grace in the eyes of the Catholic God than did English slaves in the West Indies and the southern American colonies; but the latter did have one advantage over the former, in that they managed to live longer.

In the long run the planters in the Caribbean were to find that by creating such a large slave society they were undermining the whole nature of the English style of living that they had hoped to create. The total number of slaves carried to the British Caribbean until 1807 (the year of abolition of the trade) was 1,665,000.[10] During the eighteenth century alone, 1,400,000 were transported, 660,000 to Jamaica, 300,000 to the Leeward Islands, 250,000 to Barbados. In the face of such an influx the whites constituted just a small enclave. Not surprisingly new immigration from Britain dwindled, while whites began to move out to the American colonies. Disenchantment was growing among the remaining whites partly because the slaves were not always easy to control. In eighteenth century Jamaica, for example, insurrection and rebellion were almost endemic, averaging about once every five years; some slaves escaped, taking sanctuary in the mountains from where they could continue to harass planters.

The consequences of these pressures were that the nature and quality of the planters' life was going into a decline during the eighteenth century and even more markedly in the early nineteenth century.[11] The planter hoped he could endure his stint out in the Caribbean, drinking heavily, lazing around, keeping up the pretensions of grand English living, waiting for the quick profit to be made which would enable him to return to a country estate in England, before disease and death got him in the tropics. While the black slave might die from poor conditions and hard work in the fields the white planter found survival almost as precarious; if the gin and over-eating did not end his days, malaria and dysentery might, or a hurricane, or a slave riot. Absenteeism was the favourite pastime of the successful planter, but this contributed very directly to the further weakening of the implantation of an English culture in this area. Although higher education was provided for by the founding in 1716 of Codrington College in Barbados, most planters had dwindling faith in the integrity and identity of the English-type culture that they were supposed to be fostering in the tropics but rather looked back to England as offering the true ideal and example. So their children went back to English schools while they themselves hoped it would not be too long before they were back on English soil. Consequently, with a falling white population, with increasing absenteeism, with no educated middle class emerging to manage local affairs, the whole planters' culture stood on shaky foundations — and all that remained was a seething group of black slaves, leaderless, crushed, untrained. Little wonder that the West Indies was overtaken by economic, social and political chaos in the nineteenth century.[12]

The transfer of English culture proceeded more successfully in the American setting, partly for climatic reasons, partly because there was not such a great slave influx, especially in the north. For a few years in the early history of English colonization Barbados had a strong pull on English immigration; but soon Virginia and other American colonies gained the advantage. Indeed during the seventeenth and eighteenth centuries the white population of north America grew in leaps and bounds through both immigration and natural increase. It has been estimated that the eighteenth century increase averaged out at 2½ per cent annually, in marked contrast to the position of whites in the Caribbean.[13] This white predominance, over black imports and Indian natives, allowed English values and institutions to be more firmly transplanted. This was most noticeable in Virginia where although no aristocracy was born social divisions did arise almost as rigidly as in England. Behaviour and living were modelled as closely as local circumstances allowed on the English example. Education followed the English system based on the local parish.

At the same time the American colonies as a whole did not deliberately ape the English style. Especially in the more northern colonies, where puritan and non-conformist thinking was strong, there was always some sense of anti-Englishness. In any case the local environment demanded innovation if the new settlements were to succeed fully. In some colonies social differentiation became blunted and muted; greater mobility and opportunity heralded a more equal and open society. Accordingly the English settlers in north America began to modify, diversify and adapt the English pattern. The settler pushing the frontier further into the hinterland had to rely upon his initiative and individualism; and a spirit of freedom and basic egalitarianism was thought to emerge among this band of isolated individuals confronting a hostile environment. So, in America, in contrast to the Caribbean, the white settlers were making various adaptations to the English pattern, which were to foreshadow the later development of feelings of nationalism and a desire for independence. A clear example of the contrast with the Caribbean and the growth of national feeling in north America was to be seen in the institutes of higher learning. Starting with Harvard College, in 1636, Americans encouraged the development of many such colleges and took pride in their achievements.

By the eighteenth century two patterns of transplantation had emerged in English colonies.[14] In the tropics the standard was the planter society, the few rich and powerful people dominating the whole structure yet having almost no interaction with the bulk of the labouring population. In the more temperate zone the transplanted English settlers were making a more definite impression upon the local environment, through their desire to adopt the new land as their home and through their ability to innovate and adapt upon the English example carried over originally with them. In these areas a new kind of English culture was in the making. And associated with these two patterns were two different styles of imperial political structure.

NOTES

1. L. G. Tyler (ed.), *Narratives of Early Virginia* (New York: Barnes & Noble, 1946)(1907), p. 357; also, S. E. Morison, *The Founding of Harvard College* Cambridge, Mass.: Harvard University Press, 1935), pp. 422–23, and David B. Quinn, *The Roanoke Voyages 1584–90*, I, 368–82.

2. General — Roy Lewis and Y. Foy, *The British in Africa* (London: Weidenfeld & Nicolson, 1971). Margaret Priestley, *West African Trade and Coast Society: A Family Study* (London: Oxford University Press, 1969), provides a case study of racial relationships in the economic setting.
3. James Walvin, *Black and White: The Negro and English Society, 1555–1945* (London: Allen Lane, 1973) and F. O. Shyllon, *Black Slaves in Britain* (London: Oxford University Press, 1974).
4. Winthrop Jordan, *White over Black* (Baltimore: Penguin, 1969); G. Williams, " 'Savages Noble and Ignoble' ", *Journal of Imperial and Commonwealth History* 6 (1977–78): 300–13.
5. Re English activity in Africa, Robin Hallet, *The Penetration of Africa: European Enterprise and Exploration Principally in Northern and Western Africa up to 1830* (London: Routledge & Kegan, 1965); early trade — Kenneth G. Davies, *The Royal African Company* (London: Longmans, Green, 1957).
6. B. B. Parkinson, R. E. Hyde and S. Marriner, "The Nature and Profitability of the Liverpool Slave Trade", *Economic History Review* 5 (1952–53): 368–77.
7. Edward Long, *History of Jamaica* (London: Cass, 1971)(1774).
8. Richard B. Sheridan, *Sugar and Slavery: An Economic History of the West Indies, 1623–1775* (Baltimore: Caribbean Universities Press, 1974), and "The Wealth of Jamaica in the Eighteenth Century", *Economic History Review* 18 (1965): 292–311, 21 (1968): 46–61.
9. Richard Dunn, *Sugar and Slaves: The Rise of the Planter Class in the English West Indies, 1624–1713* (London: Cape, 1973) provides detailed examination of the labour question and the land-holding of planters, especially pp. 70–87, 96–141, 224–49.
10. The best analysis of the slave trade to the Americas is by Philip D. Curtin, *The Atlantic Slave Trade: A Census* (Madison: University of Wisconsin Press, 1969), pp. 87–89, 268; also see his *The Image of Africa: British Ideas and Action* (Madison: University of Wisconsin Press, 1964) on intellectual background.
11. Lowell J. Ragatz, *The Fall of The Planter Class in the British Caribbean, 1763–1833* (New York: Century, 1929); look at the changing fortunes of a particular family, for example Price, in Michael Craton and James Walvin, *A Jamaican Plantation* (Toronto: University Press, 1970).
12. General Sudies — Vincent T. Harlow, *A History of Barbados, 1625–85* (Oxford: Clarendon, 1926); Robert H. Schomburgk, *The History of Barbados* (London: Cass, 1971), (1774); and as a general assessment, Robert P. Thomas, "The Sugar Colonies of the Old Empire: Profit or Loss for Great Britain", *Economic History Review* 21 (1968): 30–45.
13. Daniel S. Smith, "The Demographic History of Colonial New England", *Journal of Economic History* 32 (1972): 165–83; J. Potter, "The Growth of Population in America, 1700–1860" in D. V. Glass & D. Eversley (eds.), *Population in History* (London: Edward Arnold, 1965), pp. 631–79. For a general survey, see Marcus L. Hansen, *The Atlantic Migration, 1607–1860: A History of the Continuing Settlement of the United States* (Cambridge, Mass.: Harvard University Press, 1951). Some figures on British emigration are contained in *Calendar of State Papers, Colonial Series, America and the West Indies*, for example 1661–68, no. 204 and 1669–74, no. 1101.
14. Carl and R. Bridenbaugh, *No Peace Beyond the Line* (New York: Oxford University Press, 1972), pp. 160–61.

4
Government for the Whites and by the Whites

Initially the English government had no set views on how to govern the new colonies. In the absence of precedence the government acted in ad hoc fashion, making sure that its duties and responsibilities were kept to a minimum. The most satisfactory approach seemed to be to grant charters to companies of interested investors, allowing them to trade and found plantations but also charging them with the duty of government. Chartered company government became one of the standard approaches during this period, just as it was again revived at the end of the nineteenth century when the British government was interested in tropical expansion but did not want to become deeply committed.

Three kinds of colonial rule emerged in America: where the company was virtually self-governing, with wide powers and little royal control, such as in Connecticut; where individual proprietors rather than companies were entrusted with rights of ownership and government, such as in Maryland; and where the crown could exercise real power through appointing a governor, such as in Virginia. Obviously the latter form, called royal colonies, received increasing favour from the home government so that from the later seventeenth century the trend was towards this form of government. This tied in with the English government's formulation of various economic policies, later called mercantilism, wherein the state was called upon to play a greater role of regulation in the economic life of the empire. Consequently, after the 1660s a small band of Englishmen, mainly among administrators and royal advisers, began to take an increasing interest in the empire and its control. To their way of thinking the early seventeenth century official attitude of neglect, disinterest, haphazard growth and minimal restriction should be reversed for a greater coordination between the various imperial parts, and ultimate direction and control from England.

Such views were being more clearly and definitely propounded as the eighteenth century progressed. Since 1660 committees had been assisting the privy council with advice on foreign plantations and trade. Then, in the eighteenth century the Board of Trade (created 1696) took on political and colonial functions, as well as its usual concern for the advancement of English trade. It drafted instructions to governors, collected information about the colonies and tried to ensure that royal orders were carried out in the colonies. Writers such as Josiah Child, John Cary and William Petty argued that the colonies should be governed as useful appendages to Britain — a sound, mercantilist approach.[1] By the 1750s the British government was determined that the colonies should be more efficiently and effectively governed, in the interests of Britain. The flouting and ignoring of imperial orders, and contempt for British authority should be checked and the colonies brought into one grand plan of imperial direction, based on Britain.

In the colonies, however, such views were not generally warmly welcomed. From the beginning some colonies had developed their own sense of freedom and independence. For example, early Massachusetts was quite "democratic" and almost wholly self-governing — with governor and council elected by all citizens, and subject to the wishes of a popular assembly — at a time when England was moving towards absolute royal power. The writings of civil war writers such as James Harrington, and later the doctrines of John Locke, struck responsive cords among American settlers.[2] So, in the later seventeenth century American colonies were operating a more widely-based suffrage than England, with the intention of extending political power to more people and of eliminating corruption from politics. Experiments were tried using the secret ballot. The idea took root that the people of the colonies were best protected against encroachments from outside, alien executives by supporting local representative assemblies. In all, a tradition was growing up emphasizing the natural right of colonists to look after their own affairs and of the power of the people to check the actions of governors and administrators.

Popular government in the empire began in 1619 in Virginia when a representative assembly of colonists met at the request of the governor. This popular element, although not yet fully democratic, rapidly became a treasured right of Americans and meant that inevitably serious clashes would result between these local representative assemblies and the executive power of governor and council, armed with veto rights, various royal prerogatives and the backing of the metropolitan government. English officials made a serious miscalculation about the nature of the representative bodies, seeing them merely as small local governments. But to the colonists these bodies were virtually free and responsible governments, exercising full powers, and protecting the citizens from the arbitrary and ill-informed dictates of an alien government thousands of miles away.

By and large, English politicians tended to ignore the colonies. Royal advisers, however, especially in the Board of Trade, were by the early eighteenth century becoming increasingly upset with the flouting of the mercantilist regulations.[3] So the machinery of royal enforcement was increased, through customs collectors, naval officers, vice admiralty courts. But still the violations occurred. Meanwhile, the popular assemblies were annoyed at the success of the British government in "royalizing" all except two of the colonies, and with the increasing use of royal prerogatives to flout and override the popular will.

In the 1760s the final battle between these two sources of power erupted, when the crown determined upon even further consolidation and centralization under its control, in matters such as British legislation for the collection from the colonies of revenues for defence purposes. The American assemblies were fully aware of the current British political scene, with the idea of supremacy of parliament and in particular with the exercise by the parliament of financial control over the executive and applied it to their own situation. While in mercantile theory it was sensible for London to be the fulcrum of political power, developments in America over the previous 150 years had allowed the local representative assemblies to acquire sufficient legislative power and independence to oppose violently this outside intrusion.[4] In theory the British parliament could so act; in practice it was too late, without bringing on the real challenge that ended in the victory of the Americans. Not only had English settlers taken to America the whole heritage of English politics, they and their issue had also subsequently embraced the whole corpus of English political ideas thrown up in the tumultuous years of the seventeenth century.[5] At the same time the Americans had been fashioning their own political institutions to regulate their own affairs, and they were not later to be denied this system for the sake of a greater imperial whole and of Britain. They had grown self-reliant and had developed their own sense of identity; although drawing upon an English background, they had in their relative isolation been able to forge their own national character, which by the 1770s was strong enough for them to stand up against Britain. Admittedly political grievances were not the soul cause of the American revolt, and initially Americans thought some compromise could be worked out. But the British government would not back down. It was determined that the colonists should be controlled and contained: yet, lacking the power and, perhaps, the will to do so, Britain was forced in 1783 to give independence to the thirteen colonies.

Developments in the West Indies were tempestuous but not so catastrophic. There the royal system of government was more easily established, even though some of the colonies started on a corporate basis as in north America. In the West Indies English settlers took with them full political rights and established elected legislative assemblies which, like their American counterparts, were jealous of their powers. But although there were a number of confrontations between these elected bodies and the executive controlled from London, and although sometimes a governor was murdered, these differences of opinion never resulted in a final dissolution of the imperial link. This was mainly because the West Indian legislatures were based on a much more narrow popular base than in the American colonies; indeed the former were really oligarchies, controlled by planters and working in their own selfish interests. This allowed the royal wish ultimately to be dominant, with governors reducing their dependence on the elected assemblies and increasing their own powers. The assemblies for their part failed to grow so independently as their northern counterparts.

Colonies conquered from foreign powers, such as West Indies islands and Quebec from the French, presented England with a new problem of government. Some respect was paid to the existing French system of government; for practical reasons some continuity was allowed for established institutions and practices. But the British government was also keen to make its own imprint, and obviously favoured the royal system. This meant that the colonies were to be administered by a nominated governor and his nominated council. In some areas an elected assembly was also allowed, but the British government was determined that the latter should never again be allowed to get out of control. Indeed the lesson that the British seemed to learn from the American revolt was that control from the centre should be made more effective rather than relaxed.[6] So, for example, in the constitutional arrangements made for Canada in 1791 provision was made for a strong executive, providing the imperial connection and acting as a check and balance on local representative forces. Worried by the democratic excesses of contemporary France Britain wanted to ensure that a balance was maintained in the colonies, with the executive effectively checking local forces which it was argued would act only for particular vested interests.

This desire for a tight control from London operating through royal servants was carried further in respect of colonies acquired during the Napoleonic wars. For example, in Trinidad and the Cape power resided in a governor, appointed and paid from London, without the trammels of any representative body. In the 1830s the government of these two colonies was modified to the form which became known as the crown colony system of government – a governor aided by nominated executive and legislative council, but still no representative body. This became the standard form of government in tropical colonies, where English settlement was limited, where non-English European communities might already be present and where the bulk of the population consisted of people of another race and culture.

This trend towards ultimate control from Britain was justified upon the grounds that it allowed a more enlightened form of trusteeship than would be possible through an elected body representing only a limited section of the community. Furthermore, British administrators claimed that under their care all the disparate colonies could be moulded along British lines and so begin to participate in benefits of the supposedly superior British civilization. But underlying these reasons were the ever-pressing security interests of mercantilist Britain. More direct control allowed a more effective maintenance of British power in those areas, without the fear of disruption by a quarrelsome local legislative body. In this context the desire for royal control in conquered colonies is clearly understandable.

Besides the two broad approaches of royal (or crown colony) government and a more democratic system based on some degree of popular representation, other methods of administration were used in the great variety of colonies that Britain had acquired. British imperialists had no chance of instituting a standard system of administration. For example, in Honduras a cooptive Public Meeting and elected magistrates attended to the various functions of government. In conquered colonies there was usually a period of military administration before a civilian government took over. The penal colony of New South Wales started off with a governor supported by heavy military backing. Along the west Africa coast (the Gold Coast, the Gambia) merchants operated forts from which they conducted their trading activities (mainly in slaves) and over which they were charged with administrative duties; after 1750, however, the British government began to involve itself more in the area, at least indirectly (through the grant of a subsidy).[7] This situation arose mainly for security reasons, Britain becoming concerned about the activities of other Europeans in the area. From the 1820s the British government felt increasingly obliged to interfere, bringing in the regular system of crown colony government, partly with the aim of suppressing the slave trade but also because of local disturbances.

In other words the administration of so many different and scattered colonies was a matter for which British officials had neither a preconceived plan nor any standard model. The one consistent trend that did emerge as the decades passed, especially noticeable during the eighteenth century, was the desire of the British government to bring them under a closer control. Yet, as was so clearly indicated in the case of the thirteen American colonies, this was short sighted to the extent that it failed to give sufficient attention to the desires of colonial subjects. Mercantile theory put too much emphasis upon the needs of the central metropolitan power at the expense of the colonial appendages. Some writers, however, did realize that this approach might produce tension and friction. Charles Davenant, although speaking up for the dominance and control of Britain, appreciated that national ideas would emerge in the colonies; so they should be given a wide measure of self government which would hopefully find a balance with Britain's ultimate power of control.[8] Thomas Pownall went further, perhaps foreshadowing the idea of a British commonwealth.[9] He envisaged the creation of a "grand marine dominion", held together by imperial sentiment and patriotism which transcended colonial and national rivalries. In such a creation the Americans might develop national feelings but would still want to stay a part of the empire. The pivot would still need to be London where a single colonial department would administer colonial affairs; but the colonies would also send representatives to the British parliament. So, a few imperialists were thinking of ways of coordinating Britain's empire into a long term harmonious and effective unit, giving some scope to colonial as well as to British interests. But these ideas were still fuzzy and as the American experience showed most officials were not very sympathetic. British thinking still centred on herself; the colonies were meant mainly as useful adjuncts.

NOTES

1. Joseph Child, *A New Discourse on Trade* (London, 1693), pp. 165—69, 183.
2. G. P. Gooch, *English Democratic Ideas in the Seventeenth Century* (New York: Harper, 1959)(1898), p. 305; Charles Blitzer (ed.), *The Political Writings of James Harrington* (New York: Liberal Arts Press, 1955); John Locke, *Two Treatises on Civil Government* (London: Dent, 1953)(1685) and *An Essay Concerning Human Understanding* (London: Dent, 1974)(1690).
3. James A. Henretta, *"Salutary Neglect": Colonial Administration under the Duke of Newcastle* (Princeton: University Press, 1972); Thomas Pownall, *The Administration of the Colonies* 2nd ed., (London: 1765), especially pp. 19—24; "The British Atlantic Empire before the American Revolution", *Journal of Imperial and Commonwealth History* 8 (1979—80): 1—130.
4. There is extensive literature on the outbreak of the American War of Independence which is beyond the scope of this work; for quick reference, Charles M. Andrews, *The Colonial Background of the American Revolution* rev. ed., (New Haven: Yale University Press, 1931); Charles H. McIlwain, *The American Revolution* (New York: Macmillan, 1923); Oliver M. Dickerson, *The Navigation Acts and the American Revolution* (Philadelphia: University of Pennsylvania Press, 1951); Lawrence H. Gipson, *The Coming of the Revolution, 1763—75* (New York: Harper and Row, 1954); Edmund S. and Helen M. Morgan, *The Stamp Act Crisis* (Chapel Hill; University of North Carolina Press, 1953); these are classic statements on a very extensive field of research. See review article, M. Kaplanoff, "England, America, and the American Revolution", *Historical Journal* 21 (1978): 409—27.
5. On the legal background of the eighteenth century, as seen by contemporaries, see William Blackstone, *Commentaries on the Laws of England* (London: Caddell & Davies, 1803)(1765) and of the more specific A. Stokes, *View of the Constitution of the British Colonies in North America and the West Indies* (London: Dawsons, 1969)(1783).
6. Helen Taft Manning, *British Colonial Government after the American Revolution* (New Haven: Yale University Press, 1933).
7. See E. C. Martin, *British West African Settlements, 1750—1821* (London: Longmans, 1927).
8. Charles Davenant, *Discourses on the Public Revenues and on the Trade of England* (London, 1698).
9. Pownall, *Administration of the Colonies*, p. 201.

5
Developing an Empire for England?

The central importance of Britain and the peripheral role of the colonies was clearly indicated in the attention that Britain paid to the development of her colonies during this period. In brief, no government responsibility was seen to exist. A colony was meant to pay its own way and development of its wealth through the exploitation of its resources was a private affair, left to the initiative and activity of a few individuals. The daunting task facing colonial settlers and traders was to find some staple for export to Britain and Europe. Gold was highly desired but only a little was found, in west Africa; slaves became the most important export from that area. Skins and furs provided a basis for economic growth in the Hudson Bay and Ontario areas, fish from Newfoundland, and mahogany from Honduras. Often colonies staggered until a satisfactory export could be found, such as happened in New South Wales until wool exports were welcomed in London. The two most important colonial commodities bought by Britain in the eighteenth century were sugar and timber. The former came from the West Indies so that the small island colonies there were regarded as the economic jewels of the empire. But initially, in the early seventeenth century, economic progress in those islands had been slow, as tobacco, cotton, indigo and other products were tried for export potential. The swing to sugar from the middle of the century, aided by the use of slave labour, spelled the turning point in their economic development; sugar was exported to Britain and the American colonies and re-exported to Europe.[1] Britain also needed ready supplies of timber (and naval stores) for her expanding navy. The Baltic offered a source but in mercantilist times it was deemed wise to have full control over such supplies rather than be subject to the whims of a foreign power. So the great forest stands of the Carolinas acquired a special significance to Britain; and later the same attention was paid to the great lumber reaches of Canada.[2] But, as already pointed out, the New England colonies represented little economic worth to mercantilist Britain since they competed with rather than complemented the British economy.

The economic development of a colony in this period was a matter geared mainly to the greater wealth and development of Britain rather than that of the colony itself. Raw materials and food were to be produced for Britain's use (including re-export). Yet the system did not work wholly in favour of British growth; in some cases the power needs of Britain did result in the colony's economy being encouraged and promoted. This arose through the mercantilist device of bounties, subsidies and protection. For example, in the early eighteenth century the West Indies sugar colonies began to suffer in the face of competition from French colonies. So the British government responded in 1733 with the Molasses Act, to protect the sugar trade, especially with the American colonies. This brought great prosperity to the islands and made many fortunes. The Price family, for example, built up a huge estate, Worthy Park, employing eighteen hundred slaves.[3] In 1789 William Pitt estimated that £4 million was being sent back annually to Britain by way of plantation profits.[4] The giving of a monopoly to Americans to grow tobacco was made at Britain's expense. Likewise, bounties to the north American timber industry proved to be a costly business for Britain, although individual timber merchants in Britain as well as in Canada benefited thereby. In terms of cost and efficiency Britain would have done well to have retained her Baltic sources of supply. It was estimated in the 1820s that Canadian timber production had been over-stimulated by the bounty system at a cost of about £1 million annually to the British government. So, while in many respects the mercantile system was organized to benefit Britain there were side effects leading to the stimulation of production of certain goods in the colonies at Britain's expense.

Businessmen in the more northern colonies of America were dissatisfied with the emphasis that the mercantilist system put on Britain's interests and the restrictions placed on colonial development. They were willing to take initiatives in trade and industry. They objected to the notion that Britain should process materials supplied by the colonies; instead they wanted to build up their own secondary industries (especially of iron products). They objected to the restrictions placed upon their ability to trade with whomever they liked; instead all goods to foreign countries were meant to be re-exported through London, reducing their returns on colonial exports and adding to the costs of foreign imports. In fact, this restrictive system did not work perfectly and many of the colonists were finding in the eighteenth century that the system could be breached; sometimes too the British government found concessions had to be made. But even when the government tried to enforce the rules more rigorously, the evasions and floutings continued. Local initiatives and entrepreneurship could not be contained or destroyed, especially in the northern colonies, in marked contrast to the West Indies where the mercantilist system was more meekly accepted. In the north industries were slowly developing, the ship-building industry was prospering, trading (via smuggling) was much more open than the rules allowed. With rising productivity and cheap and improved distribution, a snowballing effect set in — of improved economic organization, of greater specialization and diversification, and overall increased production. American shippers found that they were not disadvantaged by mercantilist shipping regulations; indeed, they handled over one half of America's overseas commerce. So the northern colonies were developing an economic viability all of their own, sometimes irrespective, sometimes because of mercantilist regulations.[5]

In other words, economic development was not necessarily hindered or dampened by the system; indeed, sometimes it helped, while sometimes the development progressed regardless of mercantilism. The British government found the practical application of mercantilist principles to real colonial situations to be difficult; often the principles were imperfectly or incorrectly conceived, many times they were loosely or only partially applied, sometimes they were ignored or modified. So the mercantilist system appeared as a patchwork. More often than not it helped Britain; it sometimes helped colonial development; but it could also create ultimate economic weaknesses.

The long term, harmful aspects of mercantile imperialism were beginning to be felt in the West Indies from the end of the eighteenth century.[6] Absenteeism deprived the area of the entrepreneurship and initiative that characterized the economic development of the northern colonies. Furthermore, only minimal economic diversification took place. Each island relied upon one basic export crop which left it economically vulnerable when bad times set in, through crop failure, competition or changing consumer interest. Furthermore, whatever capital the islands were generating was often being lost through repatriation to Britain so that no new capital expansion could take place, even if there were someone able to undertake it. So, the slave economies ran down to catastrophic levels by the 1840s.

A similar predicament faced other tropical and sub-tropical areas. The southern American colonies followed the West Indian pattern, although to a lesser degree. They were basically a mono-culture, geared to exporting one or perhaps two primary produce crops, with little industry, and only a limited base of entrepreneurship. All such areas were to be bedevilled by a lack of industrialization beyond the most elementary levels of processing. Even so, it was possible for some limited forms of development to take place in those areas, although mainly along exploitative lines. The long term development of the country was not taken into account, but short term financial gains could be made, and not only by entrepreneurs based in Britain. In west Africa, for example, the slave trade brought benefits not only to British slavers but also to local leaders. At the height of the trade (about 1785) the Gold Coast was exporting about ten thousand slaves annually, with local chiefs and merchants participating in the profits of the system. As a result their wealth and power increased considerably, one notable example being the Brew family of Cape Castle.[7] But unlike the entrepreneurs of north America such people in west Africa had neither the inclination nor perhaps the ability to set their wealth and power to further and different developmental uses. Instead they just allowed further exploitation of this one resource, human labour, to continue, to the extent that some communities in Africa became impoverished through loss of population. Consequently tropical areas generally remained economically subservient to the greater needs of Britain; local forces were not sufficiently strong or skilled to take bold, new initiaitives on their own account. In any case, unlike the north American colonies, they did not have a preponderance of white settlers, people who were sufficiently familiar with and willing to take such new initiatives.

In the closing decades of the eighteenth century problems with the mercantilist system were becoming increasingly apparent to British politicians. The difficulty of effectively enforcing the system in America and the subsequent revolt highlighted such problems. In any case the mercantilist system, while allowing that most economic benefits should flow to Britain, also contemplated that certain burdens should be put upon Britain, particularly in the form of administrative and military costs. It suited the purposes of the British government to pay and provide for the governor and other such servants of a royal colony since they provided the vital link carrying British policy from London to that colony. Yet with a growing number of colonies the cost of colonial administration was rising, a matter which greatly displeased the British Treasury. Frequently it was found that new colonies could not stand on their own feet if they did not have a valuable export staple. Consequently at various stages the British government had to provide financial support to colonies such as Newfoundland, Nova Scotia, Quebec, Florida, Bermuda and the Bahamas.

Of greater significance than administrative costs were the military responsibilities that Britain had to undertake. Sometimes these were costs incurred in waging mercantilist wars, for the greater glory of Britain, such as the capture of Jamaica. But by the eighteenth century an increasing proportion went to local defensive operations — forts and garrisons in northern America, protecting the settlers against the French and the Indians; naval bases in the West Indies as security against sea attacks and pirates; patrols by the navy to check France and Spain. Of course, some of these costs were really attributable to Britain, being in the furtherance of her world-wide interests and power. In an age of great power struggles Britain's very survival required her to keep increasing her armed strength, especially the navy. The war of Jenkins' ear in 1739 cost Britain £31 million, the seven years' war 1756–63 £71.5 million, and the American war of independence about £100 million.[8] So, although the cost of protecting the colonies was a sizeable portion of the total defence bill met by Britain, it is difficult to differentiate exactly colonial costs from general foreign policy expenditure.

It has been estimated that between 1714 and 1788 the American colonies cost the British Treasury over £40.5 million. Naval, military and other such defence costs took up the bulk of this sum, £32.5 million. Administrative costs ran to £4.5 million, and compensation and relief to loyalists affected by the American revolution amounted to £3.5 million. The colonists were being provided, at no cost to themselves, with the benefit of British naval and military protection. A British politician claimed in 1767 that the cost of troops in America had risen to almost £400,000 annually. Indeed the cost of America was escalating rapidly, from £70,000 in 1748 to £350,000 in 1764; in the early 1760s the British army in America more than doubled, to 7,500 men.

A complete balance sheet of economic benefits that were gained by Britain out of her empire and the cost of running and maintaining that empire can probably never be accurately worked out, mainly because of limitations in relevant statistics. Various estimates have been made, although it is a topic that has generated considerable discrepancy and argument, because of the different assumptions that different theorists have made. One writer has argued that the profits made from sugar (and the slave trade) in the West Indies contributed significantly to the eighteenth century economic development of Britain; an opponent argues the reverse, that British development was retarded by the cost of the Indies (through sugar tariffs and the cost of Caribbean defence); indeed, it is claimed that money invested in the West Indies could have been better spent at home, especially in terms of social returns. This kind of debate has also arisen with respect to the American colonies. In the mid-eighteenth century many colonists objected to mercantilist imperialism on the grounds that it was hindering American development while promoting the British economy; and historians since then have produced supporting evidence. But fairly convincing arguments have also been produced moderating such claims. It has been calculated that the per capita annual costs which the mercantilist system imposed on American colonists for the decade 1763–72 was $1.20. To be set against this were the benefits per capita derived through protection and so forth, amounting to 94 cents. On balance, the per capita loss suffered by such colonist because of mercantilism was 26 cents. This was at a time when the average per capita income was about $100. So the burden endured by the colonists (for the benefit of Britain) was just over one per cent of the colonial national income, certainly no crushing disadvantage and no great hindrance to the prospect of economic development in the colonies.

In other words, mercantilism did not work to the exclusive benefit of Britain; colonies were not unduly stifled by the various restrictions; some could even take advantage of the system. Likewise for Britain there was not unbridled benefit from the system; the question of imperial costs became a matter of mounting concern from the second half of the eighteenth century. Josiah Tucker complained that colonies distracted Britain from the pursuit of her true economic interests. Adam Smith mounted a more determined campaign of criticism, arguing in 1776 that although Europe was Britain's best market British eyes had been deflected, foolishly, to the American empire.[9] He claimed that empires were expensive, swallowing up capital (mainly for defence) that could have been put to better use elsewhere. Only a few individuals benefited from the operation of mercantilism, while the masses of Britain paid higher duties on foreign products and footed the bill for colonial defence and administration. Instead, Smith suggested that Britain create a free-trading structure, with Europe, America, the whole world; the colonies could be let go, if need be. So long as Britain was competitive she would retain her colonial markets and America, and make valuable inroads into Europe.

No immediate action was taken by the government along these lines; indeed it thought in almost reverse terms, to hold on to the empire, by force if need be, and to strengthen imperial bonds. But in the nineteenth century the criticism of the system mounted. One writer figured in 1836 that Britain annually paid out over £8.5 million on account of the colonies — administration and defence costing over £5 million, and colonial monopolies over £2.7 million. Sir Isaac Coffin complained to the House of Commons in 1822 that Canada cost Britain £500,000 per year while contributing not even 500 pence; the timber trade benefited Canadians to the extent of £300,000 each year.[10] In similar fashion the purchase of sugar from the West Indies was a costly item for Britain; for example, averaging out the 1835–41 bills she could have saved £5.5 million annually by buying sugar on the world market at the prevailing price. And this deficit was not compensated for by large exports to those colonies. At that stage the West Indies made a further charge upon the British Treasury in the form of compensation (£18.5 million) for the abolition of slavery. Colonial costs seemed to be ever mounting. The establishments in Australia were an annual drain; it was not until 1833 that New South Wales' revenues balanced expenditure. The disturbances in the two Canadas in the 1830s meant further defence costs for Britain. Special projects, such as the Rideau Canal in Canada, called for British assistance. Emigration schemes made various calls upon the British Treasury. And there were the annual costs of the regular establishments, such as defence installations in places ranging from Jamaica to Van Diemen's Land, from the Cape to Gibraltar.

In the wake of this rising criticism it was not surprising that from the third decade of the nineteenth century the British parliament began progressively to dismantle the web of commercial restrictions that had grown up under mercantilist inspiration.[11] The job was completed by 1860, with the last vestiges of tariffs and protection swept away. Probably the strongest argument leading to the advance of free trade was not the factor of cost but the rising force of industrialism. With Britain acquiring in the eighteenth century an industrial know-how and infrastructure not even contemplated by other nations, and under the pressure of theories by Adam Smith and others that British manufactures should be able to compete in markets anywhere, parliament in the early nineteenth century began to respond to this industrialist philosophy of free trade. Britain's industrial lead would give her the power, if trade was free and open, to swamp markets right around the world, whereas the mercantilist system restricted these opportunities. British machines could quickly and cheaply replace the hand-work of labourers everywhere.

Britain had not made her mercantilist empire into an economically self-contained unit; indeed, she had not seriously tried to do so. Trading figures given above indicate that such an objective was not near to being realized. The example of the United States indicated quite clearly that possession of colonies was not a necessary attribute of trade, for even after the successful revolution British trade with that area continued strongly. Adam Smith seemed correct to call into question the whole worth of colonies. Yet in one respect they still had value: on a per capita basis they more than justified their existence in terms of imports. In 1838 each Australian colonist was buying British manufactures worth £10/7s/0d; the lowest colonial purchaser was the Canadian (£1/7s/0d), but even this far outstripped foreign purchases — United States, 10s/0d per head, Holland and Germany, 4s/10d per head.[12]

The early nineteenth century saw the fading of the mercantilist system and its replacement by an era of free trade. In both worlds Britain was dominant. Out of mercantilism Britain had been able to forge a base of power that allowed her to dominate the nineteenth century world-scene. Part of that base consisted of her empire acquired by bouts of bravery, recklessness and dogged determination. Yet the empire was not the sum total of British power; whether in mercantilist or free trade times Britain could hardly afford to rely solely upon her colonial possessions to acquire and maintain the position of dominance. This position was boosted by economic power gained through trade and financial nous, and rested upon the possession of a sufficient military (mainly naval) capability. And underpinning this rise to dominance was the belief in the superiority of British civilization which pushed various subjects to capitalize upon the weaknesses and inadequacies of others, to seek advantages wherever possible, to take calculated risks for gain and to thwart possible rivals.

Britain stood predominant, made powerful and rich through her enterprising subjects operating successfully the mercantilist approach. The full extent of the significance of the infiltration into India was not yet realized. Indeed, problems in the operation of the East India Company sometimes left the British government in distress; financial scandals involving company officials, almost endless fighting against other Europeans or

Indian rulers, occasional financial weaknesses by the Company, threw burdens onto the British government which some politicians would sooner not pick up.[13] Yet India could serve to compensate for losses in the west. The American revolt weakened Britain across the Atlantic, and in mercantilist terms brought a great loss of face. Sagging prestige could herald falling mercantile power. But British triumphs elsewhere, British expansion in other directions could compensate for this set-back.

Yet in the 1760s and 1770s India also looked to be a liability in some respects. Charges of maladministration, financial intrigues, and a severe famine — in 1770 reducing Bengal's population by almost one-third — posed a challenge to Britain perhaps not as severe as the American humiliation but nevertheless of sufficient proportions to warrant an assertion of firm authority. The government replied with stronger legislation, bringing the British parliament (and cabinet) into more direct supervision over affairs in India in 1773 and 1784. Pitt's India Act of the latter year meant that the Company, which once operated as the administrator as well as an economic agent, had to retract effectively to a commercial, trading capacity; administrative duties now came under closer British control. The ensuing governor-general, Cornwallis, brought the elements of British authority to India in an efficient bureaucracy, a full court structure and an organized tax system.

So, while British power in the Americas was being checked, British authority in India was firming. The chartered company was giving way to official British control. And elsewhere, too, British power was growing. Some historians, notably Vincent Harlow, have argued that the loss in America brought a direct swing in British policy to the eastern part of the globe.[14] Certainly in the later eighteenth century one can see British tentacles (mainly economic) creeping into the orient. Already foundations of British authority were being laid in Ceylon (1796),[15] and the Malay Straits (Penang, 1786, Province Wellesley, 1800, both acquired by the East India Company).[16] The China trade was opening up in the early nineteenth century.[17] The successful waging of the Napoleonic Wars by British troops brought other possessions such as Mauritius in the western Indian Ocean.

This intrusion into the east was made with commercial objectives in mind — the mercantilist principle still ruled. Just as initial entry came in the form of the East India Company so during the eighteenth and early nineteenth centuries the British presence was associated most clearly with traders and shippers. For example, Alexander Dalrymple in the second half of the eighteenth century looked hopefully for wealth from Borneo and other lesser known parts of the East Indies.[18] So hopes of economic advantage predominated.

Yet the swing to the east should not be too deliberately emphasized. More significantly it should be noted that both the British political and economic elite thought in world-wide, expansive terms; the traders, shippers and investors set the basic pattern which the politicians tended to follow. The former having grown powerful and rich through taking economic advantage, saw in the closing decades of the eighteenth century and at the turn of the new century that more opportunities lay in casting their net as widely as possible. In simple terms, "the world was their oyster, for the taking". So they operated in the east — in India, the Malay Peninsular, China — but they operated further than that. Latin America was also theirs for the asking; and so British investors began to seek their fortune there. Similarly the Pacific: the wealth of that area was hardly appreciated in the closing stages of the eighteenth century; yet it was worthwhile at least to have a presence there. So New South Wales was taken, for various reasons. It was a penal refuge, but it was also seen as a base for operations in the whole area, it linked Latin America and China, it checked French or other foreign power, it might have economic potential and it certainly provided a supply base for British traders to other areas (especially the east).[19]

So British interests were not deliberately swinging to the east as a result of their discomfiture in America; they were plumbing the possibilities of that new market, but they were also keen to follow up any advantage anywhere — the orient, the Pacific, America. The *modus operandi* was to be mainly through economic infiltration. The vital economic and political agents of mercantilist Britain had succeeded in vanquishing their opponents. The Spanish, Portuguese, Dutch and French had not been able to maintain their own against growing British power. Relying primarily upon naval strength, British political might had been able to check and contain the continental rivals. In equivalent vein the aggressive entrepreneurship of British merchants and investors had outbid their competitors. So British naval and civilian shipping could range far and wide, asserting British political and economic power respectively.

The British had actively sought to build up this power, both economic and political. So a world-wide trading network was being fashioned by the turn of the nineteenth century, and a world-wide colonial empire was in the making. Yet the former had probably been fashioned more skilfully and successfully than the latter. The British economic agents learned well how to operate in the mercantilist world, but they also were sufficiently astute (or lucky) to realize by the end of the eighteenth century that the world economic scene was undergoing a significant change, that new rules were to come into operation, and indeed British economic agents helped materially to shape the new rules. But in the political arena, British agents had not been quite so successful or clever. They had come unstuck in north America. Their approach had been to shape the rules to suit whatever situation existed, which worked well enough in ordinary times but could prove unsatisfactory if a crisis arose. It could also lead to a diffusion of imperial power as the American example illustrated. This ad hoc approach was to receive some serious rethinking as a result of the American experience, with the result that the nineteenth century brought the framing of more exact and settled rules.

The decades from Tudor times through to the early nineteenth century were marked by an almost continual growth of English (and British) power. The home island had become more united, the population was growing, its economy was rising, industrialism was beginning during the eighteenth century, the navy received only momentary set-backs and kept outclassing rivals, colonial possessions were being acquired (with the addition of more manpower), and most importantly British economic influence was seeping into all corners of the globe. Such success, such rising prosperity was almost necessarily bound up with an exuberant confidence, a bold assertiveness in the inherent capacity of the British citizen. Such a belief, such a bravado was to carry the British imperialist to daring assertions of power as the nineteenth century progressed.

NOTES

1. Noel Deerr, *The History of Sugar* (London: Chapman & Hall, 1947).
2. Arthur M. Lower, *Great Britain's Woodyard: British America and the Timber Trade* (Montreal: McGill-Queen's University Press, 1973).
3. Michael Craton and James Walvin, *A Jamaican Plantation* (Toronto: University Press, 1970).
4. J. Rose, *William Pitt and the Great War* (London: Bell, 1911), p. 370.
5. The economic relationship between the American colonies and Britain and the development of the former is well analyzed in the following: James F. Shepherd and G. M. Walton, *Shipping, Maritime Trade and the Economic Development of Colonial North America* (London: Cambridge University Press, 1972); James F. Shepherd and S. Williamson, "The Coastal Trade of the British North American Colonies, 1768—72", *Journal of Economic History* 32 (1972): 783—810; Gary M. Walton, "The New Economic History and the Burdens of the Navigation Acts", *Economic History Review* 24 (1971): 533—42 and 26 (1973): 687—88; cf. Peter D. McClelland, "The Cost to America of British Imperial Policy", *American Economic Review* 59 (1969): 370—81 and "The New Economic History and the Burdens of the Navigation Acts: A Comment", *Economic History Review* 14 (1973): 679—86.
6. Lowell J. Ragatz, *The Fall of the PLanter Class in the British Caribbean, 1763—1833* (New York: Century, 1929).
7. At the general level of effect upon Africa, see J. D. Fage, "Slavery and the Slave Trade in the Context of West African History", *Journal of African History* 10 (1969): 393—404; at the particular level (the Brew family), see Margaret Priestley, *West African Trade and Coast Society: A Family Study* (London: Oxford University Press, 1969).
8. See the seminar article by Robert P. Thomas, "A Quantitative Approach to the Study of the Effects of British Imperial Policy upon Colonial Welfare: Some Preliminary Findings", *Journal of Economic History* 25 (1965): 615—38, which

analyzes the profits from trade and shipping and sets off the costs of administration and defence; also see K. Knorr, *British Colonial Theories, 1570–1850* (Toronto: University Press, 1963), pp. 233, 148–68, 317–28, 351. Both Lilian C. A. & C. M. Knowles, *The Economic Development of the British Overseas Empire* (London: Routledge, 1924), pp. 93–95, and Herman Merivale, *Lectures on Colonization and Colonies* (London: Oxford University Press, 1928)(1841–42), p. 237, give eighteenth century estimates. No accurate balance sheet can be provided but the above sources provide considerable evidence on costs.

9. Adam Smith, *An Inquiry into the Nature and Causes of the Wealth of Nations* 6th ed., (London: University Paperbacks, 1950)(1776); E. A. Benians, "Adam Smith's Project of an Empire", *Cambridge Historical Journal* 17 (1974): 249–83.
10. Coffin, *Hansard*, 2nd Series, 6 (1822): col. 1076; and see Knorr, *British Colonial Theories*, pp. 318–28, re Canadian and West Indian costs.
11. Robert L. Schuyler, *The Fall of the Old Colonial System: A Study in British Free Trade, 1770–1870* (London: Oxford University Press, 1945); Judith Blow Williams, *British Commercial Policy and Trade Expansion, 1750–1850* (Oxford: Clarendon, 1972).
12. Herman Merivale, pp. 248–49.
13. R. Mukherjee, *The Rise and Fall of the East India Company* (Bombay: Popular Prakashan, 1973); Holden Furber, *John Company at Work* (Cambridge, Mass.: Harvard University Press, 1948); Mark Bence-Jones, *Clive of India* (London: Constable, 1974); Keith Feiling, *Warren Hastings* (London: Macmillan, 1954); P. J. Marshall, *East India Fortunes: The British in Bengal in the Eighteenth Century* (Oxford: Clarendon, 1976); K. N. Chaudhuri, *The Trading World of Asia and the English East India Company, 1660–1760* (Cambridge: University Press, 1978).
14. Vincent T. Harlow, *The Founding of the Second British Empire* (London: Longmans, 1952); cf. D. L. Mackay, "Direction and Purpose in British Imperial Policy, 1783–1801", *Historical Journal* 17 (1974): 487–501.
15. Lennox A. Mills, *Ceylon Under British Rule, 1795–1932* (London: Cass, 1964) (1933).
16. Nicholas Tarling, *Anglo-Dutch Rivalry in the Malay World 1780–1824* (Cambridge: University Press, 1962); Kennedy G. Tregonning, *The British in Malaya: The First Forty Years, 1786–1826* (Tucson: University of Arizona Press, 1965).
17. Michael Greenberg, *British Trade and the Opening of China, 1800–42* (London: Cambridge University Press, 1969)(1951).
18. Howard T. Fry, *Alexander Dalrymple (1737–1808) and the Expansion of British Trade* (London: Cass, 1970).
19. Brian C. Fitzpatrick, *British Impèrialism and Australia, 1783–1833: An Economic History of Australasia* (London: Allen & Unwin, 1939); also note economic penetration into New Zealand at the end of the eighteenth century.

PART TWO

Riding to a Crest on Free Trade

1820s–1880s

6
Comfortable Power

After the French revolutionary and Napoleonic wars British power was undoubtedly supreme throughout the world. The war yielded rich and vital territories which, added to an existing large empire in north America, the Caribbean, India and New South Wales, made Britain an imperial giant in a world where the other imperial powers were diminishing in stature. In mercantilist terms this empire made Britain unchallengeable since she could fall back on such huge (although uncounted) population reserves. This manpower could be backed up with the strongest navy in the world, after the Napoleonic wars left Britain as sole mistress of the seas. Apart from these obvious manifestations of strength Britain could draw upon another base of power which throughout most of the nineteenth century was to assure her the position of being the greatest imperial power in the world — an industrial lead over all other nations. Through a fortunate concatenation between the innovative skills of scientists and the surplus capital of entrepreneurs the impetus was given to Britain in the later stages of the eighteenth century that allowed the rise of an industrial economy. This was based upon the use of steam-power to drive machines so that the face of Britain moved from one of small-scale domestic manufacturing in villages closely linked to a rural life to rapidly growing cities, centred on factories, turning out machine-made goods. In this economic transformation Britain stood at least one generation ahead of any other nation. British machines churned out a wide variety of cheap textiles and iron and steel goods far in excess of the domestic market. So Britain turned to the whole of the world as her market-place, abandoning the more closed and inward-looking ideas of the mercantilist world (which in practice had never worked as a fully self-contained unit).

Britain's imperial power throughout most of the nineteenth century rested on this combination of large empire (and consequent large population), large navy (with strategic bases) and, probably most important, an industrial lead. Until the last two decades of the century this power was not under serious challenge by any nation, in any of the three respects.[1] With such an unchallenged supremacy, British policy in imperial matters could take a somewhat relaxed attitude towards the assertion of power; knowing that it had such reserves the British government generally did not feel under any compulsion to assert itself overtly or behave aggressively, except when a real challenge did arise in particular local circumstances. While she was unchallenged she could adopt a low, almost defensive posture in world affairs. In like manner, backed up with such a sense of security and ultimate control, British thinking could accept ideas of freedom and liberty. It is not surprising that it was in nineteenth century Britain that a liberal philosophy was formulated and gained adherents. In such a strong nation it was easy to tolerate a variety of philsophical creeds preaching individual freedom and responsibility, greater political democracy, free trade, self-government and nationalism for oppressed people. In the eighteenth century, with the rival nations still struggling for dominance, it seemed sensible policy for the government to seek tight and centralized control over all aspects of its power — colonies, navy, trade and people. But by the 1840s Britain, with no possible threat anywhere, could afford to adopt a more liberal policy. Free trade, freer colonies and the free movement of British subjects could all bring advantages, insuring the maintenance of Britain's supreme power; the possible disadvantages seemed slight.

As to the government of an empire in an age when the dominant philosophy stressed liberalism and freedom there was some sense of contradiction in the very possession of colonies. Some people did rail against the continuance of Britain's hold over the possessions across the seas. Richard Cobden and other "little Englanders" urged that the colonies should be allowed to go their own way,[2] but such ideas, although loudly announced, never became a majority view. The bulk of public opinion agreed that there was no point in deliberately giving up or abandoning the existing empire; retain what there already was, since it was thought to be an integral part of Britain's power. At the same time a loosening of the framework was seen as desirable and practicable. As Lord Grey said:

> I consider, then, that the British Colonial Empire ought to be maintained, principally because I do not consider that the Nation would be justified in throwing off the responsibility it has incurred by the acquisition of this dominion, and because I believe that much of the power and influence of this Country depends upon its having large Colonial possessions in different parts of the world.[3]

Imperial philosophy moved in the direction of London exercising an increasingly light control over and minimal interference with colonies showing sufficient political maturity. This somewhat passive approach was adopted in the belief that this was the best means of ensuring that Britain maintained a continuing influence over such colonies; if too' heavy a control was maintained the colonies would eventually feel constrained to make a deliberate break with London, by force if necessary, a repeat of the problem with the thirteen American colonies. The solution was to grant representative government to colonies of growing maturity, followed up with self-government or responsible government, and to encourage colonial federation among the smaller units so that a more self-reliant polity could emerge.

This approach was adopted at different stages during the nineteenth century for the various white settlement colonies. These were the territories — the colonies in Canada and Australia, New Zealand, Cape Colony and Natal — where political maturity was believed to be rapidly developing because the white settlers carried with them the essence of the British system.[4] The pattern of development in these places was to establish firmly the representative principle; in some cases the colonies started off with crown colony or military government status and so the first move was to expand the legislative structure by adding firstly unofficial and later elected members. Once representative government was firmly instituted the next step was in the direction of establishing the principle of responsible government. In theory, British control was still complete; British legislative supremacy could not be challenged.[5] The Colonial Office could review, even disallow, colonial legislation. But in practice, the British parliament spent minimal time considering colonial matters while the Colonial Office avoided interference, favouring the granting of greater responsibility to the colonial legislatures.

The desirability of granting more local control arose out of problems being experienced in Canada in the 1830s; pressure groups there were asking for greater powers to be given to the elective legislative body, including control over the executive branch. Apart from this colonial initiative a pressure group ("colonial reformers") had arisen in Britain. In the 1830s spokesmen such as Edward Gibbon Wakefield were urging a greater measure of freedom and responsibility for the colonies, local control rather than inefficient superintendence from the Colonial Office.[6] Both pressure groups came together, their ideas receiving specific formulation in the Durham Report of 1839; although addressed to these special Canadian problems it later came to take on a general significance.[7] With the aim of preserving the British connection (and also of swamping the French influence) Durham advised that the local Canadian population should assume more responsibility over local affairs and that the executive should be made responsible to the popularly elected assembly. Here was the essence of self-government and responsible government; and from this starting point the colonial peoples of Canada, and later the other white settlement colonies, assumed an increasingly wider range of self-governing powers. Actual implementation of these ideas proceeded at a different rate in the various colonies, starting with Nova Scotia in 1848, most colonies obtained responsible government in the 1850s but some, such as the Transvaal, Orange Free State and Southern Rhodesia, did not reach that status until the twentieth century. The lesser the degree of white settlement, and the later the acquisition of the territory, the slower the granting of responsible government.

Hand in hand with this movement towards self-government went an imperial acceptance of at least some degree of colonial nationalism and independence. This was wise policy for an imperial government that wanted to maintain a continuance of ties with its colonies. Especially in Canada after the mid-century there was a rising sense of Canadian nationalism which, if thwarted by a heavy-handed control from London, could only have hastened the desire by the colonials to make a complete break.[8] Instead, the Colonial Office was willing to make increasing concessions to the demands of rising colonial politicians for more independent action. It was expected, however, that whatever separation took place would not be complete but that strong links would still be maintained with Britain. At the same time the Colonial Office furthered schemes of colonial federation or unity, fearing that small, independent colonies trying to function on their own could only collapse, leading to an inevitable British bail-out.[9] So, the confederation of Canada was endorsed in the 1860s, and schemes of federation were contemplated for South Africa and Australasia. Colonial nationalism was seen in Britain as a force that could be used to aid rather than destroy British imperial power.

Allied to this policy of greater freedom and independence for the white colonies was the desire of the British government to transfer more defence responsibilities from its shoulders on to those of the rising colonial nations. The British Treasury, ever worried about costs, produced figures showing what an unfair burden was placed on British taxpayers for the defence of the empire, while the colonial contribution was almost non-existent. Herman Merivale, a trenchant critic in the 1850s, complained of frontier wars in the Cape, Canada, New Zealand and India which were ever costing but never ending. By the 1860s exasperated British officials argued that consonant with responsible government in colonial legislatures was self-reliance in local defence.[10] An 1861 Select Committee of the House of Commons figured that the defence of the empire — involving over forty thousand troops, as well as maintaining garrisons and naval bases — cost Britain £3.2 million whereas the colonies paid only £369,000; and of the later amount, only £73,000 found its way to the British Treasury, the rest being spent in the colonies.[11]

The result was a gradual reduction or withdrawal of the garrisons, from Australia, New Zealand, the West Indies, Ceylon, the Mediterranean and Canada. But little success was achieved in the South African area where a turbulent, expanding frontier meant the need for a continuing British presence. In the late 1870s, for example, wars in that region cost Britain over £6 million.[12] Meanwhile, the withdrawal was accompanied by a colonial response of patriotic nationalism. Volunteer forces were formed, first in Canada and spreading elsewhere, as a partial replacement for British protection. Nevertheless, the British umbrella was not removed in its vital aspect. The British navy still swept the seas clean for Britain and her colonies, and to the colonies this was more important than the necessity of providing some local military force. At this stage, Britain was still willing to shoulder the burden of naval defence.

While the British government could afford to think in relaxed terms with respect to the white settlement colonies, while the imperial mind might bask in an overall sense of power and security, the importance of a show of force was not underestimated or neglected. It was accepted by British statesmen that if Britain was to maintain her position of supreme power she needed to possess real naval and military strength and to display, even to exercise it on suitable occasions. The possession of the strongest navy was seen as essential for Britain as a world power with her maritime empire. Such a navy required bases and so throughout the century extra territory of strategic significance was acquired, even when official policy was not very keen on extending land frontiers into the interior of continents. The bases, such as the Cape, taken during the French revolutionary and Napoleonic wars, became invaluable cogs in the mechanism of naval supply as the century progressed. And more bases were acquired to help maintain the web of British trade and influence as it circled the world. Penang, Singapore, Labuan and Hong Kong came to provide the stepping stones allowing British commerce and power to spread into the east Asian region. Likewise, Aden became a lynch-pin for British trade and defence after the Suez Canal was opened, and provided Britain with an access route to India and the East apart from around the Cape. Also, in the later nineteenth century British imperialists kept an eye on Pacific developments to ensure that they were not excluded from having some strategic bases there. Meanwhile, the acquisition of Cyprus in 1878 gave Britain a base of influence in the eastern Mediterranean. In other words, even during the period of unchallenged supremacy the British government made sure that sufficient bases were obtained, scattered strategically around the world so that British naval power might be easily and effectively used in any ocean and so that British commerce might have ready access to markets anywhere in the world. In the second half of the century these strategic considerations were improved by the laying of land telegraphs and undersea cables to the scattered corners of the globe. By the end of the 1870s cable links hooked Britain not only to north America but to India, Australasia and South Africa.

Official concern for the acquisition of new territory was largely restricted to strategic bases. Until the 1880s British policy was generally disinclined to seek the acquisition of vast tracts of hinterland. In one sense that fitted in with that strand of official thinking favouring a rather loose and free imperial structure; on such an approach the acquisition of further territory seemed an unnecessary step, especially in the absence of any real threat to Britain's power. Furthermore, figures were produced at various stages in the *Parliamentary Papers* showing how costly and burdensome were colonies. So in a period of non-colonialism — rather than anti-colonialism which some commentators believe existed — it seemed strange that vast slabs of empire were being added in the mid-nineteenth century. Considerable expanses of hinterland in west and southern Africa came under British control, along with more slabs of the Indian sub-continent. Moves in the Pacific — New Zealand and Fiji — were also made although here strategic factors were partly involved.

The basic initiative for these acts of expansion came not so much from London as from local pressure points. For example, white settlers moving out from Cape Colony pressed on further inland, regardless of official disapproval, ever seeking new opportunities and fortune, in the same way as settlers from the eastern seaboard of New South Wales moved outwards, almost irresistibly, from the limits of settlement that officialdom tried to fix.[13] Or in west Africa a British presence crept slowly inland, in an informal, protectorate manner rather than as a matter of direct, colonial control.[14]

In India British authority continued to increase throughout the first part of the nineteenth century.[15] Sometimes this started out somewhat informally. Governor-General Wellesley devised the system of subsidiary alliances at the turn of the century. This amounted to a kind of tributary relationship wherein Britain offered protection to an Indian ruler and in return certain financial or land concessions were made to the Company. Furthermore the ruler had to accept a British resident (who would advise on administration, and thereby allow a continuing growth of British authority), and, as well, the ruler had to arrange troops for British use. The Nizam of Hyderabad signed one such treaty in 1798. Sometimes force was needed to subdue less compliant rulers, such as in the second and third Anglo-Maratha wars (1803–5, 1817–19). An aggressive, expansive approach was taken by certain of the governor-generals who, having wide powers as well as the advantage of remoteness from London control, could strike decisively and present a *fait accompli*. Slowness in communication from London meant that the man-on-the-spot could usually have his own way. The Sind, after becoming a subsidiary state in 1838 because it straddled what the British authorities believed to be a vital north-western defence link, was annexed by Napier five years later; he took the simple, bold step because he chose to, with the security factor advanced as the principal justification. Likewise the Punjab seemed a vital area, necessary to protect the Indian heartland; so, after bloody battles against the Sikhs in 1846 the area fell increasingly under British control and was finally annexed in 1849.

British authority would not be brooked in the Indian sub-continent. The eastern frontier, looking fragile, began to fall under British sway in 1826 after British military action. Then in 1852 Lower Burma was annexed, and thirty-six years later Upper Burma; in both cases, limited

British military intervention was used. But not all accretions of territory were by such direct means; the system of subsidiary alliance could lead to a weak state coming under ultimate British control. Also, Governor-General Dalhousie brought into play the doctrine of lapse, wherein British authority could be instituted in a state where a ruler left no natural heir. British India kept growing by both direct and indirect means, and in both cases decisions by the local governor-commander shaped this forward, expansive policy. In India, more than anywhere else, British expansion showed aggressive overtones, and primarily because of the desire of many of the local British leaders to consolidate power there — to remove difficult Indian leaders, to reduce weak Indian leaders, sometimes to replace inefficient local leadership, to subdue a troublesome frontier, mainly in the name of the security of British power. It was in the north-west, on the Afghan periphery, that British policy showed aggressive determination but was unsuccessful. Fearing a growth of Russian influence there — and it was feared by the British that this could pose a threat to the whole British presence in India — Governor-General Auckland mounted a campaign of submission in 1839. By the end of 1841 it ended in disaster and the 16,500 troops withdrew; many had already died in battle or because of the harsh winters. This exercise was to be repeated in 1878—80 and was again to prove costly.

The consolidation of British power in India, especially under Wellesley and Dalhousie, put Britain in a supreme position there. Perhaps not surprisingly the government decided that the role of the Company, which had been fading since the later eighteenth century, should be ended. In 1858 Queen Victoria proclaimed the end of Company rule; its trade monopoly in India had already ceased forty-five years earlier. Instead a secretary of state for India was appointed to supervise the governor-general and his administration; but the governor-general still retained significant authority, as signified by the addition of the title of viceroy in 1861.

The direct action by British agents which marked a number of the Indian advances was not so common in other parts of the world — in the Pacific, Africa or south-east Asia.[16] For example, in Fiji the breakdown of the indigenous political system, and the consequent rise of lawlessness and even anarchy played an important part in leading to final British action. The government in London resisted pressure for annexation through the 1850s and 1860s, but yielded in 1874 when no other satisfactory alternative seemed likely to restore order. Again, New Zealand was annexed in 1840 partly because of this factor of lawlessness. Similar conditions helped determine British action in west and southern Africa and the Malay Peninsula during the third quarter of the nineteenth century. Official policy from London generally took a limited attitude towards expansion, preferring to avoid it as much as possible. Local British groups, however, were to provide most of the pressure for action.

Frequently it was conditions of lawlessness and anarchy, arising from the breakdown of an indigenous political system trying to accommodate white encroachment within its traditional structure, that led to an advance of British authority into new areas of Africa, the Pacific and south-east Asia. So, while official policy from London might take a limited attitude towards expansion, even for strategic reasons, local white forces in the colonial enclaves scattered around the world generally took a more positive attitude towards the need for British expansion. The man on the spot, feeling himself more threatened and insecure than an administrator in Whitehall, saw, or imagined he saw, security problems of grave and immediate import. Sometimes this was because the indigenous population was unsettled, being either angry at white intrusion or unable to control a disintegrating society; sometimes it was because a European nation seemed to be posing a threat, occasionally real but mostly presumed.

Most of the mid-century continuing expansion was inspired in the periphery, out on the frontier, and generally for reasons of local strategic consideration. A threat, real or supposed, to the small band of white settlers, traders or officials became the motivation for military or administrative expansion, pushing out the threatened frontier further away from the nucleus of the existing British presence. Alternatively the basic impelling force was the voracious appetite of rugged, individualist settlers who, facing what they considered to be a relatively powerless and primitive indigenous population, felt they could sweep all before them. So long as adjoining lands looked inviting and offered opportunities for development and prosperity, and while there was a relative power vacuum in those lands, the small band of determined Europeans was prepared to move directly, even aggressively, to assert their own assumed power and cultural superiority, until stopped by another strong military force or culture.[17]

British imperialism operated under a dual approach — directives from London and initiatives from the periphery — because there were two different views as to the position of Britain's power in the imperial setting: a more secure one reposing in London, a less assured one generating in the colonies. Meanwhile, as the century progressed there was an increasing flow of people from Britain who supposedly might strengthen the spread of British culture and civilization around the world. In fact, this flow was not working in that fashion; indeed, over time the migrations helped to weaken British power around the world. Along with the current philosophical strand emphasizing more freedom and liberty for the individual was the notion of free movement of persons. Whereas in the world of mercantilism power was counted partly in terms of retaining and increasing a nation's population, the nineteenth century liberal approach towards imperialism considered such a point largely irrelevant. Rather people should be able to move freely and live wherever they choose; in any case, the loss of a few British subjects to a foreign country seemed to be trivial, considering that Britain had such a large and ever-growing empire.

To many British thinkers at the beginning of the nineteenth century the serious problem facing the British nation was the size of the home population. Malthus' predictions on over-population and fears as to dire consequences therefrom caused some British politicians and administrators to consider schemes for reducing this supposed population burden. In fact the underlying problem was one of unemployment but the immediate worry of the governors was possible violence and disorder. R. J. Wilmot Horton devised some state assistance plans to "shovel out paupers" in the 1820s but these embraced only a very small number of people.[18] More significant were the "scientific" theories of colonization propounded by Edward Gibbon Wakefield. While accepting that people should be able to emigrate anywhere Wakefield saw long-term advantage to Britain if emigration to colonial areas could be systematized by adopting a correct balance between capital and suitable migrants.[19] He hoped that his theories would produce the dual advantage of development in the colonies and alleviation of economic and social problems in Britain, but attempts to follow his approach, in South Australia and New Zealand, did not live up to expectations.

These efforts to encourage migration within the empire were only a secondary part of the total flow of people out of Britain. Hopeful emigrants did not automatically make the empire their first choice. Rather, throughout the nineteenth century the United States provided the greatest allure while the empire always took a minority. Between 1861 and 1900 British migration to the United States lay between 5,000,000 and 7,500,000 whereas to Australasia it was only about 1,100,000 and to Canada about 800,000 (some of whom crossed the border into the States).[20] And in earlier decades the United States always held an easy lead over other areas. Also, in the 1840s and 1850s the famines of Ireland drove hundreds of thousands to seek a new life in the United States.[21] The exodus from Ireland reached staggering proportions; for example, it is estimated that by 1921 over 1,800,000 Irish-born people were living elsewhere (in the United States, Britain and empire), a figure equivalent to forty-three per cent of Ireland's population at that time. Most of the people going overseas made their way as paying individuals and not as state-assisted emigrants. This meant that they could decide where they wanted to go, and so chose the United States, where opportunities for advancement appeared greatest and where for some there was an escape from British rule. Yet the developing white colonies, and even the tropical ones and the areas of British informal influence, were crying out for settlement but receiving only a trickle of people from Britain, except in times of good fortune such as the rush to the gold-fields of Victoria in the early 1850s.

British power was, in fact, being weakened through this migration to foreign lands. Yet it was a matter of no great concern at the time. The British basked in the calm sense of security and supremacy, so much so that very seldom did they feel the need to flex the imperial muscle — or make the leonine pounce — in furtherance of Britain's position. Expansion might have been taking place — "through our man on the veld" — but this was not seen as essential, indeed, sometimes not even desirable, so far as the man behind the desk in Whitehall was concerned. British power was sufficient — "leave well alone". All the world was Britain's oyster; let the traders and investors go to it.

NOTES

1. C. J. Bartlett (ed.), *Britain Pre-Eminent* (London: Macmillan, 1969); Ronald Hyam, *Britain's Imperial Century, 1815—1914* (London: Batsford, 1976); C. C. Eldridge, *Victorian Imperialism* (London: Hodder & Stoughton, 1978) and *England's Mission* (London: Macmillan, 1973); Bernard Porter, *The Lion's Share* (London: Longmans, 1975).
2. Richard Koebner and H. D. Schmidt, *Imperialism* (London: Cambridge University Press, 1964).
3. Henry G. Grey, *The Colonial Policy of Lord John Russell's Administration* (London: Bentley, 1853) 1: pp. 11, 17—18.
4. William P. Morrell, *British Colonial Policy in the Age of Peel and Russell* (Oxford: Clarendon, 1930), *British Colonial Policy in the Mid-Victorian Age: South Africa, New Zealand, the West Indies* (Oxford: Clarendon, 1969); John M. Ward, *Colonial Self-Government, the British Experience, 1759—1856* (London: Macmillan, 1976).
5. D. B. Swinfen, *Imperial Control of Colonial Legislation, 1813—65* (Oxford: Clarendon, 1970); Robert L. Schuyler, *Parliament and the British Empire* (New York: Columbia University Press, 1929), chap. vi; general — A. G. L. Shaw (ed.), *Great Britain and the Colonies, 1815—65* (London: Methuen, 1971); P. Burroughs, "The Determinants of Colonial Self-Government", *Journal of Imperial and Commonwealth History* 6 (1977—78): 314—29.
6. Edward G. Wakefield, *A View of the Art of Colonization* (Oxford: Clarendon, 1914)(1849), pp. 224—321; other contemporary writers — George C. Lewis, *An Essay on the Government of Dependencies* (London: Murray, 1841); John A. Roebuck, *The Colonies of England* (London: Dawsons, 1968)(1849); Sydney S. Bell, *Colonial Administration of Great Britain* (London: Dawsons, 1968) (1859).
7. Charles P. Lucas (ed.), *Lord Durham's Report on the Affairs of British North America* (Oxford: Clarendon, 1912); Ged Martin, *The Durham Report and British Policy* (London: Cambridge University Press, 1973), also his general article, "Was there a British Empire?", *Historical Journal* 15 (1972): 562—69.
8. Charles W. Dilke, *Greater Britain* (London: Macmillan, 1869); Alpheus Todd, *Parliamentary government in the British Colonies* (London: Longmans, Green, 1880); more recent, classic statement — Arthur B. Keith, *Responsible Government in the Dominions*, 2nd ed., rev., 2 vols. (Oxford: Clarendon, 1928).
9. Bruce A. Knox, "The Rise of Colonial Federation as an Object of British Policy, 1850—70", *Journal of British Studies* 11 (1971): 92—112.
10. Herman Merivale, *Lectures on Colonization and Colonies* (London: Oxford University Press, 1928)(1841—42) pp. 236—37; also Robert M. Martin, *History*

of the Colonies of the British Empire (London: Dawsons, 1967)(1842) gives statistical abstracts from the Blue Books of the colonies, including military costs.

11. "Report from the Select Committee on Colonial Military Expenditure", H. of C. No. 423, Great Britain, *Parliamentary Papers* (hereafter *Parl.Pap.*) 13 (1861): 69, and note earlier reports, for example for 1829—47, in H. of C. No. 56, *Parl.Pap.* 32 (1849): 93; for 1853—57, in H. of C. No. 240, *Parl.Pap.* 17 (1859, sess.1): 1; accounts (military) for 1859, H. of C. No. 114, *Parl.Pap.* 17 (1859, sess.2): 11; also, W. B. Tyler, "Sir George Grey, South Africa and the Imperial Military Burden, 1855—60", *Historical Journal* 14 (1971): 581—98.

12. "Statement . . . , 1870—71, for Military Purposes in the Colonies . . . ", H. of C. No. 38, *Parl.Pap.* 42 (1870): 369; "Return of Annual Cost of Colonies, 1859—68 and 1869", H. of C. No. 80, *Parl.Pap.* 49 (1870): 481; "Cost of Colonies, 1869—73", H. of C. No. 194, *Parl.Pap.* 51 (1875): 667; re colonial defence, look at a case study, Desmond Morton, *Ministers and Generals, Politicians and the Canadian Militia, 1868—1914* (Toronto: University Press, 1972).

13. J. S. Galbraith, *Reluctant Empire: British Policy on the South African Frontier, 1834—54* (Berkeley: University of California Press, 1963).

14. J. D. Hargreaves, *Prelude to the Partition of West Africa* (London: Macmillan, 1963).

15. B. B. Misra, *The Central Administration of the East India Company, 1773—1834* (Manchester: University Press, 1959); P. Sunderlal, *British Rule in India* (Bombay: Popular Prakashan, 1973); Cyril H. Philips, *The East India Company, 1784—1834* (Manchester: University Press, 1961).

16. W. D. McIntyre, *The Imperial Frontier in the Tropics, 1865—75* (London: Macmillan, 1967); W. R. Johnston, *Sovereignty and Protection* (Durham, N.C.: Duke University Press, 1973); Nicholas Tarling, *Piracy and Politics in the Malay World* (Melbourne: Cheshire, 1963) and *British Policy in the Malay Peninsula and Archipelago, 1824—71* (Kuala Lumpur: Oxford University Press, 1969).

17. On general nature of free trade imperialism (mid-nineteenth century), see D. K. Fieldhouse, *Economics and Empire, 1830—1914* (London: Weidenfeld & Nicolson, 1974); and more especially John Gallagher and Ronald Robinson, "The Imperialism of Free Trade", *Economic History Review* 6 (1953): 1—15.

18. R. J. Wilmot Horton, *Lectures on Statistics and Political Economy as Affecting the Condition of the Operative and Labouring Classes* (London, 1832), lectures 1, 4, 8, 10; also, various official reports, such as "First Report From Select Committee on Emigration", H. of C. No. 404, *Parl.Pap.* 4 (1826), and second and third reports in *Parl.Pap.* 5 (1826—27): 2, 223; also, H. J. M. Johnston, *British Emigration Policy, 1815—30* (Oxford: Clarendon, 1972), chaps. i, iv, ix, x.

19. Wakefield, *Art of Colonization*, letters 12, 13. For statistics look at annual "General Report of the Colonial Land and Emigration Commissioners", *Parl. Pap.* 1842—73, including Irish figures.

20. Stanley C. Johnson, *A History of Emigration from the United Kingdom to North America, 1763—1912* (London: Cass, 1966)(1913), especially pp. 344—52; W. A. Carrothers, *Emigration from the British Isles* (London: Cass, 1965) (1929), p. 305.

21. Marcus L. Hansen, *The Atlantic Migration, 1607—1860* (Cambridge, Mass.: Harvard University Press, 1951), chaps. vii, x, xi; and the Colonial Land and Emigration Commissioners reports above, for 1847—48 and 1852—53; William K. Hancock, *Survey of British Commonwealth Affairs* (London: Oxford University Press, 1937) 2: pp. 1, 28, 158, 351.

7
Free Trade and Settlement Colonies

The lynch-pin of British power in this period was commercial supremacy. While it was felt necessary for Britain to have the biggest navy, and a string of strategic bases, while she possessed the largest empire and population, the essence of British wealth — and power — was firstly trade, and secondly investment. Through developing the first industrial base Britain became the trading giant, for whom the whole world was considered an outlet. Economic advisers and traders thought far beyond selling just to the home or colonial markets. By mid-century the factories of Britain could produce goods to saturate those markets with ease and still have plenty of iron and steel products for export to America and Europe and cheap textiles that could compete more than favourably with Indian home weaves. In the first half of the nineteenth century the British parliament increasingly adopted the free trade ideas of Adam Smith, accepting the approach that restrictive trading barriers should be broken down in favour of one open international trading unit where trade goods could move freely for sale in the most suitable market. This had a certain inbuilt advantage for Britain with her industrial and technological lead. Her manufactured goods could easily swamp the like products of other countries while in a free trading world Britain could shop around for raw materials from the cheapest market.

In principle a world of free trade did not require a huge empire since a colony would provide no commercial advantage over a non-colonial area. Yet Britain maintained, and increased, her empire, partly because it provided a very ready outlet.[1] While Britain generally bought her imports from wherever they were cheapest, such as wheat from the United States or Russia rather than from Canada, it was found that certain commercial advantages flowed to Britain through the possession of an empire. Chief among these was the stability of colonial markets and the near monopoly conditions that Britain was able to exercise in those areas. So, the Australian colonies did not require much cultivation to ensure that they bought British. Yet, in a free trade world, such a monopoly could easily be whittled away. From mid-century Britain was increasingly to find that Canadian trade turned towards the United States. Still, in a number of Britain's small export industries the colonies proved to be the biggest customer for articles such as clothes and shoes, books and confectionery.

Britain's power arising from trading wealth was based more heavily upon the rest of the world than upon the empire. During the free trade period foreign trade easily dominated colonial trade, in both exports and imports. As to the former, Germany, Holland and Belgium were the biggest purchasers of British goods, followed by the United States. Between 1814 and the 1880s the colonial share of British exports fluctuated between a low of twenty-two per cent and a high of thirty-five per cent of the total.[2] At first the West Indies colonies were the best customers, taking about one-half of exports to the colonies, but from the 1830s India was the biggest customer; also, while both the West Indies and Canada were declining as major markets the Australasian group rose to prominence by the 1850s. As to imports into Britain, again the colonial share was small, usually being between twenty and twenty-five per cent of the total. The United States was Britain's biggest source of imports, followed by Germany, Holland and Belgium, and then an empire source, India. From mid-century Australasian exports were rapidly gaining on those from India. Clearly Britain was taking full advantage of the system of free trade, selling in and buying from the most favourable market. An empire was by no means essential to establishing trading wealth and power.

This fact is made more obvious when Britain's most valuable exports are analyzed. Manufactured textiles were the biggest export earner, yet until the 1880s the colonies seldom took more than thirty per cent of the total; similarly, with iron goods and hardware, the colonial share, although fluctuating somewhat, averaged out at about thirty per cent. Equivalently, Britain's essential import requirements of food, raw materials and minerals showed that generally the empire played only a minor role in comparison with suppliers from the rest of the world. Wheat was the biggest food import but the empire share, although rising, had reached only twenty per cent by 1880. As to total food imports the empire contribution remained fairly steady between the 1850s and the 1880s, at just under twenty per cent. But in one important foodstuff, sugar, the empire source was undoubtedly the largest in the first half of the nineteenth century; by the 1880s, however, the empire produced less than thirty per cent of Britain's sugar imports. In certain foodstuffs, such as rice and spices, where the import bill was not high the empire contribution constituted a near-monopoly. As to raw materials, the colonial supply lay around thirty per cent between the 1850s and the 1880s. Cotton was Britain's biggest buy, the bulk coming from the United States and the empire selling only eight to nine per cent. As to timber products the empire share fell below fifty per cent after full free trade was introduced mid-century. In contrast, however, rising imports of wool saw a strengthening of the colonial hold, up to eighty-seven per cent of total imports in 1880. Certain small-value raw materials such as tin, jute and indigo showed a preponderant colonial source.

While Britain did not look to the colonies as a major trading partner, many of the colonies for their part tended to see economic advantage in retaining an imperial link. Britain provided both a ready source of colonial needs and a convenient outlet for colonial products. India, South Africa and New Zealand looked almost automatically to Britain as their first and major supplier. But some colonies by mid-century were beginning to experience the first strivings of economic nationalism, meaning a partial weaning away from economic dependence upon Britain. Canada began the trend of looking elsewhere for economic partners and in the later nineteenth century some of the Australian colonies were placing very large import orders with countries outside Britain. Yet, while in a mood of growing economic maturity colonies began to look all over the world for the supply of their needs, there was still a close bond between the colonies and Britain with respect to the destination of colonial export products. India, most of the Australasian colonies, New Zealand, Ceylon, Cape Colony and most of the West Indies colonies sold the greater proportion of their exports to Britain; Canada, however, stood apart by not looking first to Britain as an outlet for its goods.

British traders accepted, perhaps too readily, the security which empire markets provided. Consistent with the principles of free trade they did not spend much effort in consolidating those markets but rather concentrated upon obtaining profitable outlets through the whole world, as one giant free-trading unit. So they sought to preserve existing economic links with traditional markets in Europe and the United States and as well devoted attention to seeking new economic advantages in areas hitherto outside the British trading net. As the nineteenth century progressed British economic influence spread further afield, into the far east and Latin America, creating an "informal empire".

This meant that economic expansion did not depend upon the creation of a territorial or political empire; it was not necessary for the land of economic exploitation to be formally annexed to the British crown. Indeed, many British traders and investors preferred the absence of official British control, since the latter so often involved bureaucratic interference, bungling and even restriction; the authorities would bring control and regulations upon the not always lawful activities of the traders. Mostly these agents of economic expansion were happy with a minimal British presence, just sufficient to preserve order so that trade and investment could take place safely. They agreed with a sphere of British influence being mapped out if European powers were setting themselves up in competition, especially in the economic field; or the British traders and investors were ready to accept a British consul if a local ruler was proving obstructive to their economic efforts; or occasionally the British economic interests would ask for a gunboat to be sent in, to threaten and perhaps punish a difficult local group, especially if the latter had turned against the

British economic presence and become destructive of British property and lives. But by and large British traders and investors did not particularly want full British colonial authority to be instituted in the new areas of their economic endeavour — Asia, the Pacific, Africa, Latin America; so long as the local rulers could ensure that British interests could operate there, they preferred only a limited, vague, official British presence hovering in the background, to help protect life and property and keep the trade routes open.

British economic relations with China could be taken as an example of this growth of informal British power. Initial penetration arose out of the activities of the East India Company. Then private traders, such as the Rathbones and Swires, moved in and they, backed up by an official British strategic presence in Hong Kong after 1841, began to insinuate a greater British influence into mainland China as the century progressed. By the 1870s British-Indian-Hong Kong trade with China was at a peak, supplying ninety per cent of China's imports and taking seventy per cent of its exports. Meanwhile Britain was also pushing open markets in Brazil as well as tapping supplies there and in Cuba and Peru.

Shipping was a related aspect of trade where Britain also showed supremacy during the nineteenth century. Apart from the strength of the naval forces Britain led the world during the nineteenth century in commercial shipping. The link with the sea was a time-honoured one in British minds, and it was heightened both by the possession of overseas territories and by the dictates of an international free trade economy. From the 1840s onwards there was an expansion of private shipping, culminating in the emergence of famous passenger and freight lines such as the Peninsular and Oriental, Cunard, and the African Steamship Company.[3] And there was also a host of lesser, local shippers, providing trading services for inland rivers such as the Niger, opening up areas (such as the African Lakes Company on Lake Nyasa), or plying the coastal routes of the Australian colonies. All of these helped keep the trade of the empire, and of the world, flowing in Britain's favour.

The empire of free trade, operating fullblown from the mid-nineteenth century, looked well beyond the retention of an empire established upon mercantilist ideals. The open, expansive approach of free trade meant that industrial Britain needed firstly to keep a foothold in the expanding markets of Europe and the United States as both areas entered industrial phases, and secondly to exploit new areas of the world for materials that could be processed in Britain's factories, as well as to maintain the safe trading bloc which the empire provided. The formal empire provided a safe backstop for British power, but in a world of free trade Britain could build up an informal empire of economic influence wherever opportunities presented themselves. Indeed, from the middle of the century British manufacturers and traders began searching harder for new markets for

British goods because, while British industrial production was rising, traditional markets in Europe and America, although still strong, were not expanding significantly in the face of increasing domestic industrial production in those two areas. Also, new sources of supplies were being sought as Britain increasingly found herself short of essential foodstuffs and raw materials; British food production was failing to meet the needs of an increasingly industrial and urbanized population while British factories had an ever voracious appetite for minerals for processing. So, with the removal of the last vestiges of the protectionist system the economic motive loomed larger in the spread of British power, at least in the sense of furthering the dissemination of a British economic influence, perhaps shadowy and indefinite, into many corners of the world which had hitherto been outside the traditional British fold of empire and established trading partners.

British power as measured in terms of overseas investment followed the broad pattern set by overseas trading. Again, the empire was not the major recipient of the surplus capital generated in industrial Britain. Again, it was foreign countries, mainly Europe and the United States, that attracted the attention of those British financiers who were interested in overseas investment; of course, as with trade, many investors were concerned only with expansion of the home market and did not look overseas. Figures for the early nineteenth century are very rough but the United States was the major beneficiary.[4] It is estimated that in 1838 British investment there amounted to $174 million; it helped cover that country's national debt, bought government securities and was ploughed into canals, cotton and banks. The cotton bust of the 1840s halted confidence but by mid-century British money was again flowing freely, especially into pushing railroads across the great American prairies.

Europe also provided worthwhile opportunities to British financiers. As Belgium and France undertook industrialization major improvements in communications became necessary and, as with the American case, British money flowed in for the construction of European railways — by 1854, about £35–40 million in French railways and £25–30 million in Belgian. In addition there was considerable British investment in the government securities of France and the traditional ally, Portugal. By the 1820s a new area, Latin America, was attracting the interest of the more speculative British investors. There had previously been some links between Britain and Brazil through the latter's gold which Portugal used to pay its debts. When the independence phase swept through south America in the 1820s British money flowed in almost immediately. A mini-boom arose, with £25–30 million being invested, but collapse came virtually as quickly as the boom had started.

While exact figures cannot be given for much of the century it is apparent that overseas investment was a continuing phenomenon, and not

FREE TRADE AND SETTLEMENT COLONIES

an aspect of capitalist development arising in the last three decades of the century after industrialism had generated excess profits that could no longer be profitably used in the further industrialization of Europe or north America. Between 1815 and 1830 it is estimated that Britain sent abroad £100 million while by 1854 the total invested outside Britain stood around £234–282 million. Throughout the century British industrialists and traders had been generating finance for investment at home and abroad, and there was no necessary link between British surplus capital and British imperialism, either formal or informal.

By the 1870s statistics on investment became more detailed, although not complete; so variations do exist, depending upon the assumptions of the different statisticians. In 1870 British investment in foreign countries was almost double the amount in the empire; Europe and the United States were still the leading recipients and, among empire countries, India. As to the type of investment, government bonds were preferred (especially United States bonds), while among joint-stock companies and commercial undertakings railways (especially Indian) attracted most interest. The dispersal of British overseas investment in 1870 is shown in table 2.

Table 2. British Overseas Investment, 1870 – by Place and Type.

Place		Type			
		Govt. bonds		Joint-stock coys Commercial coys	
Europe, Near East	£230m	USA	£160m	India	£105m
USA	£200m	Europe	£109m	Europe	£ 50m
Latin America	£ 85m	India	£ 55m	USA	£ 40m
		Latin America	£ 48m	Australasia	£ 39m
Total foreign	£515m	Near East	£ 38m	S. America	£ 38m
		Australasia	£ 34m	Canada	£ 20m
India/Ceylon	£160m	Rest empire	£ 16m	Foreign banks	£ 10m
Australasia	£ 74m				
Canada/Nfld	£ 20m				
Rest empire	£ 16m				
Total empire	£270m	Total	£459m	Total	£326m

Total £785 million

Source: Adapted from Alex H. Cairncross, *Home and Foreign Investment*, 1870-1913 (Cambridge: University Press, 1953), p. 182.

The dominance of foreign investment over colonial investment persisted until the 1880s but during the previous three decades the empire was rapidly increasing its share at the expense of the foreign sector. Until mid-century little investment interest centred on the colonies. Then a switch took place, as India, Australasia and Canada began to move into a developmental phase, again with emphasis upon railway and public works construction. Anglo-colonial banks were set up, and also investment and land companies. All three institutions were to play a part in helping to expand the empire, increase imperial trade and undertake colonial development. On the one hand railways, canals, telegraph links and water supplies were being constructed; on the other, more sales for British manufacturers were being created, especially in iron and steel goods, rails, rolling stock and engines. At the same time new sources of food and raw materials were being opened up for consumption or processing in Britain. So these investors were acting as one of the lynch-pins in the whole structure of British imperial expansion, and this was true for those investing in foreign countries as well as in the colonies. But colonial investment brought more benefits to Britain, in the purchase of British goods or in the employment of British overseers and technicians. Investment in foreign countries did not necessarily bring such a return.

The returns to the British investor were not generally very exploitative. Certainly in selected cases fortunes were easily made; but there were also devastating defaults, mostly in Latin America. For the 1870s the average dividend was 5.4 per cent with an average increase in capital value of 0.7 per cent; the total annual yield for the decade averaged £52 million. Foreign government bonds (especially of the United States) paid better than colonial ones, hence the preference for the former. Foreign rails also paid better than colonial although in this case more money was invested in the latter. Among the best yields were Portuguese government bonds, land and mortgage companies and colonial banks; but in each case the amount invested was very limited. The average yield on British investment is given in table 3. Overall, the returns were fairly modest, although generally paying a little better than equivalent domestic investments. This provided the inducement to turn overseas, but at the same time greater risks were involved, especially in the case of foreign, as opposed to colonial, countries.

Table 3. British Overseas Investment, 1870s — Average Yield.

Type/place	Market value	Dividend	Type/place	Market value	Dividend
Government bonds			US rail	£40m	5.7%
USA	£160m	6.1%	European rail	£35m	5.3%
Russia	£ 50m	5.9%	S American rail	£10m	5.1%
France, Holland	£ 30m	5.4%	Indian rail	£80m	4.8%
Turkey	£ 20m	5.8%	Canadian rail	£10m	1.9%
Portugal	£ 6m	8.8%	Land, mortgage coys	£ 5m	10.0%
Mexico	£ 3m	—	Colonial banks	£10m	8.4%
India	£ 55m	4.3%	Foreign banks	£ 5m	7.2%
Rest of empire	£ 50m	5.0%	Telegraph/cables	£15m	6.6%

Source: Adapted from Alex H. Cairncross, *Home and Foreign Investment, 1870-1913* (Cambridge: University Press, 1953), p. 229.

While British traders and investors were spinning a web of economic links around the world, in Europe and north America, in Latin America and the east, in the empire and Africa, the British government generally did not move immediately or directly to protect such economic interests and was not keen to extend or promote officially new economic footholds. Individual British subjects were creating an informal empire of economic interests (alongside the existing formal empire) but the government felt no direct obligation to act on behalf of those interests. Economic imperialism existed, but not because of direct governmental policy. Rather, just as the British government was adopting a fairly loose hand with respect to the administration of the white settlement colonies, so it took a fairly casual approach towards the exercise of authority and power in areas where only an informal, economic influence had been established.[5] Consistent with the rationale behind free trade was the British government's belief that its prime duty in the mid-nineteenth century was the encouragement of conditions of free trade, for all nations and all people.

This meant that British power might be used to break monopolies and closed trading systems so that the whole world could be opened to trade; and it might be used to preserve conditions of free trade and open competition. Seldom, however, was British power used to intervene on behalf of the economic interests of British manufacturers, traders or investors. The state's role was not conceived as a tool of business; its aim was to open the field to all, to allow fair competition and favour none. On those occasions when Britain officially intervened it was generally not so much in response to pressure from injured bondholders or traders as to correct an injustice and establish the rule of international law. Markets were opened, treaty rights maintained and British lives protected; but the cause of individual British profits and capital was generally not prosecuted by the exercise of British power and authority. Once markets had been opened up, British traders and investors were on their own; it was left to their own competitive spirit and initiative to take advantage of the opportunities so created, to expand, to create more trade, to build up networks of agencies, banks, insurance and communications, to obtain profits.

Obviously the British government, even if it had desired it, would not have been able to assert much political influence in Europe or the United States as a result of British economic penetration there, because most of the governments were fairly strongly established and economic patterns had long been regularised. But even in the areas more recently brought within the sphere of British economic influence the British government generally chose to assert little or no political influence. In Latin America, the east and the Levant, even where governments were fragile in comparison with the British polity and weak economies often barely managed to function, Britain asserted a very limited political role. Up to the 1880s the imperialism of free trade did not operate as the economic arm of political or territorial imperialism. Areas of economic or informal influence were not seen in government eyes as stepping stones to be brought sooner or later under direct British control.

The main explanation for this approach was that the British government was possessed of a sense of confidence and self-satisfaction. As in the political arena, the government considered that the economic manifestations of its power did not require an aggressive or expansive approach. Satisfied with the supremacy of its power, confident of Britain's industrial lead, government policy could be summed up simply in the desire to maintain that power, to maintain the status quo. With no threat existing to Britain's industrial, trading or financial position there was no need to adopt a forward, expansive policy. British trade expected to benefit more than any other nation if free trade conditions operated, and it was assumed that Britain would accumulate more surplus capital for overseas investment than any other nation. Britain could well afford to adopt free trade since it seemed she would prosper more than anyone else.

British investment in the middle of the century brought a number of developmental advantages to the formal empire. The settlement colonies of Canada and Australia during the first half of the nineteenth century had made only slow progress in achieving economic viability. Canada, however, was helped by the operation of mercantilist preferential duties in favour of its timber, so that by the mid-century, when the duties were withdrawn, the industry was sufficiently established to stand unsupported. For example, in 1854, timber constituted five-sixths of the value of total Canadian exports. The Australian colonies, like all new colonies, struggled at first until wool provided a basic export upon which economic security could rest. Even so, in the first half of the century development proceeded only slowly, as the vast interior plains were opened up to sheep. It was a similar story for New Zealand, Cape Colony and Natal — only very limited development, based on a few primary product exports such as whale oil, timber, wool or skins.

The pace of development quickened considerably after the 1850s, although not as an immediate result of the full introduction of free trade. The impetus of change came more directly from the inflow of capital for development projects. Prior to this period whatever development there had been in the colonies was attributable almost wholly to the efforts and skills of local enterprising settlers. The British government offered no financial help, unless an export involving mercantilist preference was involved, while the British investor gave scarcely a glance to the empire. But the second half of the nineteenth century saw a change on the part of the investor, although not of the government. The British capitalist sent out finance to the colonies, and with that, technology and management. Sometimes factories were set up, but most of the capital flowed into the building of railways, the provision of municipal services and the opening up of land. The improvement of communications, within the colonies and with Britain, received prime consideration, mainly because of the boost this would give to trade. From the 1850s railways were being rapidly constructed; for example, between 1852 and 1858 fifteen hundred miles of track were laid in Canada, most of the money coming from Britain.[6] The flow of money to Australasia was at first centred on land development but after the gold discoveries of the 1850s a rush of railway construction took place. The biggest recipient of imperial investment, however, was not a settlement colony. India readily soaked up British capital, again mainly for railways; by 1872 the nominal value of Indian railway securities quoted on the London market was estimated at £90 million.

At the same time the development of the colonial economies that took place in the later nineteenth century should not be seen as something primed wholly by the input of British capital. The establishment of successful growth economies depended upon combining local initiative and resources with outside capital and know-how. The one without the other was most likely to produce a rather unstable economy and an uncertain future. So, for example, the discovery of gold in Australia produced some local men of capital who played a role in encouraging new schemes; in addition, there was a work-force that was prepared to supply hard labour and initiative, taking advantage of the country's variety of resources, especially sheep and gold. To this was added an influx of British capital and technical resources; the result was a burgeoning economy.

Entwined in this story of growth was a rising sense of economic nationalism on the part of colonial settlers. Just as in the political sphere the colonies were assuming more responsibility and control over their own affairs, so in the economic setting there was a call for economic policy to be geared to colonial rather than British needs. This trend first appeared in Canada about mid-century when certain wealthy and influential individuals started to look beyond Canada having a role simply as supplier of cheap food and raw materials to Britain. They began to urge the build-up of local industries and the creation of protective barriers against Britain and other more industrialized countries which could swamp Canada under free trade policies. They also wanted to be able to make trading arrangements with whichever foreign countries they chose, especially with the United States. As the century drew to a close these nationalistic strivings had become more pronounced, and had spread to Australia. The ultimate significance of this trend was that it showed that colonial capitalists were emerging, determined to establish a sound and growing economy, anxious to assert local control and enterprise, willing to use outside help and finance but not to be subservient to it.

The developments that took place in the settlement colonies in the later nineteenth century were a tribute firstly to local initiative — to the desire for self-development — and secondly to British (and foreign) capital. Basically, it was the local settlers and colonial governments that had to accept the responsibility for and undertake the planning and execution of developments within the economy. In Australia's case development received a real boost in the second half of the century because of the gold discoveries in New South Wales and Victoria in the 1850s, in Queensland in the 1870s and in Western Australia in the 1890s. At the same time the Australian economy always had a vital backstop in the wool industry which continued to increase as settlement spread ever inland, decade upon decade. As the century drew to a close some diversification took place, into other primary products, further mineral exploitation, and a little industrialization. In Canada, timber remained a prime export, attention moving in later decades to the huge forest stands in the west. The input of British capital, aided by some American and local money, helped open up the vast prairies, through the construction of railroads and other communications. Consequently in the later nineteenth century wheat and other primary products began to cut down on the export dominance of timber. In New Zealand, Cape Colony and Natal economic development moved much more slowly, at least until the 1880s. Some capital did flow there but in the absence of a mineral boom or a flourishing export staple development plans were quite limited.[7]

While the Australian and Canadian economies appeared in a more successful light than the South African and New Zealand cases, for all of them development was conceived in terms of hard work and enterprise on the part of settlers, and capital from British private investors.[8] As for the British government, it had no role to play. Government philosophy was not to assist in colonial development. This was especially true in the heyday of free trade. While in mercantilist times one might regard subsidies and protection as forms of official aid to the development of colonial economies, in the nineteenth century the prevailing attitude was to stress individual, as opposed to public, effort. Local settlers and colonial governments should undertake colonial development; British investors and traders might assist but the British government should not directly or actively interfere. The government saw its duty as an enabling one, to open the world to trade and maintain that system; it was not prepared to take a planning, directing or even encouraging role. The exploitation of resources, the development of industries (primary and secondary) and the conduct of trade were left to the individual worker. This formula did achieve some success in settlement colonies; but in the case of more tropical areas, where hardly any British settlement had occurred, the formula was less applicable. Those areas did not have enough white settlers — people imbued with western ideas of development and the exploitation of resources — to provide sufficient impetus and initiative for such development schemes to be planned and undertaken. And in the absence of such schemes there was no call for British capital. A few indigenous inhabitants in tropical colonies did have some desire for development, some even possessed capital, but they were too few in number, and one wonders how well acquainted they were with the nature and methods of western development to be able to carry schemes through to a successful fulfilment. Together with the tropics, the slow pace of development in India during the nineteenth century might be explained in these terms. Although considerable British capital went into the country, there were not enough white settlers to push ahead schemes of economic development; admittedly there were some Indian entrepreneurs who did undertake development but only in a limited fashion.

NOTES

1. General — John Gallagher and Ronald Robinson, "The Imperialism of Free Trade", *Economic History Review* 6 (1953): 1—15; D. K. Fieldhouse, *Economics and Empire*, 1830—1914 (London: Weidenfeld & Nicolson, 1974). On general British economic scene — Donald Winch, *Classical Political Economy and Colonies* (London: Bell, 1965); Bernard Semmel, *The Rise of Free Trade Imperialism* (Cambridge: University Press, 1970).
2. The following trade figures are a composite — relying primarily upon Albert H. Imlah, *Economic Elements in the Pax Britannica* (Cambridge, Mass.: Harvard University Press, 1958), note p. 129, and Werner Schlote, *British Overseas Trade* (Oxford: Blackwell, 1952); also, Alex H. Cairncross, *Home and Foreign Investment, 1870—1913* (Cambridge: University Press, 1953), pp. 180, 189 and John H. Clapham, *An Economic History of Modern Britain* (Cambridge: University Press, 1926—38) 2: pp. 229—30. The primary statistics come from various trade reports, mainly "Trade, Navigation and Commerce, Trade Accounts of the United Kingdom", *Parl.Pap.*, annual (1833—) and "Reports on Trade and Commerce from Her Majesty's Ministers and Consuls", *Parl.Pap.*, annual (1854—), for example for east Africa-Zanzibar.

    Note especially the composite trade statistics in "Trade . . . 1841 to 1850", *Parl.Pap.* 52 (1854): 1; also colonial trade in "Accounts . . . 1846 to 1852", H. of C. No. 15, *Parl.Pap.* 65 (1854): 329; and trade figures with the principal colonies, USA and Brazil in "Accounts . . . 1850 to 1855", H. of C. No. 351, *Parl.Pap.* 55 (1856): 373. For a comparison between the value of exports to the colonies and foreign countries, see "First Report of the Royal Commission on Depression of Trade and Industry", *Parl.Pap.* 21 (1886): 189.
3. Francis E. Hyde, *Cunard and the North Atlantic, 1840—1973* (London: Macmillan, 1975).
4. Again, as with trade, figures are composite; most useful are Leland H. Jenks, *The Migration of British Capital to 1875* (London: Cape, 1927), pp. 85, 99, 193—209, 324—35, 413; also, Imlah, *Economic Elements* and C. K. Hobson, *The Export of Capital* (London: Constable, 1914), pp. 96, 128, 136.
5. On general nature — D. C. M. Platt, *Finance, Trade and Politics in British Foreign Policy, 1815—1914* (Oxford: Clarendon, 1968) and "The Imperialism of Free Trade: Some Reservations", *Economic History Review* 21 (1968): 298—306, and follow-up, 26 (1973): 77—91.

    As a case study — S. Sideri, *Trade and Power: Informal Colonialism in Anglo-Portuguese Relations* (Rotterdam: University Press, 1970); and W. M. Mathew,

"The Imperialism of Free Trade: Peru, 1820—70", *Economic History Review* 21 (1968): 562—79.
6. J. S. Mills, *The Press and Communications of the Empire* (London: British Books, 1924), pp. 19, 42, 48.
7. The scope of development in the respective colonies is beyond the aim of this book. The progress of the colonies can be followed in annual reports to the Secretary of State (starting [728], *Parl.Pap.* 29 (1846): 573); later these became "Reports to the Secretary of State for the Colonies on the Past and Present State of Her Majesty's Colonial Possessions, transmitted with the Blue Books" (starting [1595], *Parl.Pap.* 62 (1852—53): 361 and thereafter annual). Equally useful are the "Statistical Tables Relative to the Colonial and Other Possessions of the United Kingdom" (starting [2127], *Parl.Pap.* 51 (1856): 289 and thereafter annual.

Comparative figures are contained in the series "Statistical Abstracts for the Several Colonial and Other Possessions of the United Kingdom in Each Year" (starting for 1851—63 in 3508, *Parl.Pap.* 55 (1865): 433 and thereafter annual). From the 1868—69 session onwards the abstracts cover the previous fifteen year period.

Short economic summaries and brief statistical information are contained in the annual *Colonial Office List* (published annually in London since 1852).
8. As a sample of basic works on economic development in the settlement colonies, look at William T. Easterbrook and H. G. J. Aitken, *Canadian Economic History* (Toronto: Macmillan, 1956); Craufurd D. W. Goodwin, *Canadian Economic Thought* (Durham, N.C.: Duke University Press, 1961); Brian C. Fitzpatrick, *The British Empire in Australia* (Melbourne: University Press, 1941); Colin G. F. Simkin, *The Instability of a Dependent Economy: Economic Fluctuations in New Zealand, 1840—1914* (London: Oxford University Press, 1951); D. H. Houghton, *The South African Economy* (Cape Town: Oxford University Press, 1964).

8
Problems in the Tropics

Although Britain's tropical empire was continually expanding throughout the nineteenth century it was largely neglected — by the British government, by British investors and by most British traders. Indeed, until the end of the century it was mainly a small band of merchants who kept hold of the imperial ties for Britain in tropical enclaves in Africa and Asia, while in the West Indies and Ceylon that job was performed by a handful of planters. Apart from a few strategic locations the tropical empire presented no real interest to Britain in terms of power or of political development. Likewise in economic matters, apart from sugar and a few export products of small value such as spices, the tropics provided no strong allure to British businessmen. Hence the overall neglect.

One area that endured not only neglect but a positive decline was the West Indies. From boom in the mid-eighteenth century these colonies went into a continuing decay from early in the next century, aided by the ending of the slave system and competition from other producers. The move in 1833 by the British parliament to end the use of slave labour throughout the empire brought a serious labour shortage to those sugar producers, while the problem of the resultant falling production was complicated by the rise of Mauritius as an efficient sugar exporter.[1] By mid-century the West Indies colony was in a severe decline although, contrary to the fears of many, Britain's move to free trading principles had very little to do with this.

The result for this area in political terms was that most of the island colonies had to abandon the political forms that had developed there over earlier centuries and replace them with a more simple structure. The financial difficulties of the governments, along with the fears held by propertied people that the underprivileged masses, the former slaves, would increasingly resort to violence, led to demands for strong executive government to be introduced.[2] This was accompanied by an abandonment of the representative elements in the lower houses. In the later part of the nineteenth century most of the West Indies governments moved in this direction, adopting what became known as the crown colony system of government.[3] So these areas moved against the tide of greater local control and responsible government that was occurring in the settlement colonies. Rather they sank back into the typical mould of bureaucratic, centralized control that was applied to many tropical colonies in the nineteenth century. Only in Barbados, the Bahamas and Bermuda (and partly so in Jamaica after 1884) did an elected lower house function.

This system of government, centralized in the governor and his executive council, assisted by a nominated legislative council and directed from London, was introduced into Trinidad, St Lucia and Ceylon in the early 1830s and from the middle of the century was extended to most of the tropical areas, to the four west African colonies in the 1840s–50s, Hong Kong in 1843, the Straits Settlements in 1867 and Fiji in 1874. Obviously from a London viewpoint this system worked reasonably well. The tropical areas did not possess a sufficiently large white population to entrust representative government to the people; in the West Indies case the settler group had become too entrenched and often corrupt. A strong executive, linked to London, seemed the most efficient and reliable way of ensuring that enough British authority could be asserted without too much effort or cost. It should be noted that while these tropical areas did not bestow on Britain great wealth or power there was no inclination on the part of the British government to dispose of them. Admittedly the abandonment of west Africa was considered in 1865 but no action was taken. There was no intention of reducing British power as expressed by empire; at the same time there was no desire to be burdened down by costly or troublesome colonies. So a minimum administration, with London controls, was set up and a popularly elected element, which could behave disputatiously, was excluded.

The crown colony system was not the only type of administration that was used in tropical areas. While there was some move towards uniformity under that system there was still considerable diversity. In some cases a unique form of government was devised, arising from the local background; British Guiana persisted with the Dutch constitutional structure while in Sarawak a personal fiefdom was created by James Brooke.[4] As a carry-over from the mercantilist system administration by merchants was resorted to in various areas. For instance, a crude government by merchants was not finally abandoned in the Gold Coast until 1843.[5] Meanwhile, a fairly typical scene of tropical imperialism was being enacted in the middle of the century in the Oil rivers of the Niger basin – a creeping imperial influence pushed on under the banner of trade.[6] British merchants were penetrating the area, mainly in search of palm oil; the area was still under the control of different local chiefs. The increasing white presence, however, led to increasing tension and problems of jurisdiction. So a hesitant first step was taken by imperial officialdom, by placing a consul there; in other areas a high commissioner was installed.

The rather limited practical authority of these officials was boosted by a batch of legislative powers, mainly concerning jurisdiction over British subjects in foreign countries, the Foreign Jurisdiction Acts. In time, in

African and Pacific areas, this legislation provided scope for a much greater intrusion of British authority. The legislation was effective so long as some kind of protection relationship was established between the local "sovereign" and Britain; this allowed British scrutiny over the foreign affairs of that territory. Its internal affairs were also affected with respect to the settlement of judicial problems concerning British subjects. From this starting point the local British officer went on later to acquire further powers — advising the chief, especially in financial and land matters. Increasingly the local ruler came under the sway of British administrators, increasingly the latter's independence was whittled away. The plum was ready for the picking, if so desired.

Through the nineteenth century, however, the foreign jurisdiction system generally operated in a loose fashion, without introducing very much British interference in local affairs; it was in the twentieth century that the greater control followed. In earlier decades the British government relied upon the legislation mainly to punish violence and create conditions of order and harmony between a local tribe and a British interloper, generally in the shape of a trader. This was informal imperialism at work — the exercise of a light jurisdictional authority in foreign lands which had a friendly trading relationship with Britain. In this fashion a growing imperial presence was gradually being insinuated into the hinterland of the west African colonies, the Niger basin, southern Africa beyond Cape Colony and various Pacific islands.[7]

A modification of this approach was operating in Asia. Starting with some of the Indian princely states and then spreading to the Malayan peninsula (firstly in Perak in 1874) the "resident" system was put into operation.[8] A British resident or adviser was placed at the side of a local ruler, to assist him especially in financial matters. Again it was based upon the assent of that ruler to some degree of protection from Britain and superintendence over the foreign affairs of his country. Again the British government invoked this form of authority when there had been some degree of penetration by British traders and when civil order was breaking down, creating conditions of lawlessness, anarchy and violence. So an informal British presence was inserted which could later be magnified into a more direct control.

These two methods of indirect imperial influence — foreign jurisdiction and residency — were quite consistent with the prevailing British ethos of free trade. Both had been devised primarily as a response to a growing British economic presence, mainly traders in search of new products for Britain. Both were intended to provide a bare minimum of British authority so that peaceful conditions could reign, allowing the free operation of trade in the area. The British presence meant that these areas could be opened up to world trade, without any particular preference being given to British traders; but the British presence meant that British traders could not be excluded or disadvantaged by the local ruler or a European rival. By contrast the crown colony system of government did not so easily fit into the free trade framework. Its very emphasis on control from London seemed to negate the aspect of greater freedom that was commonly associated with the prevailing liberal philosophy. The main explanation for this apparent exception is that the British government considered more freedom quite inapplicable to her tropical colonies; it could only lead to anarchy and chaos. That would mean a disruption of trade, as well as a diminution of Britain's existing power. So the crown colony system was seen as the most efficient and least costly means of allowing the maintenance of free trade and the continuation of the status quo. In any case, the crown colony system was regularly used at an early stage in the political development of most of the settlement colonies; it operated as a useful preliminary stage in the process of acquiring greater political maturity and independence. Nevertheless, during the nineteenth century, the higher political development of most of the tropical colonies was not even remotely contemplated.

The little interest that did exist in tropical areas lay mainly in their economic potential. Even so, it was only a handful of British traders and planters who ventured to spend any effort in trying to exploit the riches of these places. As to the West Indies interest faded away almost completely, with the sugar industry in a very depressed condition. Some small attempt was made to diversify the economy of the islands but with little success. Some British interest, however, was focused on west Africa from the middle of the nineteenth century. This centred on the "legitimate" trade in palm oil and palm kernels, in opposition to the previous mercantilist profits made out of the trade in slaves. The ending of the British slave trade in 1807 meant that British merchants had to look to the exploitation of Africa's raw materials rather than its bodies. By the 1830s the answer seemed to be palm products, growing in the inland reaches of the Volta river in the Gold Coast, in Sierra Leone and in the Oil rivers east of the Niger delta. This last area, and the Niger hinterland, was to become the most significant source.[9]

The pattern of exploitation that operated during the century was a variation on the method of development being applied in the white settlement colonies. Whereas in the latter case success arose through a combination of local initiatives by white settlers and British capital and techniques, in the African case the successful combination consisted of African middlemen and entrepreneurs obtaining the raw products from African producers and using British merchants for trading outlets, shipping and management expertise. This interaction of African producers and middlemen with British traders and shippers allowed a successful economy to develop in west Africa, but with one important failing. Too much dependence was placed upon one product and only minimal diversification was attempted. Nevertheless, the establishment of a flourishing palm export industry was important for the fact that it showed that development was not a prerogative solely of British settlers. The initiatives taken by some indigenous people were vital, while a few individuals, such as John Sarbah of the Gold Coast, became very powerful and wealthy entrepreneurs, the equal of their leading European rivals.[10]

In the later decades of the nineteenth century the colonies of the Gold Coast and Sierra Leone and the Niger area were operating a favourable export trade concentrating upon palm products, supplemented with small amounts of other products, such as cotton, rubber and groundnuts. For most of the time considerable initiative and control lay in African hands but from the 1880s their grasp was loosening and economic control was passing to alien hands. An increasing intrusion of British traders and shippers began to swing the pattern of trade to sea routes and to a greater dependence on the commercial and financial practices of the west.[11] African entrepreneurs, small traders and producers alike found themselves increasingly subject to the pressures, and whims, of British traders on the coast, or even British shippers, merchants or bankers based in London. At the same time British factories were able to export quantities of cheap manufactured goods, such as textiles, thereby squeezing out the various specialized craft industries that had been a part of traditional Africa. Furthermore, the trend was under way — which was to become common throughout all colonial areas — towards the growing of a single export crop.

This pattern, of the destruction of local industry (and self-sufficiency), was repeated around the world. The most startling results were in India. At the beginning of the nineteenth century Indian cottons could sell much more cheaply in Britain than similar locally-made goods. This led to various protective devices being instituted by the British parliament and consequently Indian cotton exports to Britain dwindled.[12] At the same time, as industrialization progressed, British cottons began to compete successfully in the Indian market; the machine-made goods began to replace Indian handicrafts. The Indian industry declined significantly, being squeezed out of even the domestic market; this had significant social consequences by the mid-century in that it led to the depopulation of the towns which had manufactured and traded in those goods.

Increasingly, in both India and the other parts of the empire, this growing reliance upon British manufactures had important side-effects — an erosion of local self-sufficiency, the undermining of traditional domestic markets and industries, and the diminution of the local entrepreneurial role. To succeed these colonial areas had to accept the economic dictates of industrial Britain, meaning the production of essential raw materials, while the way of survival for an indigenous entrepreneur was to model himself as fully as possible on the style of a British capitalist.

While British economic links with tropical Africa centred mostly on west Africa, with the Gambia as an exception because of French ties, there was a rising British interest in east Africa in the second half of the century. This centred on Zanzibar, an old-established trading base.[13] Trade with Britain almost doubled in the 1860s—70s, mainly in cloves and ivory from Zanzibar in exchange for cotton goods from Britain. Even so, this trade was only one-sixth the value of west African trade, but there was potential for expansion, into the mainland adjacent to Zanzibar. Also, British economic penetration into central Africa was just beginning.

More significant than either the developing African trade or the withering West Indian economies were the opportunities to exploit the markets and resources of the east. Still trying to dominate the scene at the beginning of the nineteenth century was the East India Company but by 1857 it was a spent force, another failure of the mercantile system. Nevertheless, it had helped to establish Britain in a prime position of influence over the economies of the whole region, not only in India but also the Malay peninsula and extending as far as China. The China trade provided the real enticement — thus the acquisition of a string of strategic stepping stones and supply bases earlier in the century, including Singapore, Labuan and Hong Kong. The first and last became important trading bases in their own right, flourishing under a combination of Chinese merchants and a few big British trading firms, such as Guthries in Singapore and Jardines in Hong Kong. Again, as in the west African case, it was shown that non-Europeans could operate successfully alongside western entrepreneurs; and in the Asian case the Chinese were not eventually displaced or reduced in importance as happened in west Africa.

Meanwhile in Ceylon a successful plantation economy was established after the inland kingdom of Kandy had been pacified by 1815. Between the 1830s and the 1880s a flourishing export staple was found in coffee.[14] At first indigenous growers participated predominantly but by mid-century an increasing investment of British capital meant the diminution of the indigenous contribution and the development of a plantation system under the control of a few British growers. These changes were accompanied by a decline of local agriculture and a breakdown of traditional land and economic practices. While these destructive consequences flowed on from imperial intrusion into the traditional system of Ceylon certain positive aspects of western-style development were also occurring. Following the pattern in the white settlement colonies communications in Ceylon were considerably improved; roads were built and in 1864 a railway was commenced. Also, the ancient system of irrigation was restored and improved. So Ceylon experienced, much earlier than any other tropical area, the kinds of development project that were being undertaken in white settlement areas to improve their economic potential. The most obvious explanation for these occurrences in Ceylon was the fact that a group of white planters lived there who were contributing to the success of the island's economy; the development schemes that were undertaken were of greatest benefit to the white planters, while also helping the economy overall to flourish.

As to Oceania, the British took very little economic interest in it until the closing decades of the nineteenth century.[15] Before that there was only a handful of British traders scattered through the myriad of islands. For a while some had luck in the sandalwood trade; a few colonials from the Australasian colonies sailed around there plying a precarious trade. Some Queenslanders and other colonials engaged in a partly legitimate and sometimes illegitimate trade in labour, obtaining the services of islanders to work in the fields "back home". But, overall, Oceania did not amount to much in the world trading stakes and so British interest was minimal. The most attractive area was Fiji and in the second half of the century some British settlement did take place there, trying first cotton and later sugar. Some copra trading also occurred but up to the 1880s the south Pacific islands remained basically untapped, except for those tiny specks of "land" popping out of Pacific waters and covered with guano.

For the tropical colonies during the nineteenth century western-style development was not really considered as a serious possibility. From the capitalist viewpoint in London, the requisite human resources — white settlers with an understanding of the nature of development — were not present in sufficient numbers to undertake responsibility for carrying out projects to improve the economy. To the western mind the indigenous people of tropical areas had over the previous centuries ignored the efficient development, or exploitation, of their land and its natural resources; they had engaged in only the barest minimum of agriculture or mining, their industries remained at a domestic, craft level, and their trading patterns were limited. So little reliance could be put on them to be able to carry out western-style developments in the way that British migrants going out to settle colonies like Canada were doing. So to the imperial mind the vital job of the British government in the tropical domains was to ensure that conditions of free trade pertained; those areas must be brought within the international network and maintained in it. It was then assumed that only a scattering of British traders and shippers would become involved in trying to exploit the wealth of those areas; and it was also assumed that there would be a number of failures in the search for a profitable export commodity. Obviously only the most speculative of investors would be willing to seek a fortune in the unknown potential of the "wilds of Africa" or the mysteries of the east of the waters of the Pacific. The consequence was that such areas existed within Britain's free trade empire to supply a limited range of raw materials, having only moderate and not premium value; in return the tropics could soak up some of the excess manufactures of the British factories, but even in this respect the market provided only a restricted demand.

By the 1880s, the heyday of British free trade, the tropical domain was still almost completely undeveloped, with some exception in the case of Ceylon. Overall, the imperialists had failed to realize that the indigenous entrepreneurs might be used as a base for development. At the same time, it must be acknowledged that the number was not very large and it was not certain how well they fully understand the intricacies of the western commercial system, its financial manoeuvrings and the purport of development. Probably the few successful indigenous merchants who did operate within the western trading framework thought mainly in terms of the easy exploitation of whatever local resource was in keen international demand, without giving any serious consideration to long-term or large-scale development.

Until the 1880s free trade was dominant, and Britain's empire was thought of largely in trade terms. The settlement and tropical colonies existed first and foremost for trading opportunities and advantages. Their development followed for the purpose of increased trade, and since the temperate areas had more to offer they received first attention. Yet free trade meant much more than links between Britain and empire; it embraced the whole world. So even the settlement colonies fell into second place when compared with the trading advantage and investment opportunities available in foreign countries. The empire contributed to the supremacy of British power around the world but it was only part of the whole equation. British power rested firstly on her international industrial-trading-financial lead; then came the empire, as secondary evidence of the extent of British power.

NOTES

1. A. Toussaint, *History of Mauritius* (London: Macmillan, 1977).
2. Hume Wrong, *Government of the West Indies* (Oxford: Clarendon, 1923); Henry Woodcock, *A History of Tobago* (London: Cass, 1971)(1867); "Fourth Report from the Select Committee on Sugar and Coffee Planting in the East and West Indies and the Mauritius", H. of C. No. 184, Part II, *Parl.Pap.* 13 (1847–48): 1; also, sugar, etc. imports into UK, in "Account . . . 1831 to 1855 . . . ", H. of C. No. 209, *Parl.Pap.* 55 (1856): 587.
3. General — Martin Wight, *Development of the Legislative Council, 1606–1945* (London: Faber, 1946).
4. Nicholas Tarling, *Britain, the Brookes and Brunei* (Kuala Lumpur: Oxford University Press, 1973).
5. G. E. Metcalfe, *Maclean of the Gold Coast* (London: Oxford University Press, 1962).
6. K. O. Dike, *Trade and Politics in the Niger Delta, 1830–85* (Oxford: Clarendon, 1956); John E. Flint, *Sir George Goldie and the Making of Nigeria* (London: Oxford University Press, 1960); Colin W. Newbury, *British Policy Towards West Africa* (Oxford: Clarendon, 1964). "Report from the Select Committee on the West Coast of Africa", H. of C. No. 551, *Parl.Pap.* 11 (1842): 1; 12 (1842): 1.

7. W. R. Johnston, *Sovereignty and Protection* (Durham, N.C.: Duke University Press, 1973).
8. C. N. Parkinson, *British Intervention in Malaya, 1867–77* (Singapore: 1960); Charles D. Cowan, *Nineteenth Century Malaya* (London: University of Malaya Press, 1961); Clive M. Turnbull, *The Straits Settlements, 1826–67* (London: Athlone, 1972); Constance M. Turnbull, *A History of Singapore, 1819–1975* (Kuala Lumpur: Oxford University Press, 1977).
9. Dike, *Niger Delta*; A. G. Hopkins, *An Economic History of West Africa* (London: Longman, 1973).
10. R. E. Dumett, "John Sarbah . . . ", *Journal of African History* 14 (1973): 653–79; B. Ratcliffe, "Commerce and Empire: Manchester Merchants and West Africa, 1873–95", *Journal of Imperial and Commonwealth History* 7 (1978–79): 293–320.
11. P. N. Davies, *The Trade Makers: Elder Dempster in West Africa* (London: Allen & Unwin, 1973).
12. P. J. Griffiths, *The British Impact on India* (London: Macdonald, 1952).
13. R. Coupland, *The Exploitation of East Africa, 1856–90* (London: Faber and Faber, 1939).
14. L. A. Mills, *Ceylon under British Rule* (London: Cass, 1964)(1933).
15. William P. Morrell, *Britain in the Pacific Islands* (Oxford: University Press, 1960); John M. Ward, *British Policy in the South Pacific, 1786–1893* (Sydney: Australasian Publishing Company, 1948); John D. Legge, *Britain in Fiji, 1858–80* (London: Macmillan, 1958).

9
The Soul of Empire Civilization

The Imperial mind that emerged during the heady free trade days was necessarily complicated. Obviously a variety of views was expressed as to the nature and meaning of Britain's supremacy, yet nearly all presupposed the idea that British culture and civilization had reached a pinnacle to which other people could, perhaps should, aspire. There were boons and benefits to be gained if other people chose to follow the British way. With respect to migrants going out to British colonies it followed naturally that they would take with them the British style of life. The British parliamentary system was thought to be the model which those settlers should gradually put into operation for themselves; and the British capitalist and free trade system automatically operated in those colonies. The migrants also took with them the basic individual rights and freedoms which were assumed to be the birthright of every Englishman. So, for example, the notion of freedom of speech and freedom of the press, attributes which had emerged in Britain slowly over the centuries, were quickly transplanted in the settlement colonies. Nineteenth century colonial newspapers were generally zealous in their freedom to criticize and even to defame while governments found it hard to muzzle the press effectively for any length of time. This tradition was being transferred to tropical areas also by the end of the century.

British culture, while appreciative of the qualities that a good schooling could bestow on citizens, did not give education such priority as it acquired in the twentieth century. Certainly some good schools and universities existed in Britain but class notions prevailed in a way that meant education was not conceived of as a universal right. The middle class enjoyed the benefits of sound and rigorous instruction — so did the upper class, to the extent that it chose to indulge. Some small degree of mobility, through scholarships, was allowed to children of lower orders. The public school system, with its emphasis on discipline, valour and duty, was commonly regarded as the ideal training for one who intended devoting his life to imperial service. If the qualities of bravery in behaviour, firmness in decision and a degree of understanding of the problems of others could be inculcated at school, the problems of administering a huge empire across the seas would be made so much the easier.

In the colonies, however, the British estimate of the value and purpose of education received some modification as the nineteenth century progressed. Indeed, in some of the white settlement colonies initiatives were taken in schooling, the adoption of which occurred at a later stage in Britain. So whereas generally the colonies were the inheritors of the British example, in educational matters some of the colonies were able to bestow on Britain a new model. The British approach gave a minimal role to the state in the provision of education. Rather, churches and independent bodies were supposed to offer instruction, for charitable or mercenary reasons; and it was expected that many children would miss out. In the colonies, however, a more serious attempt to offer educational opportunities seems to have been made, allowing, of course, for the considerable diversity of the empire.

A cross-sectional survey of education in the 1830s reveals the kind of progress that was being made.[1] In nearly all cases the role of the church was predominant; sometimes there was a little state aid. In a number of cases the extent of school attendance was higher than in England; but the quality of education was not so high as that of the superior establishments in Britain. For example, in Lower Canada the catholic church provided most tuition in French, but some protestant schools also operated, trying to insinuate a British influence. In 1832 it was reported that one out of every three school-age children was at school and about one-half of these attended free. In New South Wales the church of England was the main provider, with a little state assistance. Secondary schooling was very limited. In Cape Colony education was only slowly developing. There were village schools, most of which were free; some existed for Dutch children, a few were free for coloured children while some private schools were run for Hottentots.[2] In the West Indies the church of England and the parish had most influence. White children tended to receive first treatment but some provision was made for black children — sometimes in day schools, or evening schools, and commonly in Sunday schools. The missions were active in black education, receiving some government support in this task. Advance to higher education was quite restricted, apart from attendance at Codrington college in Barbados, or a journey to Britain (which was preferred by those who could afford it).

As the century progressed improvements began to creep into the educational system of various white settlement colonies, which in a number of respects put them in advance of the situation in Britain. Whereas the British philosophy of government shirked from encouraging greater involvement on the part of the state a number of the colonial citizens considered that education was an appropriate responsibility for the state. In the same way as colonial governments were undertaking the construction of railways it could be argued that the provision of a state system of education was a further means of improving the lines of communication in a colony and of developing its resources. The *laissez-faire* approach towards government responsibility did not seem so appropriate for burgeoning colonies. So in Canada and Australasia the trend in the second half of the century was for government policies to be enunciated towards the provision of free, compulsory and secular education at a primary level, obviously with the state taking main responsibility and the churches or private bodies fading into second place. This approach was confirmed in Australia between 1871 and 1885. Where these colonies were moving in advance of Britain was in the aspiration of attaining universal literacy, mainly through the funding of education by the government rather than leaving education to be a matter of voluntary or individual effort. Admittedly achievement of this goal took some time. Less progress was made by the settlement colonies in secondary education which in most cases was still left to the goodwill of charitable and independent institutions. But during the nineteenth century the colonies did begin to provide tertiary instruction locally, although there was a preference by the sons of the colonial gentry to be "finished off" in England, either at university or law school.

Imperial education continued to show considerable diversity throughout the nineteenth century. While English-speaking students gained most benefit from the various developments that were taking place, allowance was made for other educational approaches. So, for example, the French catholic system persisted in parts of Canada although with somewhat stultifying consequences. The education of other racial groups also received some attention in some colonial cases. Probably the most advanced was in New Zealand where provision was made for Maoris to attend regular government schools; in addition special Maori schools were set up by the state. Religious organizations also provided for Maori education. In Cape Colony the missions made some attempt to cater for black education and on the frontiers the mixing of white and black children in the same classes did occur. Other parts of southern Africa looked almost solely at the provision of education for white children.

As to non-white areas, education was promoted most in India and next in west Africa. Even in Company days some Company patronage of Indian education was undertaken, for example at the Calcutta Madrassa and the Sanskrit College. After 1813 the British government began directing money (about £10,000 annually) towards the education of Indians, the aim obviously being to start the westernization of a select group of indigenes, so that they could occupy a rung (albeit low) in the developing administrative civil service. Such an approach reflected a reaction against the feelings of one group of British intellectuals, named the Orientalists. This small band, led by Sir William Jones, saw the value of traditional Indian society and sought to promote a greater understanding of the people. This group who sought not to devalue the Indian heritage met stronger opposition from a westernizing group. James Mill and Thomas

Babington Macaulay in the 1820s and 1830s carried further the depreciation of India's Hindu and Muslim past and sought rather to modernize the society according to British precepts and values.[3] Macaulay's Education Minute of 1835 aimed at creating a small but reliable Indian elite, educated in the western approach, to become the modernizing tools of the British *imperium*. Bengali Hindus sought to take advantage of this British "patronage", so becoming minor clerks for British rule.

The supremacy of British culture, of western education (especially its science and technology) was implicit in these moves, and many aspiring Indian intellectuals concurred. The provision for the establishment of three Indian universities in 1857 was made with such values in mind. Elsewhere, mainly in west Africa, similar although lesser moves were being made in the early nineteenth century; again, the accepted basis was the superiority of western education and values.[4] Missions such as the Church Missionary Society and the Wesleyans were busy in bringing education to places such as Sierra Leone. And this was not just at an elementary level. As early as 1827 a secondary grammar school was set up in black Africa, at Fourah Bay, Sierra Leone. In fact, blacks in west Africa were better cared for in education than their counterparts in Natal during the nineteenth century, although even in the former case it was only a small group of children (mainly sons of chiefs and other important leaders) who were participating. The problem facing the educators was that the task was so huge and the assistance from the government so slight that only a very small percolation of British education to indigenes was occurring throughout the century. Most of the effort was taken up by voluntary agencies, primarily the missionaries. So, overall, the education of the empire was a boon received primarily by the children of white settlers; only a small number of non-white subjects gained access to this key to British civilization.

The health of the empire followed a similar pattern. Tropical health was unheard of. Again, the problems were immense — India with its teeming millions, with famine and poverty, with endemic diseases like cholera and dysentery, with a sagging urban industry which was causing an exodus to the countryside and consequent strains upon the agricultural economy. No easy solutions were available, especially when the prevailing government philosophy was inclined against long-term planning or large-scale government funding and administration.[5]

Most imperial concern centred upon the life of the whites. It was expected that any Englishman who stayed too long in the tropics would die — "the mad dogs and Englishmen" syndrome. Just as white planters in the West Indies had found out earlier, so sailors on slave patrol off west Africa, and governors and army troops on shore, found during the nineteenth century that life in the tropics was a precarious proposition. Between 1825 and 1845 the annual death rate of the above sailors was

54.5 per 1,000 — in one year, 1829, it was 255 per 1,000 — while in the West Indies it was only 18.1 per 1,000 and in Britain a mere 9.8 per 1,000. On shore it was even worse, with malaria, yellow fever and the plague quickly picking off the few available whites. Between 1814 and 1878, eighteen of the sixty governor/administrators of Sierra Leone died in service, either in the colony or on their way home. As to the armed forces of west Africa, early in the century most were criminals, persuaded to volunteer for service there as an alternative to punishment — a punishment worse than death? Between 1822 and 1865 troops were sent in from the West Indies; even they found it difficult to cope. Local troops, recruited after 1865, proved the most satisfactory, from a health and survival point of view.

In colonies of temperate climate the example of Britain was followed. Like education, health affairs were regarded as a matter of local responsibility with the government taking little initiative; it was only in the latter part of the nineteenth century that the British government began to involve itself more directly in health matters and colonial governments followed suit later. So for most of the period only slow progress was made in colonial health although there was an ever-increasing awareness of the meaning of public health, of problems of sanitation and cleanliness. As early as the 1860s a system of swamp drainage and elementary sanitation was under consideration for the rather unhealthy town of Lagos. Increasingly colonial legislators followed British legislation on housing, vaccination, venereal diseases and so forth; again, it was mainly in white settlement colonies that these issues aroused public concern while in coloured areas the masses were ignored.

Two boons of British culture — education and health — transferred to the empire with only moderate results during the nineteenth century. For more progress to have been made in either would have required much more initiative on the part of the colonial governments (and the imperial government also); instead self-help was the accepted position. Furthermore, in practice only a limited range of people received the benefits of British civilization. While British settlers seemed to reap most of the results, the coloured races of the empire were largely ignored or excluded. This was in part a reflection of certain British racial attitudes of the time: these displayed much diversity with most white settlers standing at one end of the spectrum and most officials and missionaries at the other.

Official British policy during the nineteenth century has been characterized mainly under the label of humanitarianism, but within that category there was some divergence of approach.[6] Major backing for official policy came from various missionary groups which emerged in the late eighteenth century, such as the Methodists, the Baptist Missionary Society, the London Missionary Society, the Church Missionary Society and the British and Foreign Bible Society. In spite of their individual differences they were all fired with the zeal to save and convert in the name of christianity, and while they preached the worth of the individual human being their approach presupposed that western man was superior to the pagan beings of other continents.[7] The missionaries went out to new lands safe and sure in their belief of the essential validity of the western system. They were impelled by an aggressive cultural imperialism, the belief that the christian religion, and with it western culture, offered the true answer to living and the determination to offer this salvation to those unfortunate beings who were indulging, mostly out of ignorance, sometimes out of wilfulness, in heathen and savage ways.

Alongside this spiritual task, of converting and civilizing, there was the more secular approach of certain politicians and philanthropically-minded people who decided that a grand (and perhaps divine) mission had been cast upon British shoulders — to civilize the savage natives of the world, to show them the supreme heights of existence that had been created in Britain and to implant that example in foreign lands so that the local inhabitants might copy, perhaps even rise to the British level. Yet this outwardly humanitarian concern for other people had obvious harsh and negative aspects. Too much did the agents of cultural imperialism attempt the direct imposition of their views and values, especially religious, without showing any sympathy for or understanding of the traditional culture of the indigenes. Indeed the missionaries and other agents too blithely assumed that these people had no culture to speak of; very few westerners tried to come to any comprehension of the ways of indigenes, let alone consider that both groups could be considered as equals. The prevailing mood of European learning accepted without question that the apparent superiority of western technology offered positive proof of the total superiority of western civilization.

Another aspect of the humanitarian approach was expressed in the idea of trusteeship and protection of the "lesser" races of the world. This idea gathered strength as the century progressed but it was always underpinned by a sense of patronizing paternalism. The other people were thought of as children to be taught and disciplined; the imperialists had certain duties to perform for and on behalf of those other people — to civilize them primarily through christianity, through their incorporation within the world of legitimate trade and through the operation of sound British administration. From these beginnings it was assumed that the other hallmarks of western civilization could later develop.

This humanitarianism received specific application in two notable cases. Firstly, there was the establishment of the colony of Sierra Leone for former slaves, as already discussed. Secondly there was the more important humanitarian objective of eradicating slavery. Success came in stages.[8] In 1807 the British parliament ended the slave trade by British ships and diplomatic and naval moves ensued to persuade other nations to follow suit. Then in the 1820s public pressure mounted, through bodies follow suit. Then in the 1820s public pressure mounted, through bodies such as the Anti-slavery Society, to try to improve conditions for Africans by abolishing slavery totally. The parliament responded in 1833, ending slavery throughout the empire. But humanitarian concern did not rest at that juncture. In 1835—37 the condition of Aborigines in British settlements was investigated by a select committee of parliament;[9] this allowed prominent humanitarians, such as Thomas Buxton and Saxe Bannister, to vent their rage over the outrages that were being perpetrated on other races by British settlers in the various colonies. Surveying the condition of Aborigines in South Africa, Canada, Newfoundland, New South Wales, Van Diemen's Land, New Zealand, Pacific islands and Sierra Leone the report lamented the depredations that had followed upon the intrusion of white settlers into these lands. The Aborigines had suffered white aggression and injustice, most particularly in South Africa where war had resulted with the Kaffirs. In the hope of effecting a more humane policy for other races it was recommended that new territories should be annexed only with the sanction of parliament; private individuals could not independently acquire land from indigenes. Furthermore, it was urged that the British government, in future dealings with tribes, should proceed on the assumption that they were civilized nations, even if in appearance they seemed savage.

Yet an ambiguous stance was taken in response to these recommendations. Although the humanitarians might urge that a spirit of equality should pervade dealings between the British and Aborigines, in practice this was often unrealistic and frequently a protective attitude was adopted. No matter how laudatory it was to claim that the signatories were full equals it had to be accepted in fact that most tribes did not really understand the meaning and implications of a treaty. Furthermore a number of British imperialists felt that only if the British government exercised paternalistic and protective prerogatives could the survival of many of these indigenous peoples be assured. So in certain circumstances negotiations provided various restrictions upon the indigenes, with respect for example to their offer of lâbour, or their purchase of "ardent" spirits, or even the alienation of their land. In these cases it was clearly assumed that these people could not look after themselves in open negotiations. In 1836 the Aborigines Protection Society was formed in awareness of these difficulties.

The humanitarian approach, in other words, was caught in a dilemma — on the one hand arguing for the equality of different societies, and on the other trying to protect a society which might fall easy prey to the wily machinations of aggressive, individualistic westerners. This dilemma was further compounded by some division of opinion among humanitarians about the need for colonization and civilization in hitherto "neglected" areas. A minority flatly denied the value of colonization or of the introduction of any white contact; rather they urged "hands off". The bulk of humanitarians, however, thought that white influence was desirable, although on a restricted basis, such as through missionaries. So, civilization could come to these people, leading to the elimination of barbarous customs, slavery and other unsavoury aspects of life in those societies.

Throughout the nineteenth century missionaries were active agents of British imperialism. The travels of David Livingstone in central Africa have received greatest exposure but they were merely one example of the world-wide sweep of Christian teachings. The arrival of the London Missionary Society in the New Hebrides in the 1840s and 1850s merits just as much attention, as do the numerous bands of other fearless zealots who forsook Britain for the saving of heathen souls.[10] Today their achievements are still largely unassessed or misassessed. In their desire to change one set of beliefs and one way of life for another, the missionaries are now denounced as desecrators of society and violators of individual rights. Certainly the missionary's dedication to conversion may have been based upon a misplaced sense of cultural superiority, but he was able also to achieve certain positive effects, not least of all being the amelioration of distress and trauma caused by the confrontation of the two cultures. The missionary was placed in the unenviable position of having to bridge the gap between the two ways of life. The tribesman, having come into contact with western culture, was almost invariably tantalized by material aspects of western ways. So he was willing to accept the presence of the missionary, with his stories of Christ and injunctions on moral behaviour, in return for access to knives, or calico, or rifles or beads. The missionary found himself cast in the role of not only a disciple of Christ but also an agent of trade and subaltern of imperialism. In the latter roles he tried to present a subdued image, avoiding the excessive rapaciousness of some British traders and the aggressive impetuousness of some British imperialists. Yet he nearly always found the effect of his entry reduced by the presence of bit-actors — undesirable refugees from British civilization, drunken whalers and whoring sailors. It was hard for the missionary to make dramatic impact upon his audience, the people of a traditional society, when there were so many other actors on stage, playing the lie to the story of the supremacy of British culture and civilization.

Very few missionaries saw themselves as active agents of British imperialism, rather that was a secondary, but unavoidable task. To achieve the main objective of conversion it was necessary for the missionary to reveal other aspects of western civilization, material and spiritual. For communication the missionary found he had to be a teacher, offering instruction in the English language as well as learning to understand the local tongue. He offered a new style of living, brought different ideas on elementary health (some of which worked, some did not), and helped suppress some "undesirable" practices. So, in a host of ways the missionary represented the British imperial presence. He could help to pacify an area, thereby making it easier for the British trader to operate, or he might be the advance-guard of a more official British presence; or once that presence was established he might be a relay-station in the network of British jurisdiction and control.

In India too missionaries tried to have an impact upon local customs, after the Baptist Carey settled near Calcutta in 1792. Overall they achieved little. Probably the greatest effect upon Indian traditions and customs came with the administration of Lord Bentinck (1828—35), who set out to suppress widow-burning, robbery and sacrificial murder by religious sects and infanticide.[11] This was another aspect of the process of westernization.

British humanitarian interest in other people received support from a number of important dignitaries in the British colonial administration, such as James Stephen,[12] Lord Glenelg and Sir George Grey. But as the century progressed this official concern focused increasingly on the sense of imperial mission, as typified in the mid-century by the ideas of Earl Grey. To him the British rule brought the blessings of peace, order and stability instead of chaos and anarchy, it brought freedom rather than oppression and tyranny. Some British imperialists were even becoming convinced that God was on their side, since Britain had been allowed to win the largest empire ever and her civilization seemed to stand almost at the pinnacle of perfection. So it was reasoned that the British had been charged with the task of governing and raising up the inferior races put under their care. By the 1870s and 1880s this paternalistic sense of imperial mission had become the dominant official manifestation of the earlier humanitarian concern for the welfare of other races. Increasingly Britain's sense of duty was being expressed in such a way as to swamp whatever initiatives or responsibility these other people might have wanted to take.

British policy towards other races, as expressed by most missionaries and humanitarians, and frequently by imperial officials in London, did show some awareness of the problems of other cultures. Certainly it was only an imperfect and inexact awareness, sometimes it was falsely based, and it was pinned to the facile assumption that the British way of life was superior. Yet it must be remembered that the state of learning in this field was very elementary; the discipline of anthropology had not emerged in its own right. So some of the statements of policy were based upon ignorance rather than an overt assertion of British racial supremacy. But distinctly harsh and violent racist sentiments were commonly displayed by British settlers in the colonies, both temperate and tropical, with desires for land and labour.

Through the nineteenth century the settlers in Canada, Australia and New Zealand generally showed a reckless disregard for the welfare of the

Aborigines of those lands; sometimes the whites also resorted to violence to ensure that enough land was available. In New Zealand the mid-century Anglo-Maori wars arose partly over land disputes, with the whites pushing on ever forward into Maori areas. In Australia as in Canada the settlers swept on in an uncontrollable surge and although the Aborigines put up some resistance they could not match the firepower of their foes. In all three areas the original inhabitants lost not only the bulk of their land but also a sense of identity and the will to live. So their population began to dwindle significantly, not only through skirmishes and fighting with the whites but also because of the general confusion that enveloped their lives and out of a sense of resignation as they found their world overturned. In the first century of contact the number of Australian Aborigines dropped from about 300,000 to about 75,000. Guns, poison and punitive raids quickly took their toll. Meanwhile their Indian brethren in Canada found themselves in a similar position. Their loss of land meant a loss of food supplies — buffalo. The alternative was cheap, vile American whiskey, with the result of physical and psychological degradation.

The record of the white settlers in these areas was not wholly negative. For example, in Canada, although the Indians were suffering at the hands of the whites the position was even worse just south of the border. Furthermore, when by the end of the century the North-West Mounted Police and missionaries were beginning to have effect in frontier regions, harmonious relations were established, and the Indians turned increasingly to the government for protection, to become wards of state rather than full citizens.[13] Such protection, however, did nothing to help the dignity of the Indian and little to preserve his way of life. In New Zealand, an early attempt was made at combining the two races within the one system. Shortly after cession and annexation in 1840 a humanitarian influence on official policy was evident, in the policy of amalgamation. This envisaged a sharing of power, especially in administration and justice, between the few white residents and the many Maoris. Indeed the proud Maoris had gained respect in some British eyes, arising from the favourable impressions of explorers such as Cook.[14] The Maoris, however, although willing to deal with white settlers on the basis of equality soon found that the latter always insisted on getting their own way. With more and more whites flooding in, demanding more and more land, the Maoris resisted more strongly. By 1858 the number of whites had overtaken the number of Maoris; the result was war, and defeat for the Maoris. Then began a slow job of rehabilitation, starting in 1867 with the provision of four special Maori seats in the legislature.

In Cape Colony and Natal the position was complicated by the preponderance of blacks over whites, whereas in Canada and Australia a white dominance was quickly established (and in New Zealand after 1858). From a position of numerical inferiority one can easily understand racist ideas emerging in a small white community, asserting racial superiority as a defence against the more numerous black community. Also the situation in those two colonies was further complicated by the existence of another European culture, the Dutch (or Boers), who had operated a racist, slave system prior to the British occupation.[15] Those Boers that moved out into new areas, such as the Orange Free State and the Transvaal, carried their racist ideas with them, establishing a very rigid system. Some Boers, however, stayed on in the British areas and although slave practices were forbidden racist ideas persisted, with even some religious backing. Nevertheless, there did emerge in Cape Colony a strand of liberal policy towards other races. British missionary and humanitarian pressure helped to encourage legislation for the Cape which assumed a basis of equality between blacks and whites. So, for example, 1853 voting laws created a common roll, for black and white; in practical terms, however, it allowed a white advantage. Although most of the pressure came from Britain there was support among some settlers for this more liberal approach. Natal, by contrast, approached more closely the Boer states.

The white settlers of the temperate colonies showed a marked sense of their racial superiority, never doubting their claims to land which they regarded as vacant or waste; but these lands did already belong to other people, not in the western sense of being owned and conferring property rights, rather in the sense of establishing an identity for those other people and of providing a means of sustenance. In tropical lands, the whites expressed just as strong a racism, but this time based upon the cheapening of the body of the coloured man. In the early years of the nineteenth century slavery was still permitted in the empire and it continued to flourish in the sugar colonies of the West Indies. But the rise of humanitarian feeling in Britain, along with a political protest by Jamaican slaves in 1831, brought parliamentary moves in Britain to end slavery throughout the empire. After 1833 work in the tropical empire had to be carried out by free men, but immediately the problem arose as to where enough hard-working labourers could be obtained. Another sugar-growing area, Mauritius, found the solution in 1834, by bringing in coolies from India under an indenture system.[16] By 1870 over 350,000 indentured labourers had served there and the population became so mixed that by the twentieth century Indo-Mauritians constituted a majority of the population.

Indentured labourers were also tried in the West Indies. By 1928 almost 250,000 Indians had been imported into British Guiana. The usual system was to employ the labourers for a fixed term, at a low wage; eventually the labourer should be repatriated to India. Legislation provided for government regulation of the system but in practice enforcement was very lax. Although it was certainly milder than the earlier system of slave labour the indenture system also exhibited a number of degrading features and debased the value of human endeavour. India was the main source of this cheap labour which was sent around the world, to the places mentioned above, and to east Africa, Malaya, Fiji and so on.[17] It is estimated that by 1870 between one and two million Indian labourers had joined the gang of workers, helping to develop the various tropical domains of the empire. In the wake of the coolies came Indian traders and merchants, so that an Indian sub-culture frequently showed up as a concomitant of the spread of British imperial influence.

Another variation on the indenture system arose mid-century in the south Pacific. Labour was urgently needed in the Australian colonies, in some of the Pacific islands such as Fiji and Samoa, and to work the nitrate mines of Chile. Pacific islanders provided the answer and so a labour trade developed in the second half of the century, conducted not only for British colonies but also for French and German outposts in the area.

First use of island labour was for whaling expeditions and in the sandalwood trade. But as plantation economies became established in the region so the demand for island labour increased, especially for the growing of sugar in Queensland.[18] Between 1863 and 1901 over sixty thousand islanders were used in that industry. Most were brought from the New Hebrides and the Solomons but some were also harvested from New Guinea. The British government, however, continued to display a humanitarian concern for the well-being of these people, and was suspicious of the intentions of Queensland settlers. To prevent a slave economy developing in the south seas the British government passed various acts in the 1870s in the hope of establishing some kind of general jurisdiction — through a high commissioner — to control the labour trade. Pressure was also brought to bear on the Queensland government to regulate the trade, and although at first there were examples of violent and deceitful methods, even kidnapping, being used to obtain the islanders, in later years a more regular recruiting system developed wherein the islanders offered their labour willingly, knowing fully what advantages and disadvantages were in store for them. For the many who volunteered to work in Queensland for three years the attraction was metal weapons, a boxful of gaudy wares and escape from the monotony of a stagnant existence — such was the allure of western civilization. By 1885 the system was fairly well regulated and it came to an end after the turn of the century.

The assumption that whites could not, or should not, work in the tropics meant that cheap, coloured labour had to be obtained, whether in slave or indentured form, to undertake the development of the plantation economies of those areas. Yet this sense of racial superiority did not reign unchecked throughout all the tropics. In one area, Fiji, an attempt was made after 1875 to assure a proper place for the original inhabitants and to restrict a white takeover. Governor Gordon tried to preserve Fijian control over the land and to keep intact the workings of traditional

Fijian society.[19] Such an approach was well in the forefront of sociological thinking of the time, being marred only by the lack of scientific knowledge on the workings of such a traditional society.

So British racial and cultural superiority did not reign unalloyed. Official humanitarian concern could make itself felt in favour of the protection of other races. The soul of the empire might have been basically geared to the supremacy of the whites; the interests of white settlers and planters might have generally prevailed; but the empire was so large and diverse a creation that complexity and contradiction also had a place. Consequently Fijians might be protected, slaves might be freed, various protections and rights might be afforded to other races. Yet, within all the ambiguities of this confused racial picture it remains true that most of the benefits of civilization flowed to the whites. And this situation arose primarily from the assertion of the overwhelming superiority of British civilization.

The third quarter of the nineteenth century saw Britain resplendent in power. For visible signs perhaps the most outstanding was the conferring of the title "Empress of India" on Queen Victoria in 1875; Disraeli, the prime minister, pulled off another coup that year with the acquisition of £4 million worth of shares in the Suez Canal. British power rode high. But it was not just a matter of possession of the Indian empire with its teeming millions. For many, empire meant the challenge of "savage" Africa, as explorers, missionaries and traders went tentatively and hesitatingly into the unknown; for a smaller number, British power meant proselytizing among the pagan Polynesians. Many British subjects understood British imperial power to involve the establishment of another British society in the broad flat-lands of interior Canada, Australia and South Africa.

British imperialism was a multi-faceted construct. It could by no means be measured just in the economic dimensions of a formal empire. Britain's trade with her colonial possessions provided a comforting support to total British economic relations, but more important was the capacity to trade with the whole world. British investment was in a similar position. The empire was not an essential aspect of British power; it helped and supported but was not indispensible. Just as in earlier decades British power had grown through the successful operation of ideas of mercantilism, now, from the end of the eighteenth century, British economic strength and capacity was to be extended by the operation of principles of free trade. British merchants, shippers and investors had the capacity and foresight to make this change in economic thinking. They operated far and wide. India and Australia were useful for trading and investment purposes; but more important was the United States, or Europe, or Latin America. The

British trader in China, the British investor in Brazil, his counterparts in Chicago and Lisbon provided the basis of British economic strength.

This free-ranging economic power arose out of Britain's industrial supremacy. The phrase "workshop of the world" was being forged in the factories of midland Britain. The teeming millions of products being churned out of her textile factories, her iron and steel mills, her railway workshops needed teeming millions of customers. Britain's formal empire could not sop up these products; not even India's huge population could provide a sufficient market. So Britain's free trade imperialism looked to all parts of the globe, and especially the developing economies outside Europe.

Britain's economic relationships did not demand political control of the markets; rather they worked well in conditions allowing freedom of behaviour, regardless of who governed the particular territory. Yet Britain's formal empire kept growing; land kept being annexed. Even in some of the lands of British economic penetration, closer political relations with Britain were coming into being, to lead eventually to full, formal control. The reasons for such extensions of political power were multifarious. Often it was because of determined action by the local British man-on-the-spot; so frequently it was because of a threat, or presumed threat, to the continued existence of whatever degree of British power or influence already functioned in that foreign land. The loss of power, of a presence, of prestige was generally not to be tolerated. The property of a British person, the life of a subject, and especially his capacity to trade in foreign soil had to be assured and such protection might involve the show of imperial might, or even the assertion of a greater degree of official authority.

While in economic relationships freedom was the prevalent word, the political setting of Britain's empire was moving more towards formularization and even regulation. The separate establishment of the Colonial Office in its own right in 1854 was a token of this. The administrative operations of a commercial company were ceased in India which came under full, official control. The government of tropical dependencies was regularized in a more standardized fashion — the crown colony system. Even in the colonies of white settlement a degree of systematization came in, with responsible government. Yet, in this case the moves were introduced in the name of freedom. Let such areas have greater political responsibility, so that they would be happy to stay under the umbrella of British imperial power. Rather than choose the way of independence which the thirteen American colonies had taken they would remain within the British empire and grow up as models of British society transplanted into foreign parts. Little Britain reborn.

Britain and her empire released a sense of unbounded, total power by the 1870s. It could be seen in terms of industrial primacy, or trade with the whole world, or investment around the world, or supremacy in commercial shipping. It could be seen in terms of the "jewel of India" or the route to India; it could be the possession of the largest formal empire in the world. But this was not sufficient. British power encompassed those economic facets, and more. The industry, the trade, the investment, the shipping gave Britain wealth and, even more important, a sense of total power. The wealth gained through economic dominance was being used to establish a culture, a way of life for the whole world.

British power now meant the acceptance, and even the furtherance, of this British mode in other places. Obviously such wealth and economic primacy generated in the British mind a strong sense of superiority and confidence. Her power, her capacity seemed unbrooked. The success with which British settlers had moved into the lands of others in Canada and Australia and established there a flourishing mini-Britain led to the notion that Britain had a chosen role in world government, to show the "less fortunate" societies of the undeveloped world how to look after themselves.

Cultural arrogance was developing rapidly in these decades. The British way was the right, the only way. Westernization in the British fashion was the model to progress, to the future. Western education and Christianity were seen to be the key to this success; the traditional societies needed to be shaken out of their lethargy and superstition. They needed to be taught western science and technology, so that a modern, capitalist economy could be put into operation. In the long run this would bring greater profit to the operation of Britain's system of free trade imperialism.

As the decades passed by, many British administrators began to argue that the best way to save these societies from their supposed rotting stagnation was by the substitution of the British model. Their existing political structures should be allowed to decay or should be overturned. Instead, with proper British control, the societies could be modernized and made more efficient. It was acknowledged that this would be a long task, but it would bring benefits to Britain, and the local societies, in the long run. The British sense of racial superiority explained that success came so easily in the white settlement colonies because the agents responsible were British subjects. With Indians or Maoris a more patient tutelage would be necessary; as to Australian Aborigines or Canadian Indians, the effort did not seem worthwhile.

By the end of this period, by the 1870s, British power was bursting out; it was confident and proud. But it was also ready to become both more assertive and defensive. For it was about to be tested. The first part of the nineteenth century showed a British power where reality and appearance somewhat coincided. The Britisher could swagger confidently and was rarely challenged. So he did not really need to assert his power. By the end of the third quarter the world scene was changing. He would now need to use that power. Little England had become Greater Britain, but it must now preserve that position. Perhaps the Anglo-Afghan war of 1878—80 was a portent of the problems British power would encounter. British power would now have to be protected; the responsibilities that power brought would now have to be exercised.

NOTES

1. The annual Blue Books and reports of the respective colonies provide useful information on education; also the *Colonial Office List*. For 1830s, see Robert M. Martin, *History of the Colonies of the British Empire* (London: Dawsons, 1967)(1843), pp. 9—11, 66, 156—59, 420—21, 481—82.
2. P. Lewsen, "The Cape Liberal Tradition — Myth or Reality?", *Race* 12 (1971—72): 65—80.
3. Eric Stokes, *The English Utilitarians and India* (Oxford: Clarendon, 1959).
4. F. A. Hilliard, *A Short History of Education in British West Africa* (London: Nelson, 1957), pp. 6—7, 118; P. Foster, *Education and Social Change in Ghana* (London: Routledge & Kegan Paul, 1965); James A. B. Horton, *West African Countries and Peoples* (Chicago: Aldine, 1969)(1868).
5. A. Balfour and H. H. Scott, *Health Problems of the Empire* (London: Collins, 1924); re west Africa, A. McPhee, *The Economic Revolution in West Africa* (London: Cass, 1971)(1926), chap. viii.
6. Christine Bolt, *Victorian Attitudes to Race* (London: Routledge & Kegan Paul, 1971); V. G. Kiernan, *The Lords of Human Kind* (London: Weidenfeld & Nicolson, 1969); C. A. G. Bodelsen, *Studies in Mid-Victorian Imperialism* (New York: Fertig, 1968)(1924).
7. Roland Oliver, *The Missionary Factor in East Africa* (London: Longman, 1952); Tim Jeal, *Livingstone* (London: Heinemann, 1973); E. A. Ayandele, *The Missionary Impact on Modern Nigeria, 1842—1916* (London: Longman, 1966); A. J. Hanna, *The Beginnings of Nyasaland and Northern Rhodesia, 1859—95* (Oxford: Clarendon, 1956); P. Wright, *Knibb "The Notorious": Slaves' Missionary, 1803—45* (London: Sidgwick & Jackson, 1973); M. Craton, "Proto-Peasant Revolts", *Past and Present* 85 (1979): 99—125.
8. Roger T. Anstey, *The Atlantic Slave Trade and British Abolition 1760—1810* (London: Macmillan, 1975); Suzanne Miers, *Britain and the Ending of the Slave Trade* (London: Longmans, 1975); T. Clarkson, *The History of the Abolition of the African Slave-Trade by the British Parliament* (London: Cass, 1968)(1808); Thomas Buxton, *African Slave Trade and its Remedy* (London: Dawsons, 1968) (1840).
   Look at two seminal works — Eric Williams, *Capitalism and Slavery* (Chapel Hill: University of North Carolina Press, 1944); Frank Tannenbaum, "The Destiny of the Negro in the Western Hemisphere", *Political Science Quarterly* 61 (1946): 1—41. Also the comparative study by C. Degler, "Slavery in Brazil and the United States", *American Historical Review* 75 (1970): 1004—26; Mary Reckford, "The Jamaica Slave Rebellion of 1831", *Past and Present* 40 (1968): 108—25; review article — G. J. Heuman, "Slavery and Emancipation in the British Caribbean", *Journal of Imperial and Commonwealth History* 6 (1977—78): 166—71.
9. "Report from the Select Committee on Aborigines (British Settlements)", H. of C. No. 538, *Parl.Pap.* 7 (1836): 1, H. of C. No. 425, *Parl.Pap.* 7 (1837): 1; Saxe Bannister, *Humane Policy* (London: Dawsons, 1968)(1830).
10. For example the Melanesian mission, in D. Hilliard, *God's Gentlemen* (St. Lucia: University of Queensland Press, 1978).

11. J. Rosselli, *Lord William Bentinck* (Berkeley: University of California Press, 1974).
12. P. Knaplund, *James Stephen and the British Colonial System, 1813–47* (Madison: University of Wisconsin Press, 1953).
13. R. C. Macleod, *The North-West Mounted Police and Law Enforcement, 1873–1905* (Toronto: University Press, 1976).
14. The treatment of the Maoris is well covered; H. M. Wright, *New Zealand, 1769–1840* (Cambridge, Mass.: Harvard University Press, 1959); Alan Ward, *A Show of Justice* (Canberra: Australian National University Press, 1974); J. M. R. Owens, *Prophets in the Wilderness* (Auckland: University Press, 1974); J. Marais, *The Colonisation of New Zealand* (London: Dawsons, 1968)(1927); B. J. Dalton, *War and Politics in New Zealand, 1855–70* (Sydney: University Press, 1967).
15. W. M. Macmillan, *Bantu, Boer and Briton* (Oxford: Clarendon, 1963)(1929); C. W. De Kiewiet, *British Colonial Policy and the South African Republics, 1848–72* (London: Longmans, Green, 1929); David Welsh, *The Roots of Segregation* (Cape Town: Oxford University Press, 1971); Lewsen, *Myth or Reality*.
16. Hugh Tinker, *A New System of Slavery* (London: Oxford University Press, 1974); I. M. Cumpston, *Indians Overseas in British Territories, 1829–54* (London: Dawsons, 1969)(1953); Alan Adamson, *Sugar without Slaves* (New Haven: Yale University Press, 1972); P. C. Campbell, *Chinese Coolie Emigration to Countries within the British Empire* (London: Cass, 1971)(1923).
17. K. S. Sandhu, *Indians in Malaya* (London: Cambridge University Press, 1969); Robert G. Gregory, *History of Race Relations within the British Empire, 1890–1939* (Oxford: Clarendon, 1972).
18. O. W. Parnaby, *Britain and the Labour Trade in the South West Pacific* (Durham: N.C.: Duke University Press, 1964); D. Scarr, *Fragments of Empire* (Canberra: Australian National University Press, 1967); P. Corris, *Passage, Port and Plantation* (Melbourne: University Press, 1973).
19. J. K. Chapman, *The Career of Arthur Hamilton Gordon* (Toronto: University Press, 1964); P. France, *The Charter of the Land* (Melbourne: Oxford University Press, 1969).

PART THREE

Clinging to the Peak
1880s 1930s

10
Power in Check

Between the 1880s and the 1930s British imperial power stood at its pinnacle. During the decades leading up to the 1914—18 war the size of the empire continued to grow as new territories were added, generally with startling ease, all around the globe. The treaties arranging the peace following that war brought the empire to its greatest extent, as various mandated territories formerly belonging to the defeated states, were entrusted to Britain's care.

Yet for the British government the possession of the world's greatest empire did not bestow unbounded blessings. First and foremost among the concerns of British statesmen was the awesome task of how to preserve and protect such a huge empire. Mere possession and sheer immensity alone did not ensure an uninterrupted right of enjoyment. The key to official British thinking on this point could be summed up in an attitude of caution; it would be best for Britain and empire — and hence the world — if no-one "rocked the boat". Hopefully no contentious issues would be raised, or if they were strenuous attempts would be made to resolve them by conciliation and compromise. With luck the avaricious desires of other western countries, anxious to prove to the rest of the world their full nationhood, could be satisfactorily channelled through diplomacy and deals. In such a fashion Britain's relative position of preeminence could remain unchallenged, even though by the closing decades of the nineteenth century momentous changes were taking place in the world scene.[1]

The spirit of competition was increasing among the leading powers of the world — Germany, France, Russia, the United States, Italy and Belgium, alongside, of course, Britain. The age of capitalism had come into full flower. Now, other countries were joining Britain in relying upon economic growth through industrialization; now it was not only British traders and investors who sought profit through ventures around the globe; now eyes again fixed on imperial and military strength as an index of success and prestige. No longer did Britain stand preeminent in the scale of world power. Although she still seemed to possess more of the obvious insignia of world power than any other nation she no longer felt secure that she held an unchallengeable lead. And the events of 1914—18 and 1939 -45 showed quite clearly that another country was prepared directly to challenge Britain's supposed supremacy; and there were other times between the 1880s and the 1940s when possible threats to Britain's position either actually arose or were imagined to arise.

Britain's relative decline, or at least slip from undoubted supremacy due to growing competition from other nations, was most marked in the factor which throughout the earlier nineteenth century had made her so unchallengeable — industrialization. British dominance in a number of fields of industrial output was overtaken as the century drew to a close by the United States; and after the turn of the century by Germany. As the decades passed, Japan showed herself to be much more competitive than Britain in a variety of manufacturing fields, especially in eastern markets. Furthermore, European manufacturers and industrialists began poaching upon former British markets and performed with a more acute business acumen than their island counterpart.[2] This was true even in many British colonies where settlers often lamented the lackadaisical approach of the British supplier; in contrast, European manufactures would be supplied on time and serviced adequately. The early lead which Britain held had sometimes encouraged sloppiness and inertia in business practices, which could be fatal at a time when the competitive spirit of capitalism was flowing so strongly.

The rapid growth in the industrial capability of other countries, along with a failure to meet their competitive strength, meant that Britain was faced automatically by a shrinking world market. This problem was exacerbated, however, by a change in attitude by most of the rising industrial powers towards the system of world trade. Whereas Britain had wedded herself to free trade, a system which was very convenient and beneficial to her while she was undoubted master of the factories and mistress of the seas, the newer industrial nations saw immediate disadvantages in following the British example. Even in the initial stages of their industrialization there were obvious reasons to impair or exclude the free entry of cheap British manufactures while local factories were building up quality and expertise behind protecting walls. Similar protective devices were applied, where possible, to overseas markets, so that the possession of colonies became important since they could be made into an exclusive outlet for the manufactures of the metropolitan power to the exclusion of British manufactures. Yet Britain, operating under principles of free trade, held her colonial possessions open to all industrialists, and let the more competitive win. While British traders found themselves restricted in selling to German colonies in Africa German businessmen opened up lucrative new avenues in Britain's African domains. To this unfavourable situation was added the unfair discrimination which British entrepreneurs suffered through foreign governments generally backing and aiding their own businessmen in other countries while at first the policy of the British government did not contemplate using the resources of the foreign office or the navy to assist British businessmen expand overseas.

Without such official support British enterprise obviously found it more difficult to protect its position, let alone extend operations, in comparison with other western business concerns.

From the 1880s it was becoming increasingly necessary for a reassessment to be made of Britain's position in the world. The British public at large and even many backbench politicians were slow to accept the full implications of Britain's relative decline and of the rise of effective, forceful competition; businessmen were more aware of the situation and many sought to pressure the government to change policy more in line with the European approach. This pressure was made more insistent by the fluctuating economic crises that plagued the western world through the 1870s, 1880s and 1890s. Depressed industrial and trading conditions meant that businessmen wanted more assurance of safe markets and greater security for their operations. In their eyes the uncertainties of the economic climate needed to be compensated for by increased government protection and support. And increasingly the British government responded favourably, partly because of business pressure but more because of a reassessment of the realities of the total power situation by leading politicians and administrators, such as Lord Salisbury, Lord Rosebery and Joseph Chamberlain. Certainly the pressure from the capitalists was a factor influencing government policy but it was not necessarily the predominant one; the top policy-makers took into account the whole array of evidence indicating that Britain was having difficulty in holding her own against the rising competition of Germany, France, Russia or the United States.

The main change in policy which came into operation from the 1880s was the assertion by the British government of a more directly expansive, openly aggressive imperial policy. Leading statesmen, realizing that Britain's supremacy was under challenge, were now prepared not only to show British force but also to use it; perhaps they were endorsing the adage that offence was the best means of defence. If a frontier of the empire seemed fragile and unsettled, Britain's shrewdest move was to consolidate her position there by moving the frontier further into the hinterland; that would allow the former area to become safe, although the new periphery would become a danger spot. This process would then be repeated, with a further expansion of the frontier, and so the empire would continue to grow until stopped, normally by confrontation with the imperial forces of another European power. The matter of final boundaries would then be settled by negotiation and agreement between the two western powers. So Britain's approach of "passive" and hesitant imperialism in the earlier nineteenth century was changing by the last two decades of the century into one of much more overt and direct expansion; the competitive spirit had also entered the colonial scene, with France after 1879 setting the pace.[3]

This change in approach was expressed either through the continual extension of the frontier where indigenous people proved troublesome, through the arbitrary demarcation of vast continental and oceanic reserves where the claims of other imperialist nations were in competition, or through official diplomatic, occasionally military, assistance to protect the economic interests of businessmen in territories of informal British influence.[4] This more aggressive imperial policy was adopted in the name of protection, in the hope of preserving the status quo, of maintaining Britain's position in the world.

In Egypt, the British found their power under threat, not by foreign competitors such as the French, but internally, from nationalist strivings among the local leadership.[5] Certainly the interests of British bondholders were under threat, and certainly they were crying out for British action; but the solution of British occupation in 1882 was adopted not so much in response to capitalist pressures as to the safe retention of an essential pivot of British imperial power. So much of British power was believed to be bound up in the east — in the possession of a great empire in India and Oceania, in a flourishing trade with that empire and China — that any threat to ease of British access to the east was taken to be a fatal blow to the whole structure of British power. It was essential for Britain to be able to maintain in total security strategic routes to the east, which meant after 1875 that the British believed that they must have a say in the operation of the Suez route. The next progression was for Britain to assert control over the troublesome frontier of the Sudan in 1898—99, with the aim of securing the headwaters of the Nile; this move was also made to exclude France from influence in the area and, indeed, was one of the occasions when the competing claims of European imperialists resulted almost in forceful confrontation rather than a negotiated settlement.[6]

At the same time Britain felt it wise to maintain a second route to the east, the old, established one around the Cape of Good Hope. Yet even here security was posing problems for the maintenance of British power. The British acquisition of the Cape from Holland during the Napoleonic wars had never been happily accepted by many of the Dutch, or Boer, inhabitants. In the hope of escaping British overlordship they had fled beyond the frontiers, establishing their own communities. But by the 1870s their presence, alongside the two British colonies of the Cape and Natal, was posing problems for British administrators, for example, with respect to relations with African tribes. Then, after the discovery of gold in the 1880s, the Boer republics began to develop a strength of their own, threatening the viability of the British imperial foothold in southern Africa. There even appeared a danger that the Boer areas would come to dominate the whole area, leading to the eventual loss of the British colonies to the Boers. One solution to this threat was for the Boer republics to be surrounded by British settlement. Little encouragement was needed, for British settlers kept spreading north from the Cape, pushing British influence into Bechuanaland and the Zambezi. And arch-imperialists, such as Cecil Rhodes, envisaged a great British domain in central Africa, virtually encircling the Boers. A second solution to the Boer problem was the direct use of force which after the second Anglo-Boer war of 1899—1902 seemed to herald success for the British policy of paramountcy in southern and central Africa. The alternate route via the Cape was secure, as was the Cape's hinterland, with British imperial sway extending over Cape Colony, Natal, the Orange Free State, the Transvaal, Southern Rhodesia, Northern Rhodesia, Nyasaland and the three high commission territories of Bechuanaland, Basutoland and Swaziland.

With a similar concern for the security of the frontier and the maintenance of British imperial power the boundary was pushed out from Lower Burma into Upper Burma, and a British presence insinuated into Tibet and Persia. In the Pacific Britain moved out from her base in Fiji by arranging protectorates in New Guinea (which was later annexed), the Gilbert and Ellice Islands, the Solomons and Tonga.[7] In some cases, as with New Guinea, Tonga and the New Hebrides, expansion occurred partly as the result of a deal with another imperial power, such as Germany or France. This applied also in the case of east Africa where the Germans and the British arranged respective areas of influence. Deals were also done with the French, for example, drawing up boundaries in the Niger region and agreeing upon the future existence of Siam.

While much of this rash of British expansion in the 1880s, 1890s and 1900s flowed directly out of official concern for the preservation of existing British world power, some aggressive moves were also made for the direct protection of existing economic interests of British businessmen in areas of informal influence. This was a change from practices earlier in the century. Now aggrieved British bondholders in Latin America or disprivileged traders in west Africa could expect more official British intervention on their behalf, mainly at a diplomatic level, but sometimes involving the show or use of force.[8] Likewise in China and the Levant the British government was now more prepared to give official backing to British trading and financial interests, in a fashion similar to that which France and Germany had already been exercising. With British power under threat, in both the empire and areas of economic interest, with challenges arising both internally from problems of disorder and anarchy and externally from foreign rivals, the official response turned more readily to the display and use of force. Certainly the aggressive and expansive moves that occurred still arose partly through the initiatives of men-on-the-spot, but now their behaviour was more readily condoned, and even primed, if not actively encouraged, in London. The main restraint on the use of unlimited force where imperial claims came into direct competition was the fear of being involved in a serious war with other western nations. Where competition with indigenous people was concerned, this fear was minor. With western nations, Britain resorted to negotiation so that war could be avoided — although as shown in the eye-ball confrontation between the British and the French on the Nile in 1898, Britain was not prepared to back down easily. Now the government felt a stronger duty of protection than in mid-century. It had become imperative for the state to act more directly in the protection of all that was British: not only the lives of its subjects but also their property and economic interests, not only Britain and empire but also trading-financial outlets scattered over the world. Political, strategic and economic factors constituting British power were becoming inextricably intertwined from the 1880s in the face of these mounting challenges.

At first the main rival seemed to be France, backed up from the 1890s by Russia.[9] Then, after the turn of the century British concern deflected to the growing might of Germany, culminating in a life-and-death struggle between 1914 and 1918. Then followed a period of quiescence, when Britain still seemed the greatest power, so long as no-one bothered to make a serious challenge. In fact, American power was outstripping that of any European nation, while in the 1920s and 1930s the first non-European challenge was thrown down by Japan. The final test came in 1939—45 when British power in the western hemisphere was assaulted by Germany and in the east by Japan. Finally the fragile structure of British world-power was exposed. At the same time, throughout the whole period, challenges were being made economically, as well as on the military-strategic front. Before the end of the nineteenth century both the United States and Germany proved to be effective industrial competitors while France, and later Japan, continually chipped away at Britain's industrial and economic lead.

In military terms Britain was to find in the twentieth century that the possession of a large empire was a vital source of strength; yet this was not without problems. While during most of the nineteenth century imperial philosophy accepted that Britain should undertake the bulk of the burden of defence, especially by sea, there was discontent, especially by the Treasury, at the immensity of this responsibility. No matter how firmly attempts were made to keep down costs, new charges and new tasks always seemed to arise. Problems on the frontier of Afghanistan would not go away; nor as the century drew to a close could west Africa be ignored, with local communities such as Benin and the Ashanti giving trouble and the French military expanding. At sea the eastern Mediterranean made a continual drain upon defence funds, as did the south Pacific and China waters. The regulation of "kidnapping" in the south seas and the stopping of slavery in east Africa arose from noble motives, but cost money. Meanwhile the perennial problem of fractious groups in southern Africa, such as the Zulus and more importantly the Boers, loomed larger and proved ever more costly. By 1902 it seemed that the Boers had finally been overcome, although at a cost of £220 million to Britain, and at a loss of 22,000 British lives (out of a total of 448,000 troops).[10] War was a costly business. But even in peace Britain's costs in protecting the empire made a treasurer gulp. Means were always being sought to shelve some of the costs to other bodies, and when chartered companies such as the British South Africa Company offered to operate their own para-military force to control problems with local people the Colonial Office did not refuse. Even so, some imperial troops had to be supplied when a Matabele and Mashona rebellion broke out in the 1890s. Owning an empire gave a sense of strength and security, but the empire itself had to be made secure, and with colonies claiming impoverished treasuries this meant that the British taxpayer had to foot most of the bill to show the British flag around the world.

It was in maritime defence that the British government began to push for a real contribution from some of the colonies. Slowly, and in some cases reluctantly, the Australian colonies, New Zealand, Canada and Cape Colony/Natal came in with money either for the British navy or in some cases to build their own vessels.[11] The need for the colonies to provide for more than local fortifications and the protection of local ports was clearly pointed out in a royal commission of 1881—82, and again at the 1887 conference. It was shown, for example, that of Australia's seaborne trade of £115 million, £58 million was with Britain. Yet each New South Welshman paid only 2s/4d towards the costs of his defence, while the corresponding British contribution was 15s/7½d. So Britain sought a more equitable sharing of the defence burden. The Australasian colonies were the first to respond, agreeing to a small payment at the 1887 colonial conference; their complaisance arose because of an imagined Russian naval menace in the area.

Naval defence became immediately more expensive by the turn of the century when Britain became engaged in a deadly naval arms race with Germany. In a succession of conferences the established colonies, and the Federated Malay States, undertook a greater naval responsibility. Australia even decided to go ahead with the creation of its own dominion navy rather than continue its subsidy to the British navy. Only Canada dragged the chain.

It was during the wars of 1914—18 and 1939—45 that Britain reaped the benefits of having so much auxiliary power in the form of colonial possessions scattered around the world. In both wars the empire rallied valiantly to the defence of Britain and the British cause; this amounted not only to a positive material effort but also to cooperation in overall defence planning and working through bodies such as the Committee of Imperial Defence. In the first war, while Britain supplied 4,500,000 men in the war effort, 3,000,000 came from the empire — 826,000 from India, 418,000 from Canada, 420,000 from Australia, 146,000 from South Africa (twenty per cent of all adult European males) and 10,000 from New Zealand. The empire also came in with material assistance; for example, Canada produced sixty million shells.[12] This war spelled success for imperial defence policy. Efforts over the previous decades to shelve an increasing amount of military and naval responsibility to the colonies had finally born fruit. The colonies had complied, mainly out of a sense of growing nationalism: responsibility for defence had to be accepted as one of the burdens of nationhood. At the same time the colonies felt themselves still part of an overall imperial strategy, so emphasis was put on cooperation and ultimate direction from Britain. In any case it boosted colonial egos to be represented in imperial war conferences and cabinets. Only in the case of some French Canadians, Afrikaners and Irish was there displayed a sense of dissension from the common imperial purpose.

The willingness to contribute to the imperial war efforts had been demonstrated earlier than the 1914—18 war; some slight assistance was offered to Britain in both the Sudan campaign of the 1890s and the second Anglo-Boer war. As the twentieth century progressed, Britain's reliance upon the strength of the empire became more necessary: the mercantile notions of power measured in terms of manpower were being revived. After the 1919—20 peace settlement, with the addition of mandated territories, Britain appeared even greater than before. In terms of population and empire she was the greatest power the world had ever known. Yet underneath the appearance was a ringing hollowness. Britain had world-wide commitments yet real limitations on the amount of force she could wield, arising partly from internal economic weaknesses. When international crises, such as the great economic depression of the 1930s, occurred Britain had to approach her defence responsibilities on the cheap. Yet attempts were made to keep up the appearance; for example, the development of a major naval base at Singapore was planned after 1921, although completion came very slowly; and as its quick collapse in 1942 showed, it was wasted effort. In any case, by the 1920s British naval supremacy was ended, although this was not popularly recognized. The rise of the United States, the ending of the Japanese alliance and the Washington naval conference of 1921 signalled Britain's naval decline. Yet the aura of Victorian power persisted — an illusion not backed up by reality.

The 1920s and 1930s were fortunately quiet times for Britain so that her power was not seriously tested. Nationalist tensions in Ireland, Egypt and India were subdued while more serious international incidents in places like Manchuria or Spain were left to their own fate. For the empire countries which had helped so much in the 1914—18 war, defence lapsed into a consideration of insignificance. The spirit of cooperation waned, as evidenced by their refusal to stand by Britain against the Turks in 1922. Men in the empire, just as in Britain, hoped for an eternal peace and turned their backs on military problems. The vanity of these hopes became only too apparent in 1939 when German armed might struck out again, finding Britain and the empire quite unprepared. Yet, again there was ready rallying for the British cause.[13] The manpower contribution of Canada, Australia, New Zealand and South Africa was over 1,650,000 by 1945, while India supplied just under 2,300,000 as against Britain's 2,000,000. Canada and Australia undertook to churn out war materials, although such willingness was not wholly disinterested since it meant a boost to local industrialization.[14] Even the smaller, undeveloped colonies came to Britain's rescue. By 1945 they had raised almost £50 million which they loaned to Britain, £16 million interest-free. As well, the dependent empire provided manpower totalling more than 473,000, over three-quarters coming from Africa.

In the twentieth century the size of Britain's empire proved a boon since it could supply so many personnel in armed struggle, as well as supply food, raw materials, even money to a beleaguered "mother" country. At the same time the empire still needed to be defended, and although prime responsibility was meant to lie with Britain she was inadequately geared for such a huge task. It was becoming increasingly necessary for the individual colonial areas to look to their own defence or to look to other strong nations for protection. The imperial umbrella had too many holes in it. A concerted incursion upon any colonial area would show how easily the structure could disintegrate, as the Japanese quickly discovered in Malaya.[15] The two world wars showed that in military terms the empire operated to help protect the metropolitan power, rather than the reverse.

NOTES

1. General background — Richard Koebner and H. D. Schmidt, *Imperialism* (Cambridge: University Press, 1964); A. P. Thornton, *The Imperial Idea and Its Enemies* (London: Macmillan, 1959); W. R. Johnston, *Sovereignty and Protection* (Durham: N.C.: Duke University Press, 1973).
2. D. C. M. Platt, *Finance, Trade and Politics in British Foreign Policy, 1815–1914* (Oxford: Clarendon, 1968) and "Economic Factors in British Policy During the 'New Imperialism' ", *Past and Present* 39 (1968): 120–38.
3. Re French competition — P. Gifford & W. R. Louis, *France and Britain in Africa* (New Haven: Yale University Press, 1971); John D. Hargreaves, *West Africa Partitioned* (London: Macmillan, 1974). As to similar German competition — P. Gifford & W. R. Louis, *Britain and Germany in Africa* (New Haven: Yale University Press, 1967).
4. For general approach — Ronald E. Robinson & J. Gallagher, *Africa and the Victorians* (London: Macmillan, 1961).
5. Richard Atkins, "The Conservatives and Egypt, 1875–80", *Journal of Imperial and Commonwealth History* 2 (1973–74): 190–206; G. N. Sanderson, *England, Europe and the Upper Nile, 1882–99* (Edinburgh: University Press, 1965).

6. Compare with G. N. Uzoigwe, *Britain and the Conquest of Africa* (Lansing: University of Michigan Press, 1974). Good general synoptic approach — G. N. Sanderson, "The European Partition of Africa", *Journal of Imperial and Commonwealth History* 3 (1974): 1—54.
7. D. Scarr, *Fragments of Empire* (Canberra: Australian National University Press, 1967).
8. Platt, *Finance* . . . ; David McLean, "Finance and 'Informal Empire' before the First World War", *Economic History Review* 29 (1976): 291—305.
9. Cedric J. Lowe, *The Reluctant Imperialists* (London: Routledge & Kegan Paul, 1959); William L. Langer, *The Diplomacy of Imperialism* 2nd ed., (New York: Knopf, 1951).
10. Trevor Lloyd, "Africa and Hobson's 'Imperialism' ", *Past and Present* 55 (1972): 143.
11. Re shifting the cost of defence to the colonies, see official reports and conferences — "Proceedings of the Colonial Conference, 1887", [C.5091], *Parl. Pap.* 56 (1887): 1, especially 213—30, 254—62, 308—12, 327—28; and 1897 conference, [C.8596], *Parl.Pap.* 59 (1897): 631, especially 638—41, 646—49. Also, 1902 conference, [Cd.1299], *Parl.Pap.* 66 (1902): 451 and 1909 conference (especially on empire defence), [Cd.4948], *Parl.Pap.* 59 (1909): 335. General — M. Ollivier, *The Colonial and Imperial Conferences* (Ottawa: Queen's Printer, 1954).
12. D. C. Gordon, *The Dominion Partnership in Imperial Defence, 1870—1914* (Baltimore: Johns Hopkins Press, 1965); R. A. Preston, *Canada and "Imperial Defence"* (Durham, N.C.: Duke University Press, 1967).
13. Franklyn A. Johnson, *Defence by Committee* (London: Oxford University Press, 1960); and general assessment, Grover Clark, *The Balance Sheets of Imperialism* (New York: Macmillan, 1936) and *A Place in the Sun* (New York: Macmillan, 1936).
14. Nicholas Mansergh, *Survey of British Commonwealth Affairs* (London: Oxford University Press, 1952), 76—77, 188—89 and *Documents and Speeches on British Commonwealth Affairs*, 2 vols. (London: Oxford University Press, 1953, 1963); "The Colonial Empire (1939—47)", [Cd.7167], *Parl.Pap.* 10 (1946—47): 403 at 412, 519.
15. Raymond Callahan, "The Illusion of Security", *Journal of Contemporary History* 9 (April 1974): 69—92.

11
Economic Challenge

The challenges to Britain's economic and industrial supremacy from the 1880s were not squarely faced in Britain, and were given little consideration by individual empire countries. Indeed, a few colonies were themselves thinking of a role of rivalry, if they could succeed in establishing an industrial base of their own. The fact of Britain's relative decline was not widely recognized but there was always a core of eminent politicians aware of Britain's flagging economic performance. Among the most ardent was Joseph Chamberlain. To him the ideal solution was a closer empire economy — an imperial *Zollverein*.[1] "We peoples of the Empire should treat each other better than we treat foreigners". Chamberlain and British manufacturers were upset that the dominions did not buy more products from Britain — for example, in 1913 they bought only thirty-eight per cent from Britain but were pleased to sell her fifty-nine per cent of their exports.[2]

In the early years of the twentieth century Chamberlain favoured tariff reform, abandoning free trade in favour of a system of imperial preference. But most politicians and the public still held sacredly to free trade, with its supposedly cheaper food for the masses. But the experiences of the 1914—18 war, with closer imperial economic cooperation and the need for more government interference in the economy, helped start the erosion of the sanctity of free trade. This was heightened by the 1917—18 royal commission into natural resources urging that an imperial trade policy be worked out and by a 1918 House of Commons select committee advocating imperial preference.[3] But it took the crises of the great world depression of the 1930s to cause a final abandonment of the nineteenth century, liberal, free trade approach.[4]

At a meeting in Ottawa in 1932 official recognition was given to the idea of imperial preference. This had been adopted by individual colonies somewhat earlier. For example, Canada, wishing to offer a safe base for her rising industries brought in protective tariffs, but after 1897 arranged a preferential tariff so that British and other colonial products could gain access at a cheaper rate than foreign goods. This approach spread to other colonies. Finally Britain caved in, and after 1932 arranged bilateral trading agreements with individual empire countries, wherein reciprocal tariff preference was given. The aim was to boost intra-imperial trade — in food, raw materials and manufactured goods — at the expense of foreign competitors. But it was never contemplated that the empire would become an exclusive trading block; this was impossible. All the countries, Britain and increasingly the colonies, needed foreign trade. But the trend was to strengthen, at least temporarily, some of the closer trading links between Britain and the various empire members that had been building up since the turn of the century. 1932 confirmed the trend officially, from the British point of view.[5]

In view of the rise of foreign competitors it was not surprising that some tightening of economic links between Britain and empire countries occurred. Indeed, the closer relationship arose more on Britain's part, as she obtained fewer of her imports from foreign countries and sold more of her exports to the empire. Individual empire countries for their part were still very pleased to have a ready market for their products in Britain but a number of the more established economies, primarily those of the dominions, were looking for new market opportunities, as well as obtaining an increasing amount of manufactured products from countries other than Britain. The weaker colonies, of course, generally remained heavily dependent upon Britain.

As to Britain's imports the first four decades of the twentieth century showed a marked swing to the empire, after the relative stability of the nineteenth century. Foreign suppliers (led by the United States) still remained stronger, but were declining. The pattern of British and Empire trade over these four decades is indicated in table 4.[6]

In the twentieth century metals other than iron, steel and coal, such as copper, lead, zinc and tin, were also gaining intrinsic value, with the empire again yielding up great wealth. Before the 1914—18 war, however, Britain failed to take advantage of some of this mineral wealth and allowed foreign rivals to move in. So, Germany and Belgium bought Australian lead and zinc concentrates and the United States Canadian nickel. Germany also processed tungsten reserves from Burma, Australia and Malaya. The war showed Britain the folly of this neglect and increasingly in the 1920s and 1930s British industrialists bought directly from colonial producers rather than from German and other intermediaries. The British also became more active in the exploitation of empire wealth, such as Northern Rhodesian copper. Britain had not, however, neglected the value of Malaya's tin which dominated the world market and she was successfully exploiting this both before and after the war. The main mineral deficiency throughout the empire was in oil products and iron ore, but Britain's interest in the middle east in the twentieth century was designed to counteract the oil problem.

In the case of Britain's exports, again she looked more closely to the empire as her main outlet, since foreign markets were being lost either by her being shut out or because she failed to meet foreign competition. By

Table 4. British-Empire Trade, 1890-1938.

British Imports (%)					
1890		1910		1938	
Empire share	23	Empire share	25	Empire share	40
India	7.5	Australia	8	Canada	8.5
Australasia	7	India	7	Australia	7
		Canada	4	New Zealand	5

British Exports to Empire (%)					
1890	1901	1910	1913	1929	1936
33	37	34	37	42	49

Empire Share of Britain's Main Exports (%)				
	textiles	iron/steel	coal/coke	machinery
1913	44	48	4	32.5
1934	44	55	10	51

Source: Adapted from Werner Schlote, *British Overseas Trade from 1700 to the 1930s* (Oxford: Blackwell, 1952); Albert Imlah, *Economic Elements in the Pax Britannica* (Cambridge, Mass.: Harvard University Press, 1958) and other sources. See note 6.

the 1930s the empire was becoming the vital outlet for her industrial goods. India was the main buyer, followed by Australia although South Africa made a temporary surge in the 1930s. The main foreign buyer was the United States. The closer empire tie for British exports was not, however, reciprocated by the individual colonies. Canada, of course, was much more dependent upon the United States than upon Britain for her manufactures. But in the early twentieth century a number of the Australian colonies and Ceylon obtained more of their imports from sources other than Britain, and some of the West Indies islands were choosing American suppliers over British. As the twentieth century progressed the more established economies kept cutting down Britain's share of their imports, while there was generally some increase in the empire share as well as in the foreign share. After 1925 there was in most cases a slight British recovery but by the mid-1930s the decline set in again. Even in the dependent empire there was a growing swing away from British manufactures: Malaya, for example, looking to foreign and empire sources, Ceylon to empire sources and Hong Kong to foreign sources. By contrast, west Africa still looked mainly to Britain.

In other words, the empire overall was reducing its dependence upon British manufactures, yet Britain was relying more and more on empire outlets. Among exports of small value, such as beer, soap, books, luxury foods, Britain continued to find empire countries the major buyers. Australian women loved to parade in hats from London while eating English chocolates and sipping English tea. Among exports of high value the empire was becoming an essential outlet. Whereas one century previously textiles went out three pieces to foreign countries and one to the empire, in 1930 the destinations were pegged almost evenly. Yet British manufacturers had little reason to have long-term faith in these empire outlets. Especially among the more developed economies (of the dominions), there was a growing sense of economic independence, plans for industrialization and a search for diversified trade. Britain could not expect to maintain her share in those countries. Table 5 shows imports and exports by empire countries for 1913–37.

Table 5. Trade of Empire Countries, 1913-37.

	Imports by Empire Countries (%)						Exports by Empire Countries (%)					
	From						To					
	Britain		Rest Empire		Foreign		Britain		Rest Empire		Foreign	
	1913	1937	1913	1937	1913	1937	1913	1937	1913	1937	1913	1937
Australia	53	43	10	16	37	38	46	50	8	10	46	40
Canada	21	19	4	11	75	71	49	42	6	11	45	48
New Zealand	59	49	23	24	18	27	86	77	5	6	10	17
India	65	30	6	24	29	46	23	33	14	18	63	49
S. Africa	57	43	12	9	31	48	81	37	4	13	15	50
Ceylon	33	22	50	44	17	33	47	55	13	25	40	20
Malaya	20	15	27	17	52	68	35	16	12	21	43	63
Nigeria	67	53	17	7	17	40	57	89	—	11	43	—
Gold Coast	50	50	25	42	25	8	—	—	—	—	—	—

Source: Calculated from appropriate Board of Trade, *Statistical Abstract of the British Empire*; also see Werner Schlote, *British Overseas Trade from 1700 to the 1930s* (Oxford: Blackwell, 1952).

Among the empire suppliers, India's nineteenth century hold was broken, briefly by Australia but for most years after 1912 by Canada.[7] It should be noticed that while the empire share of British exports was rising, in many colonies the British share of colonial exports was not. In the years leading to the 1914–18 war Canada's case was unusual, with a rising British share, but this was due to more food (especially wheat) being exported from Canada's expanding frontier. In the Australian colonies there was some swing towards diversifying outlets, so as to be not so dependent upon Britain. India was both drawing into a closer trading network with Japan and undergoing simple industrialization, mainly in textiles. The latter made her an exporter, and rival to Britain in the Asian region. So while building up foreign and empire markets India was cutting down on her share of trade with Britain. From the 1890s, some of the depressed West Indies colonies tried to diversify their trade by looking to the United States and Canada; others, however, drew closer to Britain. Some of the newly acquired tropical colonies, for example in west Africa, found ready French and German markets alongside the British, while Malaya was building up a strong trade with foreign countries and the rest of the empire. Other areas, notably New Zealand and South Africa, still relied very heavily on Britain as their main outlet. After the 1914—18 war the pattern fluctuated considerably but by the 1930s the British share of exports was rising in the case of Australia, Canada and India while it stayed strong for New Zealand in both the 1920s and the 1930s; South Africa, however, was weaning itself away from Britain very decisively in the latter decade.

Britain's increasing reliance upon the empire was clearly shown in food imports. The empire's share was continually rising, from nineteen per cent in the 1890s to forty-two per cent in 1935. The depression of the 1930s and the Ottawa agreements cemented this trend. There had always been a heavy dependence upon empire sugar but even in foodstuffs such as wheat, where the empire had previously been an insignificant supplier, there was a sharp upswing, sixty-three per cent coming from the empire in 1934. That year too, imperial cows were producing over one half of Britain's butter imports while meat growers in Australasia and elsewhere were cutting into the dominance of American meat, taking thirty-two per cent of the market. In many food items where Britain's import bill was not large, for example tea and cocoa, empire countries such as India and the Gold Coast held a near monopoly on supplies.

Raw materials presented a fairly similar pattern. Cotton was Britain's biggest import, the empire's share rising steadily to seventeen per cent in 1934; this resulted partly from the numerous initiatives taken to induce greater cotton-growing in the developing colonies. The United States remained the largest exporter to Britain, while India was the main empire supplier. By contrast the empire, mainly Australasia and South Africa, had always been the main grower of wool for Britain and in the twentieth century continued to hold its share of about eighty per cent or more. In timber, however, the empire proved a disappointment, the Canadian forests never being able to meet the demand that they had earlier coped with; empire timber in the twentieth century did not reach twenty per cent of Britain's requirements. With many imports of small value the vast bulk came from the empire, such as jute and indigo from India and rubber from Malaya. Britain's mineral requirements were in many cases provided by the empire. While in the nineteenth century the gold mines of the empire had dominated the world supply (and in 1912, South Africa was providing forty per cent of world output), in the twentieth century the emphasis switched to other minerals, such as copper and petroleum, although the gold resources were still appreciated.

The empire held its greatest economic value to Britain in terms of individuals; proponents of British imperialism flourished the argument that on a per capita basis the empire was by far Britain's best customer. For example, in 1902 each Natal citizen purchased British goods worth £8/6s/6d, a New Zealander £7/5s/7d, a Cape colonist £6/19s/6d, an Australian £5/5s/6d, and a Canadian £1/18s/4d. By contrast a German was buying only 11s/8d worth of British goods and an American 6s/3d. This argument did not make allowance to the total population of the respective countries. This pattern remained in later years of the twentieth century. Likewise it was the dominions, although with only a low total population of about fourteen million, which proved the best buyers in individual terms, as against the vast masses of the dependent colonies and the outside world. Britain would have to wait until the middle of the twentieth century for the population of the tropics to become sufficiently consumer-oriented before she could more fully canvas that market.[8]

The Ottawa agreements of 1932 did not produce any dramatic, long-term swing towards closer British-empire trade. Indeed, Britain probably sought an answer to the problem of foreign competition too late, in the 1930s when the world was plagued by unemployment, slack production and minimal trade. Britain failed to hold her position in the world economy not only because her rivals were newly geared and highly aggressive but also because she continued to believe in free trade at a time when others did not adhere to it so genuinely. Then when Britain did endorse closer economic links with the empire she was to find that many of the individual members were already building up strong links outside that structure.

So the world seemed to be shrinking in on Britain's trade. This was equally evident in the areas of economic influence such as Latin America and China which Britain had been successfully opening up in the second half of the nineteenth century.[9] For example, British-India-Hong Kong trade peaked with China just after the turn of the century; by 1913 it was already under fifty per cent and it continued to decline thereafter, to under thirty-three per cent in the 1930s. Japan was cutting in on British trade and shipping with China. Indeed, Britain's overall trade decline was reflected in world shipping figures; these reached a peak in the 1890s and thereafter went into decline. Further weaknesses were revealed in Britain's trade balances. Traditionally Britain had seldom been able to chalk up a positive balance but most of the deficit arose through trade with foreign countries. Except for Canada most of the colonies, and especially India and Australia, through the nineteenth century were indebted to Britain in trade terms. But in the twentieth century the flow against Britain set in, so that by the 1930s even India and Australia were achieving either a rough balance or sometimes a positive balance. Here was further evidence of the growing economic weakness of Britain, of her growing reliance upon the empire, and the greater independence of the dominions.

As against this relative decline as a trading power Britain was still able to wield authority as a financial centre of the world. British accounts had always been balanced through invisible earnings: through being a world banker, shipper and insurer, and especially through dividends from overseas investments. The significance of the income from overseas investment is shown by its increase as a part of the national income, from four per cent in 1880 to ten per cent by 1914. The yearly income from these investments between 1870 and 1914 averaged out at £110 million; obviously it was higher at the later date (1913, £210 million on a total investment of over £3,700 million). Because of the selling of securities and bonds the 1914—18 war led to a reduction in this total but there was some recovery in the 1920s. The economic crises of the early 1930s lead to a further thinning out and revaluation but by 1938 there had been some recovery. Then the total invested amounted to almost £3,500,000,000, but the return was somewhat lower, only £142,000,000.

The pattern of investment repeated that of British trade — a growing interest in the empire as opposed to foreign countries — but this occurred in two stages. An early peak of empire investment arose in the 1880s; then there was some withering away but by the late 1920s and 1930s the empire had again become the centre of British investment interest.[10] The amount of British overseas investment in 1885, 1913—14 and 1938 is given in table 6.

The 1885 figures indicated the great interest of the British investor in opening up temperate grasslands (especially for food), thus the continuing investment in the United States and the splurge in Australia and Latin America, especially the Argentine.[11] This pattern continued into the early twentieth century, but attention now centred on inland Canada; furthermore, considerable money went to South Africa for war reconstruction and mineral exploitation. By this stage, too, the British were beginning to take some interest in the tropics, especially developing Malayan rubber. The 1914—18 war and the world depression brought contractions in total British investment and it was not until the end of the 1930s that it was beginning to approach pre-1914 levels. By this stage interest had become consolidated in favour of the empire. Canada, however, was showing signs of increasing independence, herself becoming an exporter of capital as well as falling more under the financial sway of the United States. This left Australia as the main beneficiary of British overseas funds, while among foreign repositories Latin America (especially the Argentine) had replaced the earlier concentration upon the United States.

Table 6. British Overseas Investment, 1885, 1913-14, 1938 (£m).

1885		1913-14		1938	
Total	1,300	Total	3,763	Total	3,543
Foreign	625	Foreign	1,983	Foreign	1,455
USA	300	USA	755	Argentine	368
Europe/Near East	175	Argentine	320	USA	268
Latin America	150	Brazil	148	Brazil	164
		Mexico	99	Mexico	66
		Japan	63	Chile	63
Empire	675	Empire	1,780	Empire	1,988
India/Ceylon	270	Canada	515	Australia	520
Australasia	240	Australia	332	Canada	420
Canada	113	India/Ceylon	379	India	388
Cape/Natal	35	S. Africa/Rhodesia	370	S. Africa	199
Rest	17	N. Zealand	84	N. Zealand	134
		W. Africa	37	Central Africa	73
		Straits Settlement	27	Malaya	67
		N. Borneo	6	W. Africa	55
		Hong Kong	3	Ceylon	28
		Rest	26	E. Africa	24
				W. Indies	21

Source: Compiled from: 1885, A. Cairncross, *Home and Foreign Investment* 1870-1913 (Cambridge: University Press, 1953), p. 182; 1913-14, H. Feis, *Europe, the World's Banker 1870-1914* (New Haven: Yale University Press, 1930), and G. Paish articles (see note 10); 1938, Bank of England, *United Kingdom Overseas Investments* 1938 to 1948 (London, 1950); and R. Kindersley articles (see note 10).
Note that fully accurate figures cannot be given, especially for private investment; so, while exact comparison between the figures should not be made, the trends of investment are accurate.

Over the fifty years from 1880 to 1939 the kind of investment enticing the British investor changed. This was associated with a move away from the less secure and sometimes defaulting foreign government bonds firstly to the more assured railway securities and later to the more stable colonial government bonds. The exploitation of minerals and tropical resources was also beginning to attract attention, reflected by rising British government concern in the dependent empire.

The inter-war years saw a further fall in foreign government bonds, not at all helped in the 1930s by defaults and low rates of return, while empire government bonds and municipal loans firmed as favourites. In the inter-war years railway securities also declined, especially after the big sell-out of American stock, so that now South American rails dominated the foreign holdings, equalling the empire total. Mining also took a fall in this later period although there was continuing interest in the gold, diamond and copper wealth of southern Africa. As against this, raw materials, especially oil and rubber, were attracting increasing capital; there was also an increase in investment in commercial and industrial undertakings. Private investment made up the bulk of the British flow of capital into the Argentine, the United States, Malaya and British central Africa, and it constituted a considerable proportion of the flow into Canada, west

Africa, Brazil and South Africa. For Australia, India, New Zealand and east Africa the flow of public funds well exceeded private investment. The inter-war years heralded the rise of private investment in exploiting the potential of tropical areas which the British government was to more seriously embrace in the 1940s. Table 7 shows the type of British overseas investment in 1913 and 1938.

Table 7. Type of British Overseas Investment, 1913, 1938 (£m).

1913			1938	
Total	3,763	Total		3,545
Government/municipal loans, total (30%)	1,125	Government/municipal loans, total (43%)		1,521
Empire govt.	676	Empire		1,127
		Australia		456
		India		240
		Canada		125
		New Zealand		122
		S. Africa		99
		W. Africa		19
		Central Africa		12
Foreign govt.	300	Foreign		394
Municipal	152	Brazil		83
Railways, total (41%)	1,531	Railways, total (24%)		837
Empire	306			229
India	141			88
USA	617			—
Other Foreign	467			519
Raw materials, total (10%)	389	Raw materials, total (13%)		451
mining	273			187
oil	41			124
rubber	41			82
tea, coffee	22			42
nitrates	12			16
Public utilities	185			219
Finance, land coys, bank	317			200
Commercial, industrial	216			285

Source: Compiled from: 1913, H. Feis, *Europe, the World's Banker 1870-1914* (New Haven: Yale University Press, 1930); 1938, Bank of England, *United Kingdom Overseas Investments 1938 to 194 1948* (London, 1950).

Most British investors tended to look firstly for security and so accepted a modest return.[12] Some people were of course more speculative, hoping for the lucky "strike", and sometimes big profits were made. One Transvaal gold company for the period 1936—40 turned in an average return of 505 per cent, one rubber company 300 per cent between 1911—17 and one tea company 83 per cent between 1922—26.[13] But generally modesty prevailed. The average rate of return on South African gold was 4.1 per cent for the period 1887—1932 while the average yearly return for tea in the 1890s was 4.5 per cent rising to a peak of 13.3 per cent in 1913. The most successful of the great chartered companies yielded a moderate return, and this reflected the general run of yields. The average rate of return on all investments in 1907–8 was 5.2 per cent, in 1929 5.6 per cent and 1933, feeling the effects of the depression, 4.3 per cent. Table 8 shows the rate of return on British overseas investment in 1907–8, 1930 and 1934.

Table 8. Rate of Return on British Overseas Investment, 1907-8, 1930, 1934 (%).

	1907-8	1930	1934
Government/municipal loans	4.0	4.5	4.1
foreign government	4.8	5.2	3.7
empire government	3.6	4.4	4.2
municipal – foreign	4.5	5.5	3.1
– empire		4.6	4.7
Railways	4.4	4.9	2.6
USA	4.5	6.0	2.3
other foreign	4.7	4.5	1.8
India	3.9	5.5	5.1
other empire	4.0	5.3	3.3
Raw materials	10.6	9.0	7.7
mining	11.1	8.6	10.5
oil	4.5	12.4	9.0
rubber	8.2	5.3	2.4
tea, coffee	8.4	7.1	6.2
nitrates	15.0	5.2	0.6
Public utilities	5.9	6.0	4.4
Finance, land coys, banks	5.6	6.2	3.2
Commercial, industrial	5.7	7.0	4.9

Source: Compiled from: 1970-8, G. Paish and R. Lehfeldt articles 1930, R. Kindersley article in *Economic Journal* 1933, 1934, R. Kindersley articles in *Economic Journal* 1936, and for the three dates, also see Royal Institute of International Affairs, *The Problem of International Investment.* (see note 10).

The 1907–8 figures indicated a better return for foreign investment over both empire and home investment – 5 per cent as against 3.9 per cent and 3.6 per cent respectively. Not surprisingly, the share of overseas investment was catching up on that of home investment in the latter part of the nineteenth century and the early twentieth century. Latin America, especially the Argentine, was booming, as reflected in the high rate of return for Latin American railway stocks. The exploitation of minerals was offering the best returns, especially the nitrate industry, but this took up only a small issue of capital – between 1882–96 Britain invested only £12 million in Chilean nitrates. But mining, rubber and tea also provided many rewards. Overall, government bonds were returning lower than the average.

The 1930 and 1934 figures contrasted the good and bad news of the inter-war period. By the later date foreign bonds and foreign rails had gone into a severe decline. After defaults, such as the one by the Brazilian government, British investors were swinging increasingly to the stability and security of empire loans; in 1938 they returned 3.9 per cent while foreign loans yielded only 2.7 per cent. Incomes from raw materials had obviously been hit by the economic slump but South African mining and oil were still lucrative.

From the point of view of the recipients, this flow of capital was being eagerly sought for development purposes. British investment in the dominions since the 1880s had pushed them into a situation of buoyant growth. By the 1920s Australia was hungry for more capital with insufficient of her own to carry out plans for economic diversification, industrialization, increased immigration and higher land utilization. The flow to Latin America, which reached a peak by 1928, similarly opened up the immense economic potential of the area, especially of the Argentine and Brazil. However, the problem of borrowing too freely was driven home to New Zealand in the inter-war years when the government debt in London had more than doubled, to £163 million between 1914 and 1935; repayment almost crippled the country.[14] Canada showed the greatest financial maturity. In the years leading up to the 1914–18 war Britain bought heavily into Canada's assets — railways, land, lumber and mining; but during the war local capital began buying back, and afterwards Canada turned increasingly to the United States for capital, so that during the 1920s the latter overtook Britain as the main foreign investor. At the same time, Canada began investing in outside countries, including Britain. While South Africans were able to generate some local capital, for mining and agricultural pursuits, and also took capital from the United States and the Netherlands, they still had to rely heavily upon British investment. Tropical colonies, such as Malaya and Ceylon, were also experiencing economic growth, with the help of British finance. Interest was also beginning to be focused upon tropical Africa; between 1870 and 1936 the total foreign investment there amounted to £941 million and was dominated by Britain — £102 million went to Southern Rhodesia, £75 million to Nigeria, £35 million to the Gold Coast and £46 million to Kenya-Uganda.[15]

British financial supremacy was at a peak just before the 1914–18 war; the next twenty years saw Britain trying to recover and maintain her position but, buffeted by international crises and internal weaknesses, she did not fully succeed. So she was replaced by the United States as chief creditor of Canada and much of Latin America (especially the Argentine and Chile), but she maintained her place in Australasia, India,

Africa, her eastern empire and China. Also she was investing considerably in the middle east — for oil — and other areas such as Venezuela. Overall, Britain was declining faster in trade than in investment, and while in the 1930s no one could doubt the power of the American dollar London remained as a leading financial centre. At the same time there was an element of camouflage in this situation; the British economy had serious flaws, the pound was overvalued, and Britain's relative trading decline placed strains on the financial ability of the British capitalist. By 1939, the untested economic might of the United States and the flexed muscles of Germany and Japan were to pose crucial threats to the maintenance of Britain's position as a great economic power in the world.

NOTES

1. "Despatch from Mr Chamberlain . . . re British Empire Trade and Foreign Competition", [C.8449], *Parl.Pap.* 60 (1897): 1.
2. From "Statistical Abstracts", see footnote 6.
3. "Final Report of the Royal Commission on the Natural Resources, Trade, and Legislation of Certain Portions of His Majesty's Dominions", [Cd.8462], *Parl. Pap.* 10 (1917—18): 1; also see resolutions re imperial preference in [Cd.8482], *Parl.Pap.* 23 (1917—18): 315, and the Imperial economic conference in [Cd. 3018], *Parl.Pap.* 10 (1928): 477.
4. Ian M. Drummond, *British Economic Policy and the Empire* (London: Allen & Unwin, 1972); primary source — William J. Ashley, *The Tariff Problem*, 4th ed. (London: King, 1920)(1903).
5. General background — William K. Hancock, *Survey of British Commonwealth Affairs* (London: Oxford University Press, 1940), 2, part 1; Samuel B. Saul, *Studies in Overseas Trade, 1870—1914* (Liverpool: University Press, 1960); older, general treatment — Charles C. McLeod and A. W. Kirkaldy, *The Trade, Commerce and Shipping of the Empire* (London: Collins, 1924).
6. Tables 4 and 5 on imports and exports, and analysis therefrom, are composite constructs from a variety of sources. It must be remembered that trading figures are not exact; but I have chosen to look for trends, rather than exact details. The most useful sources are Werner Schlote, *British Overseas Trade from 1700 to the 1930s* (Oxford: Blackwell, 1952) and Albert H. Imlah, *Economic Elements in the Pax Britannica* (Cambridge, Mass.: Harvard University Press, 1958). The basic primary sources are the annual "Statistical Abstracts" of the United Kingdom and empire, and "Trade, Navigation, etc." accounts, printed in the *Parliamentary Papers*. Hancock, *Survey*, has useful tables in Appendix II.
7. Most useful trading information is contained in the following official papers — "Return Showing the Imports and Exports . . . 1881—85, 1886—90 and for Each Year Since", H. of C. No. 214, *Parl. Pap.* 68 (1903): 557; a statement on 1901 empire and foreign trade, [Cd.1638], *Parl.Pap.* 70 (1903): 621; more trading statistics, [Cd.1761], *Parl.Pap.* 67 (1903): 253; return on imports from white settlement colonies, H. of C. 133, *Parl.Pap.* 56 (1907): 95 and H. of C. No. 226, *Parl.Pap.* 78 (1914): 451; imports from Australia and New Zealand, 1912, H. of C. No. 249, *Parl.Pap.* 66 (1913): 389; trade tables; [Cd.3691], *Parl. Pap.* 31 (1930—31): 1.

Useful composite figures are given in: "Statistical Tables and Charts Relating to British and Foreign Trade and Industry (1854—1908)", [Cd.4954], *Parl.Pap.*

102 (1909): 693; tables for 1900—13, [Cd.7432], *Parl.Pap.* 89 (1914): 1; and tables for 1924—30, [Cd.3737], *Parl.Pap.* 31 (1930—31): 21.
8. Ashley, *Tariff Problem*, 144.
9. D. C. M. Platt, *Latin America and British Trade, 1806—1914* (London: Adam & Charles Black, 1972); Alan K. Manchester, *British Preeminence in Brazil, Its Rise and Decline* (Chapel Hill: University of North Carolina Press, 1933); Henry C. Ferns, *Britain and Argentina in the Nineteenth Century* (Oxford: Clarendon, 1960); Richard Graham, *Britain and the Onset of Modernization in Brazil* (London: Cambridge University Press, 1968); D. C. M. Platt, *Business Imperialism, 1840—1930* (Oxford: Clarendon, 1977); re China — Francis E. Hyde, *Far Eastern Trade, 1860—1914* (London: Black, 1973); C. F. Remer, *Foreign Investments in China* (New York: Macmillan, 1933); J. Hayes, *The Hong Kong Region (1850—1911)* (London: Dawson, 1977).
10. With investment figures the picture is even less exact than trade. Again, a composite analysis is given, for the amount of investment, and returns; again, the trends are the most valid part of the analysis. Especially useful are: Alex H. Cairncross, *Home and Foreign Investment, 1870—1913* (Cambridge: University Press, 1953), especially pp. 180—89; and Herbert Feis, *Europe, the World's Banker, 1870—1914* (New Haven: Yale University Press, 1930), with comparative European figures, pp. 16, 23—24, 27.

George Paish provides useful raw figures in "Great Britain's Capital Investment in Other Lands", *Journal of the Royal Statistical Society* 72 (1909); 465—80, "Great Britain's Capital Investments in Individual Colonial and Foreign Countries", *Journal of the Royal Statistical Society* 74 (1910—11): 167—87, and "The Export of Capital and the Cost of Living", *The Statist*, supplement, 14 February 1914; R. A. Lehfeldt, "The Rate of Interest on British and Foreign Investments", *Journal of the Royal Statistical Society* 76 (1912—13): 196—207.

For investment in 1920s—30s, look at the annual surveys of Robert Kindersley in *Economic Journal*, 1929—39, especially "A New Study of British Foreign Investments", 39 (1929): 8—24, "British Overseas Investments in 1935 and 1936", 47 (1937): 642—62 and "British Overseas Investment, 1938", 49 (1939) 678—95. Also, "British Capital Abroad", *Economist*, 20 November 1937, 359—66. Very useful information is brought together by the Royal Institute of International Affairs in *The Problem of International Investment* (London: Oxford University Press, 1937), and Bank of England, *United Kingdom Overseas Investments, 1938 to 1948* (London, 1950).
11. On general interpretation, see A. R. Hall (ed.), *The Export of Capital from Britain, 1870—1914* (London: Methuen, 1968); P. J. Cottrell, *British Overseas Investment in the Nineteenth Century* (London: Macmillan, 1975); Hancock, *Survey*, also looks at investment, in the dominions.
12. Re returns, see Cairncross, etc.; also M. Edelstein, "Realized Rates of Return on UK Home and Overseas Portfolio Investment in the Age of High Imperialism", *Explorations in Economic History* 12 (1976): 283—329; M. Blaug, "Economic Imperialism Revisited", *Yale Review* 50 (1961): 335—49.
13. J. Fred Rippy, *British Investment in Latin America, 1822—1949* (Minneapolis: University of Minnesota Press, 1959), pp. 181—83; A. G. Ford, "British Investment in Argentina and Long Swings, 1880—1914", *Journal of Economic History* 31 (1971). Re gold in South Africa, see Sally H. Frankel, *Capital Investment in Africa* (London: Oxford University Press, 1938) and *Investment and the Return to Equity Capital In the South African Gold-Mining Industry, 1887—1965* (Oxford: Blackwell, 1967).
14. Hancock, *Survey*, p. 189; and Royal Institute of International Affairs, *Problem*, pp. 252—53.
15. Frankel, *Capital Investment in Africa*, p. 158.

12
A Commonwealth of Dominions

With Britain beset by rising competition the question loomed larger than ever as to the political future of the empire, in particular of the four white settlement colonies — or dominions as they were becoming known in this period — already exercising self-government in internal affairs. One answer seemed to be to close ranks, to draw together the various colonies under a more centralized control from London. But this did not impress the colonies already exercising responsible government. Instead, the idea was freely floated of a grand imperial federation, as propagated by the Imperial Federation League. A series of colonial and imperial conferences, starting in 1887 and continuing through the twentieth century, helped considerably to strengthen the strands of imperial sentiment in a loose informal fashion.[1] Imperial grievances could be aired, schemes of cooperation could be considered; some success was achieved in defence planning but detailed plans of union, either economic or political, were avoided and a heavy centralized bureaucratic control was shunned. The conferences functioned as ideal means of communication and cooperation, not of control.[2]

Colonial leaders had no desire to forego the degree of independence they had already achieved. During the mid-nineteenth century Canadian and Australasian colonies had acquired legislative control over internal matters such as fiscal and trading policies and waste lands; this came later to the South African colonies. The next step was to assert greater control over foreign affairs, and later, even to chip away at the reserve powers which the supreme British parliament possessed, for example, making void repugnant colonial legislation and having ultimate sanction over the making of constitutions. In the colonies nationalistic and independent sentiments were rising. The analogy of the adolescent reaching manhood was resorted to as colonial leaders expressed the belief in their political maturity, claiming that they no longer needed the ultimate sanction of Britain for their actions.

This growth of nationalism was spurred on in the early twentieth century by the strong development of their economies. Already the four dominions had healthy exports in primary products. In Canada industrialization and mineral exploitation were proceeding at a pace.[3] The two world wars provided a further boost to this trend, the pattern being repeated in Australia although to a lesser extent. New Zealand and South Africa were not so fortunate in industrial developments but nevertheless moved ahead strongly in primary production, and in minerals in the South African case.

The rise of these flourishing economies was boosted by growth in population. Canada, followed by Australia, showed the biggest gains, acting as magnets for British migrants. Indeed, in the matter of migration the theme of closer imperial links was quite definitely confirmed in the first part of the twentieth century, the lure of the United States finally being broken.[4] Between 1900 and 1914 Canada took 1,500,000 and Australasia 500,000 of Britain's total flow of 4,700,000. The extent of the United States' previous hold is clearly illustrated by the following figures: between 1812 and 1914 13,600,000 British migrants went to the United States while only 3,800,000 chose British North America (numbers of which also crossed to the south), 2,200,000 to Australasia and 700,000 to southern Africa. But from the early twentieth century this pattern was reversed; whereas between 1890 and 1900 only 28 per cent of migrants stayed within the empire, between 1901 and 1912 63 per cent did.

The British flow was light during the 1890s but picked up thereafter, especially after 1907. Now the majority were English and Scotsmen, rather than Irish. After the 1914—18 war migration became more organized and involved more state assistance.[5] Now immigration was conceived as a two-fold policy, one of helping British development by sending out surplus unemployed and one of helping the empire by supplying vitally needed labour for development. So joint sponsoring schemes were planned; for example, Australia provided land for migrants while both the British and Australian governments helped with passage money and better transport organization. Yet such schemes met with only minimal success, mainly because the desire of the British to live in the colonies was waning. The best year for migration between the two wars was 1920 — before the state schemes were operating — when 135,000 went out, but this in no way approached pre-war figures. On the whole, this empire settlement scheme proved a failure, most migrants still preferring to finance their own passage.

Life in the white colonies was advancing rapidly to British levels and in some respects ahead of them. The openness of opportunity, the ready availability of food and space helped produce a healthy, upstanding community, and advances in health treatment did not take long to reach the colonies. In education the emphasis upon equality of opportunity meant that many colonial children had more prospects for a good life than their British counterparts. In Australia primary level education became the perquisite of all young teenagers, while after the turn of the century increasing emphasis was put upon the furtherance of training at a secondary school level. Yet feelings of insecurity in the culture of the colonies still persisted and the ultimate in excellence was still conceived of in British terms. So while colonial universities expanded and new ones opened, Oxford, Cambridge and the Inns of Court were seen as the hallmarks of success.

The colonial was not yet prepared to assert a cultural independence and was, indeed, undervaluing the spirit of initiative that appeared in the colonies. Already there were cases of political ideas arising first in the colonies and being later adopted in Britain. Secret ballot, the payment of members of parliament, votes to women and manhood suffrage were put into operation first in outposts of the empire. Britain was not the sole originator of ideas of liberalism and democracy; the transference of ideas and institutions was not a one-way movement from the metropolitan power to the colonies.

The improvement in world communications was helping to improve life in the dominions. The railway revolution which had begun to open them up in the mid-nineteenth century persisted in later decades so that both coasts of Canada and of Australia were linked while numerous lines zigzagged across the countryside.[6] In southern Africa the rail-line pushed further north in the quest of building a Cape to Cairo backbone. Whereas in 1850 only 8,500 miles of rail had been laid, by 1895 50,000 miles traversed India and the colonies. In the twentieth century the dominions leapt aboard the petroleum-powered motor car and soon horizons were clouded with dust from bush-tracks. In the inter-war years machines took to the air; in 1932 Imperial Airways carried its first mail and intrepid passengers to Capetown via Cairo.[7] Earlier the cable system had been considerably expanded.[8] The Eastern Telegraph Company brought Australasia, Hong Kong and South Africa within easy communication of London. At the turn of the century British worries about the challenge of rival empires lead to the construction of a government-controlled "all-red" cable link to Australasia via Canada. The Marconi Company inaugurated a wireless maritime service to help shipping. And in 1927 a single company (later known as Cable and Wireless Ltd) took over the cable and wireless interests of the various empire countries. All these technological developments boosted immensely the accessibility of even the furtherest place in the empire and consequently reduced the feelings of loneliness and isolation.

Armed with the prospect of a viable economic future, an expanding population and a rising standard of living, the white settlement colonies not unnaturally were pressing for acceptance as full members of the international family of nations. To receive such recognition they had to convince foreign countries that they had weaned themselves away from "mother" Britain and now stood fully independent. In colonial minds their valiant fighting efforts in the 1914—18 war marked their full political development. Britain was prepared to acknowledge this but foreign countries were not so sure. After all, Britain had made a general declaration of war bringing in the whole empire, although Australia, New Zealand,

Canada, South Africa and India claimed that Britain's declaration was also theirs. Again, in the fighting, while the dominions maintained control over their own forces at the front, a general overall command by Britain operated. The whole effort was one of cooperation, yet under a British lead. Most importantly, Britain had made it clear before the war that she alone determined British and empire foreign policy.

At the 1919 peace conference the dominions were accorded an indeterminate status, short of full nationhood, and in their admission to the League of Nations the dominions took on a similar dual status, as individual members and as part of the empire. Sometime during the 1920s, however, the dominions probably acquired full nationhood although no precise date can be given.[9] The passing of the Statute of Westminster in 1931 put the official seal on this development through categorizing the dominions as members of the British Commonwealth of Nations. But even after that event not all the nations were exercising their full rights in foreign policy, such as diplomatic representation.

The "commonwealth" idea had been gestating very slowly as the political answer for the grown-up empire. Colonies could be granted independence without being separated completely from their imperial heritage. Colonial nationalism could be satisfied in a way that imperial unity could never manage. Aspects of the commonwealth idea had been in formulation since at least the eighteenth century. In the next century the "little Englanders" casually contemplated some sort of a commonwealth structure wherein the colonies might freely cooperate and associate with Britain. In the twentieth century the elaboration of the "dominion" concept for the self-governing colonies became one of the hallmarks of the commonwealth spirit; the creation in 1907 of the Dominions Division within the Colonial Office was token of this.

The political maturation of the dominions waited upon their assertion of full power in foreign affairs — making treaties, having their own diplomatic representation, making war and peace, in short devising a foreign policy independent of British needs. Canada took the lead in these matters; as early as 1871 she was participating in treaty making. By the 1920s the dominions were taking an increasingly autonomous stand in foreign affairs, refusing to come to Britain's call in 1922, and overall taking a rather insular view to international problems.[10]

The coming of war in 1939 indicated the individual position of the different dominions; there was now no imperial unity in matters of foreign policy or defence.[11] In South Africa a bitter debate took place on entry into the war. Eire, which had joined the ranks of the dominions as the Irish Free State in 1922, went its own way, declaring neutrality. But in Australia and New Zealand stronger emotional ties with Britain clouded the issue, politicians there talking of an automatic commitment; in any case, their defence arrangements involved close cooperation with Britain.

Throughout the 1920s and 1930s Australia and New Zealand were slow to take initiatives showing their full sense of independence in foreign and defence matters. By contrast Canada, South Africa and Eire were pushing the matter, by 1939 having already established diplomatic missions in foreign countries. Australians and New Zealanders, however, felt more vulnerable to foreign attack and so naturally felt a stronger need for great power protection. Traditionally Britain had done this, until Japan swept through the Pacific and the fall of Singapore shattered this belief. Quickly reliance was transferred to another great power, the United States.

The waging of the war between 1939 and 1945 showed how the spirit of independence had grown since 1914—18.[12] Now, with each dominion having full control over its own foreign policy and defence forces there was no imperial war cabinet. At the same time a common imperial spirit persisted and there was daily communication between London and dominion capitals. Also, dominion representatives were put on various British boards and agencies.

The constitutional changes underlying this assertion of national independence and whittling down of the supremacy of the British parliament were formulated in various conferences during the 1920s. In particular, the Balfour Declaration of 1926 (as to the nature of dominion status) and the subsequent Statute of Westminster of 1931 gave the British constitutional seal to the demands of the Canadian, South African and Irish governments for full dominion competence.[13] So, for example, the governor-general of a dominion came to be acknowledged as a representative of the crown and not of the British government. So the powers of disallowance and reservation (admittedly seldom used) were practically wiped out. In future, British legislation applied in a dominion only at the latter's request and consent while dominion legislation would not be invalid because it was repugnant to a British statute. Even so, a few limitations on constitutional competence persisted — for example, in some of the constitutions creating federations, especially where it was intended to protect or entrench certain interests or rights. On the other hand South Africa took up a position of extreme constitutional independence, acquiring in the 1930s the right to secede or become a republic.

The dominions (Canada, Australia, New Zealand, South Africa, Irish Free State, and Newfoundland for a few years) were accepted by the British government as states of full autonomy and equality with Britain. The Commonwealth of Nations was seen as this group of nations freely associating and linked by a common allegiance to the crown. But in fact all was not in harmony. The Irish Free State (later Eire) was never satisfied with the solution which the British government devised in the 1920s for the Irish troubles and in the 1930s it increasingly went its own way. In South Africa Afrikaner nationalism was growing in intensity and, taking advantage of the status of independence, brought in racial policies discriminating against black Africans and Asians; this marked a growing moral disunity within the commonwealth.[14]

Meanwhile, the spirit of dissension was sweeping through India. Indian nationalism had been developing throughout the nineteenth century. Although full equality between Indian and European had been promised in 1858, in practice it did not pertain. A vernacular press, which had been printing without restrictions since 1835, became increasingly critical of British rule after 1882. Three years later an organization to represent Indian political interests was formed, the Indian National Congress. At first this body spoke out moderately, as the elite band of educated middle class Indians hoped to insinuate themselves fully into the British system. But by the turn of the century rising disillusionment with British control led to the emergence of a more extreme, nationalist splinter-group.

The British government did not contemplate conferring self-government upon India, as it had upon the white settlement colonies, for some considerable time in the future. It was expected that a slow path of political education would be necessary before Indians would be able to govern themselves to the satisfaction of the British. A start was made in 1882 when Lord Ripon instituted an elected majority for local municipal boards — local self-government. But political extensions at the higher levels of government came more slowly — for example, with Indian representatives elected indirectly to the provincial and central legislatures in 1892. At the executive level, Indians were put on to the Council of India and the Viceroy's Executive Council in 1907 and 1909 respectively. Further extensions of the electoral principle were made in 1909, but the British government was making such political concessions too late to satisfy the demands for self-government which increasing numbers of Indian nationalists were making.[15]

In 1919 further political powers were transferred to Indians, but still the British government insisted upon the sharing principle, that at the provincial level authority be shared between British officials and Indians' elected representatives. Yet by this stage Indians, after helping in Britain's war effort, and after hearing widespread discussion on nationalism at the peace conference in Paris, were demanding an equivalent status with the white settlement areas. British repression, as at Amritsar in 1919 when hundreds of Indians were shot, only fanned Indian discontent higher. Gandhi, leading a non-cooperation campaign and schemes of civil disobedience, was helping to frustrate British administration. The British government made further concessions in 1935, but still not enough to satisfy Indian demands. Dominion status was promised, whereas Indians felt it should be instituted. The British government, however, was still able to withstand a concerted opposition from Indian nationalists because the principle of separatism had been growing through the twentieth century. By promising separate representation to Muslims, and other groups, the British were able to forestall independence, with Hindus and Muslims generally unable to cooperate fully in their demands for political power.

Yet the Indians, although divided, were making the British presence difficult to maintain. By their nationalist strivings the Indians had pushed the course of political development faster than most British authorities had ever contemplated. The Indians were asserting that they too could exercise a full political maturity equally with the white settlers of the British commonwealth.

NOTES

1. Maurice Ollivier (ed.), *The Colonial and Imperial Conferences from 1887 to 1937* (Ottawa: Queen's Printer, 1954); Richard Jebb, *The Imperial Conference* (London: Longmans, 1911); John Tyler, *The Struggle for Imperial Unity 1868–95* (London: Longmans, 1938); John Kendle, *The Round Table and Imperial Union* (Toronto: University Press, 1975).
2. General — William K. Hancock, *Survey of British Commonwealth Affairs* (London: Oxford University Press, 1937), I. H. Duncan-Hall, *Commonwealth* (London: Van Nostrand Reinhold, 1971); Arthur B. Keith, *Speeches and Documents on the British Dominions, 1918–31* (London: Oxford University Press, 1932); Nicholas Mansergh, *Documents and Speeches on British Commonwealth Affairs, 1931–52* (London: Oxford University Press, 1953); "Special Issue on the First British Commonwealth", *Journal of Imperial and Commonwealth History* 8 (1979): 1–192.
3. Re Canadian initiatives, Robert L. Borden, *Canada in the Commonwealth from Conflict to Co-operation* (Oxford: Clarendon, 1929); Carl Berger, *The Sense of Power* (Toronto: University Press, 1970).
4. Hancock, *Survey*, I, pp. 28–29, 153–59; John D. B. Miller, *Britain and the Old Dominions* (London: Chatto & Windus, 1966), pp. 17–19; L. Gallaway and R. Vedder, "Emigration from the United Kingdom to the United States, 1860–1913", *Journal of Economic History* 31 (1971): 885–97; C. Newbury, "Labour Migration in the Imperial Phase", *Journal of Imperial and Commonwealth History* 3 (1974–75): 234–56.
5. J. A. Schultz, "Canadian Attitudes Towards Empire Settlement 1919–30", *Journal of Imperial and Commonwealth History* 1 (1973): 237–51; "Report of the Inter-Departmental Committee on Migration Policy", [Cd.4689], *Parl.Pap.* 10 (1933–34): 599, also, report of royal commission on natural resources, [CD.8462], *Parl.Pap.* 10 (1917–18): 83–85.
6. J. S. Mills, *The Press and Communications of the Empire* (London: British Books, 1924).
7. Robert McCormack, "Imperial Mission", *Journal of Contemporary History* 9 (October 1974): 74–97, re air route to Cape Town.
8. See reports on cables, [Cd.1065], *Parl.Pap.* 11 (1902): 199, see later developments in "Report of the Imperial Wireless Telegraphy Committee, 1924", [Cd.2060], *Parl.Pap.* 12 (1924): 635.
9. Robert M. Dawson, *The Development of Dominion Status, 1900–36* (London: Cass, 1965)(1937); Arthur B. Keith, *Dominion Autonomy in Practice* (London: Oxford University Press, 1929) and *The Dominions as Sovereign States* (London: Macmillan, 1938); Gwen Neuendorf, *Studies in the Evolution of Dominion Status* (London: Allen & Unwin, 1942).

10. On Canadian assertions of national identity, see George Glazebrook, *Canada at the Peace Conference* (London: Oxford University Press, 1942); John S. Galbraith, *The Establishment of Canadian Diplomatic Status at Washington* (Berkeley: University of California Press, 1951).
11. Nicholas Mansergh, *Survey of British Commonwealth Affairs* (London: Oxford University Press, 1952), re external policy, 1931–39; review article, D. Carlton, "The Dominions and the Gathering Storm", *Journal of Imperial and Commonwealth History* 6 (1977–78): 172–75.
12. Gwendolyn M. Carter, *The British Commonwealth and International Security* (Toronto: Ryerson, 1947), Heather J. Harvey, *Consultation and Co-operation in the Commonwealth* (London: Oxford University Press, 1952).
13. Kenneth C. Wheare, *The Statute of Westminster and Dominion Status* (London: Oxford University Press, 1953), pp. 62–99; Philip J. Noel-Baker, *The Present Juridical Status of the British Dominions* (London: Longmans, 1929).
14. Rheinhold Hoernle, *South African Native Policy and the Liberal Spirit* (Johannesburg: Witwatersrand University Press, 1945).
15. C. H. Philips, *The Evolution of India and Pakistan, 1858–1947* (London: Oxford University Press, 1962); Anil Seal, *The Emergence of Indian Nationalism* (Cambridge: University Press, 1968); Ram Gopal, *How India Struggled for Freedom* (Bombay: Book Centre, 1967); R. C. Majumdar, *History of the Freedom Movement in India* (Calcutta: Mukhopadhyay, 1962); M. N. Das, *India under Morley and Minto* (London: Allen & Unwin, 1964); review article — T. Raychaudhuri, "Indian Nationalism as Animal Politics", *Historical Journal* 22 (1979): 747–63; J. R. McLane, *Indian Nationalism and the Early Congress* (Princeton: University Press, 1977).

13
The Sentiment of Imperial Glory

For a period — the 1890s — the more aggressive attitude of the British government towards imperialism was reflected in public opinion. Over the centuries the expansion of British imperial influence around the world had not been a matter of concern or excitement for most British people. Usually interest was restricted to a small group, obviously some traders, soldiers and politicians, along with the settlers who went out to the colonies and their relatives back home. But as the nineteenth century drew to a close public interest in empire increased markedly, perhaps never becoming a plaything of the majority but certainly attaining a place of affection and pride in the hearts and minds of a good minority. The actual extent of public endorsement cannot be fully measured but the size, splendour and diversity of the empire gave a thrill to many people, especially of middle class status, as well as encouraging groups of working class people to volunteer for overseas service or to abandon a hard life in Britain for promised opportunities, perhaps even a life of ease and luxury, in Britain's far-off outposts. Certainly an imperial conference in London could not help but draw hundreds of thousands of flag-waving, hoarsely cheering, loyal subjects into the streets. And a war to whip the ignorant Boers or thrash the brutal Huns inspired an immediate response from British youths, eager to fight and die for God, queen and empire.

The rise of public interest flowed from a number of events. The enthusiasm of politicians such as Disraeli in the 1870s and Rosebery and Chamberlain in the 1890s had some public effect.[1] Institutions such as the Royal Colonial Society and the Imperial Federation League helped prime the mind for a strong British culture spreading around the world. The Royal Geographical Society, sponsoring expeditions of adventure into "darkest" Africa — and anywhere — aroused passions of pride in British valour. Furthermore authors, some writing adventure stories, others describing the empire, attracted a growing public that was at least anxious to empathize with men involved in the imperial struggle, even if they themselves were not willing to become actually embroiled in it. In the 1880s and 1890s these various influences came to a head, bringing forth a rush of public approval for the empire and its expansion. It was at this time that imperial writers had their greatest influence. While Professor Seeley explained to his students that the British empire was a natural and glorious creation, and Froude dreamed of a grand confederation of Oceana, popular writers such as Rudyard Kipling inspired readers to identify with a life of adventure, duty and morality, the ingredients of the imperial experience.[2] Within two months of its publication in 1885 Rider Haggard sold five thousand copies of *King Solomon's Mines*, so successful was the formula.

The reason for this positive response was that the authors captured the mood of frustration and despair that gnawed away in the minds of the readers. The world of the 1880s and 1890s was marked by more doubt and confusion than had existed earlier in the century. Man's ideas on his position in the world were under challenge, especially by Darwinism. Just as Britain was finding her position of supremacy challenged by rivals, so man was beginning to doubt earlier confidence in his ability to order and control his life.[3] Men now doubted previously accepted notions on the creation of the universe and man's relation with God. Equally shattering to the psyche of the individual was the growing sense of frustration and alienation that was enveloping him. As he became a creature of an urbanized, industrialized society, so he was beginning to feel himself increasingly isolated and alienated from his society and his environment. He faced a major task of self-identification. Where the novels of Haggard and Kipling (and later Conrad and Buchan) succeeded was in portraying characters faced with the problems of the world that the reader himself battled. Here was a hero, beset by a hostile environment, a man all alone, menaced by huge, impenetrable India. And the authors offered some sort of solution. Rather than bemoan such a fateful dilemma the hero went out — with boldness, a sense of rectitude and a dedication to service — to face the perils and problems larger than himself. Armed with a creed of action and duty, cloaked in the belief of his morality, he was prepared to do battle in the struggle for survival. Whether in the long run he won or lost did not really matter, so long as he acted with courage and conviction. Such a philosophy gave the ordinary reader heart, even a sense of purpose in a bewildering, changing world. Such a philosophy could be applied to imperialism, giving even to its active aggression a noble quality. Imperialist behaviour could become a means of handling the intellectual problems of man. If he was not brave enough actually to go out and participate in imperial endeavours, at least he could through reading or flag-waving share vicariously in the great imperial adventure. By embracing the imperial morality a sagging confidence and flagging conscience could be revived.

This public interest in empire reached a peak in the 1890s, pouring out in a frenzy of excitement over the Anglo-Boer War of 1899. The problems of fighting, however, soon jolted some of this unthinking enthusiasm and thereafter interest in and awareness of empire settled down to a more passive level.[4] Of course people with relatives and friends across the seas kept alive imperial inks while specialized bodies such as the Round Table busied themselves as information agencies and sometimes as pressure groups on behalf of imperial interests. Great crises such as the two world wars also brought an effusion of imperial sentiment, although this was probably stronger from the colonial end than from Britain.

Yet imperial sentiment was mainly a white preserve; other races did not participate in the brotherhood of the commonwealth.[5] Indians, for example, found themselves as pariahs of the empire, at least in white eyes.[6] Their second class status became highlighted at the turn of the century when various white colonies brought in legislation restricting their immigration. Natal set the pattern in 1897, using a literacy test for entry.[7] By the aid of language and other requirements it was possible for the colonial government always to ensure that an Indian or other coloured applicant was disqualified. Other colonies followed suit. The Union of South Africa disprivileged Asians who were seen as trading rivals to Europeans. Australia had earlier been scared by the prospect of Chinese hordes sweeping in and raking off the gold wealth of the country. Australia, New Zealand and Canada brought in legislation discriminating against Chinese, Japanese, Javanese and other Asians. The Australian people, wishing to keep out cheap foreign labourers willing to live at a low standard, propagated the dream of a "white Australia". The Indians, however, found themselves at a disadvantage even in other tropical areas. For example in Mauritius, east Africa and Fiji there was communal strife between Indians and the original inhabitants, mainly because the latter resented the position of privilege that the former acquired through becoming the economically and educationally dominant group in the community. Yet in those areas the Indians still found themselves socially inferior vis-a-vis the small band of white settlers. Although Winston Churchill, when colonial secretary, promised Asians living in Kenya that there would be equal rights for all "civilized men" nothing constructive was done by the British government.[8] It was left to the Indian government at various conferences to prosecute the cause of Indians living abroad, but nothing much was achieved, apart from the ending of the system of Indian labour transportation in the 1920s and 1930s.

The policy of racial discrimination was most clearly demonstrated in the Union of South Africa in the 1920s and 1930s.[9] The more liberal approach of the Cape — in political, land and educational rights, especially for "civilized" blacks — was being whittled away by the Afrikaners of the Transvaal and the Orange Free State; for example, in the 1930s separate rolls rather than a common roll were brought in for Cape blacks. Overall, a more segregationist situation was arising; earlier policies concerning reserves were refashioned along the lines of creating separate living areas or homelands for Africans. Land representing fourteen per cent of the area of South Africa was provided for the blacks, being about seventy per cent of the total population. About one-half of the blacks, however, lived in white areas, especially cities, providing cheap labour. Pass laws were introduced, security legislation allowed the removal of the individuals and even tribes, while economically the position of the black worker kept deteriorating.

The racial intolerance of the South Africans was copied in other white states, although less harshly. In Australia and Canada the lot of the Aborigines and the Indians respectively deteriorated further, as they were banished to the "back-blocks". Missions continued to bring a little comfort and succour while at a governmental level a heavy-handed, paternalistic policy of reservations and wardship was being moulded. Only in New Zealand was there some aura of enlightenment.[10] The Maoris, firstly through their own efforts and secondly through the tolerance of the whites, were making a comeback. Sometimes through cooperation, sometimes through protest, the Maoris were able to make their presence felt. With a rising population, through schemes of self-help and improvement, even through their own parliament and religious outlets they were able to restore a degree of cultural autonomy as well as gain a measure of respect from the whites.

The British government, still betraying a humanitarian interest, hoped to reduce the more harsh spirit of racism apparent in the white dominions. Yet the settler mentality of the dominions prevailed. White South Africans, being outnumbered by the blacks, responded defiantly with policies of putting them down. In Australia and Canada the number of coloured people was so small that the whites virtually forgot about them. Only in New Zealand, where the Maoris were too many yet not enough of a threat, could some degree of compromise and tolerance be worked out. Blighting all these racial situations was the overwhelming pride of all whites in their own achievements. British people, both at home and in the empire, were convinced of the superiority of their civilization over all other peoples, as manifest in their parliamentary and judicial systems, as well as in their technology and standard of living.

NOTES

1. John R. Seeley, *The Expansion of England* (London: Macmillan, 1883); Richard Faber, *The Vision and the Need* (London: Faber, 1966).
2. James A. Froude, *Oceana* (London: Longmans, 1886); Rudyard Kipling, various writings, such as *Plain Tales from the Hills*; Henry Rider Haggard novels, such as *Nada, the Lily*.
3. See analysis by Alan Sandison, *The Wheel of Empire* (London: Macmillan, 1967).
4. Note the rise of critics — Bernard Porter, *Critics of Empire* (London: Macmillan, 1968); note especially J. A. Hobson, *Imperialism* (London: Nisbet, 1902) and *Psychology of Jingoism* (London: Richards, 1901). Re Boer war hysteria, see Eric Stokes, "Milnerism", *Historical Journal* 5 (1962): 47–60.

5. Robert A. Huttenback, "No Strangers within the Gates", *Journal of Imperial and Commonwealth History* 1 (1973): 271–302.
6. Indian Emigration to Empire, see [Cd.5192], *Parl.Pap.* 27 (1910): 1, 24–25; "Memorandum re Indians in Kenya", [Cmd.1922], *Parl.Pap.* 18 (1923): 141.
7. David Welsh, *The Roots of Segregation* (Cape Town: Oxford University Press, 1971).
8. Robert Gregory, *A History of Race Relations within the British Empire, 1890–1939* (Oxford: Clarendon, 1972); R. A. Huttenback, *Gandhi in South Africa* (Ithaca: Cornell University Press, 1971), and *Racism and Empire* (Ithaca: Cornell University Press, 1976).
9. Phyllis Lewsen, "The Cape Liberal Tradition", *Race* 12 (1971–72): 65–80; R. Hoernle, *South African Native Policy and the Liberal Spirit* (Johannesburg: Witwatersrand University Press, 1945); Sydney H. Olivier, *White Capital and Coloured Labour* (Westport: Russel & Russell, 1970)(1929).
10. John A. Williams, *Politics of the New Zealand Maori* (Seattle: University of Washington Press, 1969).

14
Tropical Trusts

Daunted by the cost of struggling tropical dependencies the British government, especially the Treasury, hoped that the administration and development of the tropics could be undertaken by private enterprise. In the 1870s—80s approval was given to four chartered companies to act as quasi-sovereigns in certain areas. In the Niger basin a variety of British commercial concerns had been competing between themselves and with the French for the trading wealth of the palm tree. Finally under the guile of George Goldie a monopoly was established; this eventually (1886) became the Royal Niger Company. In similar fashion, central Africa was consigned to the direction of Cecil Rhodes' British South Africa Company and east Africa to William McKinnon's Imperial British East Africa Company.[1] Company rule was also instituted over the wilds of north Borneo. For the companies, the burdens of administration were to prove too onerous and for the shareholders profits too elusive. Only the Royal Niger Company showed healthy returns (about 6—6½ per cent), while the Imperial British East Africa Company folded up by 1893 and shareholders in the British South Africa Company had to wait fifty years to get a reasonable dividend.[2] Company rule helped to keep out foreign rule but failed to provide a very effective or efficient control. So in east Africa the Foreign Office was forced to enter into protectorate arrangements with the Sultan of Zanzibar and inland potentates so that by 1895 British authority was being exercised through a high commissioner over the area later known as Kenya and Uganda.[3] In the Niger case the company gave up its administrative responsibilities to the British government at the end of the century while in Southern Rhodesia the British government found itself entwined with company administration after 1896;[4] finally in 1923 company rule ceased in central Africa.

A board of directors sitting in London with prime responsibility to British shareholders could not adequately govern these overseas areas and especially could not protect the interests of other races. So the British government had to move in; yet even here there were strictures. A penny-pinching Treasury meant that only a minimal official presence (in personnel and in equipment) was provided. The Foreign Office was a more frugal organ of government in this respect than the Colonial Office, the latter requiring the display of a larger and more expensive retinue of power. The Foreign Office would get by, wherever possible, with a consul, as in the Zambezi area in 1883. By the end of the century, however, both departments were readily resorting to the device of protection and foreign jurisdiction. This allowed large parts of the interior of central and western Africa, as well as coastal eastern Africa, to come under some vague degree of British authority exercised by high commissioners or consuls. Protection treaties with the local chiefs ensured that other European nations were kept out.[5] In Malaya a variation on this approach – placing a British adviser or resident to assist the local sultan in the more efficient government of his people – was extended throughout the peninsula between 1888 and 1909; this approach was also adopted in Brunei and in Zanzibar.

This informal kind of authority was linked with a system of government later known as indirect rule. Where all the trappings of official control could not be provided, it was thought wise to work through existing organs of local power. The practice of indirect rule was fashioned in some of the Indian princely states during the nineteenth century. The resident system in Malaya after 1874 was a version of it; adaptations of it were made in the African setting in the late nineteenth and early twentieth centuries. Finally it received its most explicit formulation when Lugard as high commissioner tried to administer the huge expanses of the recently acquired Northern Nigeria with insufficient staff.[6] His experiences led him to write *The Dual Mandate* (1922), the principles of which came to be accepted as the hallmark of good government until the 1940s. The essence of administration was to preserve and build upon the virtues of existing local structures. The local people continued under the control of their own chiefs, headmen and councils; local laws and tribunals persisted in most cases, unless unduly severe treatment resulted. Chiefs were singled out for support by the imperial government: sometimes this meant bolstering a flagging ruler or even restoring or creating one. The British presence was felt through a handful of officials – the district officer or travelling commissioners, or more remotely a high commissioner or resident.[7]

While one of the aims was to retain officers and institutions already familiar to the local communities official policy also intended some changes toward British ways. So new burdens and responsibilities were introduced, especially hut taxes and other financial devices to help collect revenue to pay for administration. Taxes (in cash) were also collected in some areas to encourage the indigenes to become wage-labourers. Such changes meant, in fact that the traditional life of the community was gradually being eroded – in particular the role of the chief was increasing, in power and wealth.[8] But in time the chief himself was to find his position under challenge, as the tasks of administration multiplied and became more complicated. Gradually the chief became a rubber stamp for the district officer. In the long run, the system of indirect rule acted as the vehicle for greater imperial control. Yet not all traditional bodies were weakened in this fashion; the fairly strong system of kingship in Buganda persisted throughout the colonial period, with the British system of advice operating fairly lightly.[9] So indirect rule worked ambivalently — partially preserving and partially changing.

Imperial administrators at the turn of the century were also advocating policies of trusteeship. To justify their rule some imperialists spoke of the great mission that had been entrusted to the British to help and protect other races. The principal of trusteeship was redolent with phrases of protection and paternalism, that the coloured people who were less well endowed with the ability to govern their lives and to prosper would be looked after and assisted to find a better life through British governors. Joseph Chamberlain was convinced in the 1890s that blacks were incapable of governing themselves;[10] Negroes were "totally unfit for representative institutions" and liberal constitutions. Journalists wrote that if the British withdrew from the tropics bloodshed, anarchy and slavery would return. The British were there to civilize and protect them, eradicating traffic in domestic slaves, arms and liquor, hoping eventually to introduce British morality.

The ultimate in protectiveness arose in Fiji.[11] Governor Gordon's hopes of preserving the Fijian way of life and protecting their land largely failed, mainly because the protectors did not really know what traditional Fijian society was like. In the long run, Fijian life ossified, with little change occurring and few initiatives being taken. Such over-protection and over-paternalism was evident elsewhere, for example by Hubert Murray in Papua, so that these people were not prepared for the onslaught of "progress".[12] The one positive gain from this approach was that most land remained with the indigenes and was not alienated to Europeans.

The source of ideas on trusteeship were manifold — nineteenth century humanitarians, Exeter Hall, anti-slavery groups, John Hobson, E. D. Morel, the Fabians. The horrors of the 1914—18 war led to bitter denunciations of the evils of imperialism and to greater emphasis upon the duties of trusteeship, for both humanity in general and the dependent people. So by the 1920s the British government felt the need to dress up imperialism in a more favourable light. Exploitation of the natural resources of a territory was shown to be for the benefit not only of the metropolitan power but also for the local people. Another principle of government, emphasizing the importance of the local peoples, was enunciated in 1923 — native paramountcy.[13] Devised for the needs of Kenya, with the aim of checking the encroachment of the power and interest of white settlers, this principle became another of the basic guidelines applied throughout the tropical dependencies. Furthermore, the responsibilities arising out of the mandate system of the League of Nations had some carry-over effect to existing empires.

Yet the preservation of the interests of the indigenes was hard to achieve. Changes almost invariably flowed on from the introduction of even the slightest degree of white civilization; and more often than not these changes arose out of the demands of the local people who believed they saw advantages and benefits in the western way. So the trend was for an ever greater adoption, sometimes imposition, of British ways. This was most clear in the case of white missionaries. After the initial distrust of the people had been broken down and the chief had succumbed, the missionary's zeal would begin to make headway. So there followed much destruction of the traditional system. Yet there was never a complete elimination of earlier ways, and in the twentieth century some degree of compromise and amalgamation between a christian way and a traditional way was worked out in certain communities. Indeed, sometimes resistance and non-cooperation followed, with revivals of earlier beliefs and customs, as an indication that there were strengths and virtues in the way of life of the traditional local community which could match the supposed benefits of the western system. So, independent christian churches in Africa or the Ratana movement among the Maoris, even the cargo cults of Melanesia, were signs of this combination, of desires to both emulate the new ways and show a sense of independency and the resilience of their own traditional modes.[14] Changes were inevitably occurring, but not in a way fashioned or imposed solely by the imperialist power. Although some of the traditional leaders were willing to be pawns of the imperialist masters, there was never a wholesale adaptation of the British system. Rather the ideas and institutions of the imperialists became modified, sometimes rejected, to suit the local situation.

The British government by the early twentieth century was hoping for a high degree of uniformity in political administration in the tropics; this meant the crown colony system of government. Yet as the years rolled by the cry rose louder and louder for political development; this came not only from the few whites residing there but also from a growing number of indigenous leaders. Yet the British government thought that advance from the crown colony system should come only slowly.

Southern Rhodesia, however, was an exception. With an influx of white settlers demands were soon made for the area to be treated like Cape Colony or any other settlement area. By 1898, in less than a decade, the representative principle was introduced. The situation there was anomalous, with both the British South Africa Company and the British government participating in administration. Nevertheless, rapid political advance continued, under white pressure, until 1923 when responsible government was instituted.[15] These developments encouraged white settlers in Kenya to make similar demands, but the British government considered the white presence there less pressing and held back. The only other part of the dependent empire to reach the level of responsible government was Malta

— 1921—30 — although because of its strategic significance defence and certain other matters were reserved to the British government. The Maltese had had a representative element since 1849.

It was in the addition of elected members to the legislative council that the British government was most prepared to allow political advance in her colonies.[16] In 1881 a partially elective legislative council was created in Cyprus — not properly a crown colony at that stage — and in 1884 Jamaica saw a return of the elective principle. Similar developments occurred in Mauritius in 1885, Fiji 1904, Ceylon 1920, Northern Rhodesia 1918—24, Kenya, Southern Nigeria, the Gold Coast and Sierra Leone in the 1920s and most of the Caribbean territories between 1924 and 1936. Elsewhere, the main trend was towards establishing firmly the principle of crown colony government. The mandate of Tanganyika received this system in the 1920s but some mandates were administered along with existing colonies, for example the Cameroons with Nigeria. High commission territories in southern Africa and the Pacific, and protectorates such as Somaliland, still saw only light British control, through commissioners assisting and directing local leaders.

In colonies where different national groups lived together the British government interfered with various protective devices. Cyprus had separate Turkish and non-Turkish rolls; in Southern Rhodesia, even after the granting of responsible government, legislation concerning African interests was reserved to British control, while Africans themselves could vote if they reached the regular franchise qualifications; in Kenya and Fiji special provision was made for groups other than the indigenes or British, primarily Asian immigrants; and in some African areas Arab groups were given special representation alongside African peoples. In the interwar years moves were gradually being made affording nominated representation to non-white people; but in colonies introducing an element of popular representation, this initially worked primarily to the advantage of the small group of British residents.

The dependent colonies were slower than the settlement areas to embrace the spirit of nationalism but this was not surprising since in many cases no clear national entity had ever existed before. Yet during this period manifestations of proto-nationalism did occur, although mainly at a fairly narrow level. Inspiration for these developments came from the Indian examples. Political organizations in India, the press and their protest movements provided an impetus for political aspirants in other dependent territories, especially Africa. In the latter case loyalties still lay primarily with the tribe and for most people it was difficult to think beyond the local region. Nevertheless, some leaders were gaining a sense of resentment towards the foreign ruler and a desire for more authority in their own behalf. Sometimes actual resistance to British control broke out but it was nearly always sporadic and haphazard, and consequently achieved little. More frequently, tribal leaders cooperated with the British, although often with the intention of gaining enough British know-how to be able to reassert themselves in full control of their own people. Many of the cases of independency, especially in religion, also had overtones of a nationalist nature. The existence of an independently minded, indigenous press also helped mould an elite mind critical of Britain. Some editors in west Africa had since the 1880s unhesitatingly asserted free speech, claiming to protect their people against a possibly authoritarian government. Colonial authorities, although empowered to do so, exercised little practical censorship over this press.[17]

A more skilled leadership, with a wider perspective, was needed before a more genuine nationalist movement could be seen to emerge. The beginnings, however, were there in the inter-war years, as manifest in the National Congress of British West Africa or the Mau movement of western Samoa.

NOTES

1. Nigeria — John Flint, *Sir George Goldie and the Making of Nigeria* (London: Oxford University Press, 1960); Rhodesia — John S. Galbraith, *Crown and Charter* (Berkeley: University of California Press, 1975); East Africa — John S. Galbraith, *Mackinnon and East Africa, 1878–95* (London: Cambridge University Press, 1972).
2. Trevor Lloyd, "Africa and Hobson's 'Imperialism' ", *Past and Present* 55 (1972): 130–53.
3. Harry Johnston, *The Uganda Protectorate* (London: Hutchinson, 1902); G. Mungeam, *British Rule in Kenya, 1895–1912* (London: Oxford University Press, 1965); M. P. K. Sorrenson, *Origins of European Settlement in Kenya* (Nairobi: Oxford University Press, 1960).
4. Nigeria — J. C. Anene, *South Nigeria in Transition, 1884–1906* (London: Cambridge University Press, 1966); Margery F. Perham, *Lugard* (London: Collins, 1956–60); Michael Crowder, *Revolt in Bussa* (Chicago: Northwestern University Press, 1973).
5. W. R. Johnston, *Sovereignty and Protection* (Durham, N.C.; Duke University Press, 1973).
6. See Charles L. Temple, *Native Races and Their Rulers* (London: Cass, 1968) (1918); Frederick J. D. Lugard, *The Dual Mandate in British Tropical Africa* (London: Cass, 1965)(1922).
7. As an example of the working-out of the system, look at Nigeria — A. H. M. Kirk-Greene, *Principles of Native Administration in Nigeria* (London: Oxford University Press, 1963) and Ian F. Nicolson, *The Administration of Nigeria, 1900–60* (Oxford: Clarendon, 1969).
8. Lucy P. Mair, *Native Policies in Africa* (London: Routledge, 1936). As a general study, look at the magisterial work of William M. Hailey, *An African Survey* (London: Oxford University Press, 1938).
9. Donald A. Low and R. C. Pratt, *Buganda and British Overrule, 1900–55* (London: Oxford University Press, 1960).
10. See Joseph Chamberlain, Great Britain, 4 Hansard *Parliamentary Debates* 54 (1898): 1538–41.

11. James K. Chapman, *The Career of Arthur Hamilton Gordon* (Toronto: University Press, 1964).
12. Francis J. West, *Hubert Murray* (Melbourne: Oxford University Press, 1968).
13. "Report of the East Africa Commission", [Cmd.2387], *Parl.Pap.* 9 (1924–25): 855; Penelope Hetherington, *British Paternalism and Africa, 1920–40* (London: Cass, 1978).
14. As an example, in Rhodesia — Robert I. Rotberg, *Christian Missions and the Creation of Northern Rhodesia, 1880–1924* (Princeton: University Press, 1965); Terence O. Ranger, *The African Voices in Southern Rhodesia, 1898–1930* (London: Heinemann, 1970); R. Hall, *Zambia 1890–1964* (London: Longman, 1976).
15. Hugh M. Hole, *The Making of Rhodesia* (London: Cass, 1967)(1926); Philip Mason, *The Birth of a Dilemma* (London: Oxford University Press, 1958); Lewis H. Gann, *The Birth of a Plural Society* (Manchester: University Press, 1958); Richard Gray, *The Two Nations* (London: Oxford University Press, 1960).
16. Look at respective colonial constitutions, and M. Wight, *Development of the Legislative Council* (London: Faber, 1946).
17. Fred I. A. Omu, "The Dilemma of Press Freedom in Colonial Africa", *Journal of African History* 9 (1968): 279–98; J. Scotton, "The First African Press in East Africa", *International Journal of African Historical Studies* 6 (1973): 211–28.

15
Economic Growth

While the British government took only halting steps in the political and social advancement of the dependent empire, her interest in its economic advancement seemed more keen, although it is doubtful whether the actual results were any greater. At least in words, the British government after 1895 professed a more determined concern for the economic well-being and advancement of her tropical domains, and in actions there was some little fulfilment. The previous government policy of no assistance for development had worked well enough in the white settlement colonies where British settlers seized upon any possible initiative, but such a policy largely failed in the tropical setting. From the British government's point of view money would be made available only in cases of grave emergency, such as when a hurricane devastated Mauritius in 1884. The British Treasury was forever complaining that tropical areas were a financial burden, mainly because of defence costs, sometimes because of deficit-ridden governments. By the mid-nineteenth century the British coastal establishments in west Africa were struggling to make ends meet; the Gold Coast, although introducing a poll tax in 1852 which it hoped would yield £22,000 annually, found in 1853 that only £7,600 was paid. The British government had to come to the rescue of all four west African colonies in the 1860s and the 1870s, paying out £32,000 in 1865.[1] The British taxpayer had to fund military costs such as the Ashanti war or the West African Frontier Force (which was subduing and demarcating inland Nigeria). Still this expansion was much cheaper than the cost of subduing the Boers in South Africa. It has been estimated that the cost of acquiring and resettling 250,000 Boers was about £1,000 per person. In comparison, the acquisition of about 70,000,000 Africans between 1882 and 1898 ran out at about 3s/0d each.[2]

In the face of such running costs British politicians hesitated to spend money on colonial development. Only by the end of the century was approval given less grudgingly. The idea had been attracting growing support in the 1880s but it took colonial secretary Chamberlain's endorsement in 1895 to give it official sanction.[3] He clarified as general empire policy the previously few isolated cases of assistance, as when in 1890 Britain had set up a botanical garden in the Gold Coast to teach Africans better methods of planting and crop diversification. Now the British government might encourage and assist state-promoted economic development in the colonies, especially in matters such as railways and other communications; now the British government might stimulate capital investment, guarantee loans or try to improve mining and indigenous agriculture. This change in British attitudes was not, however, made disinterestedly, for Britain's economy had been suffering the fluctuating ravages of depression crises since the 1870s. Now it was hoped that such assistance might provide a fillip to Britain's harassed industry. So the economic development of the tropics became part of Britain's imperial trust, through "the judicious investment of British money" "for the benefit of their population and for the benefit of the greater population which is outside".

Chamberlain was greeted immediately by the bankrupt governments of the West Indies.[4] In the later years of the nineteenth century the British government was being continually called upon to bail out these governments. Chamberlain responded with various forms of financial aid: grants to cover budget deficiencies, hurricane relief, aid for the sugar industry and agricultural research, subsidies for steamships. Money was also allocated to east and west Africa, especially for communications. The Uganda railway cost Britain about £5.5 million while grants of over £5 million were paid out until Uganda and the East African Protectorate became self-supporting. In west Africa's case most money went as government loans, raised on the London market at preferential rates of interest and guaranteed by the British government. By 1914 Southern Nigeria, the Gold Coast and Sierra Leone had borrowed over £10 million, much of it going to the construction of communications such as the seven hundred mile Lagos—Kano railway.[5] The British government, however, got some return from grants to west Africa through profiting on the issue of silver coin.

In all, very little was achieved by this new policy. Under the Colonial Loan Act of 1899 only £3 million was allocated for actual development. Empire-wide schemes of assistance did not materialize; with no ground rules to follow, the disbursement of the limited amounts of money available proceeded on an ad hoc basis, much as before. The most advantageous aspect of the restated policy was in the opening up of colonial loan-raising, with Britain acting as guarantor. Colonial governments rushed in with schemes for building railways, roads and public works.[6] Indeed they acted too eagerly, only to find by the 1930s, when the price of agricultural exports slumped so low, that they were riddled with heavy debts at fairly high rates of interest. In 1939 Nigeria's overseas interest bill absorbed one quarter of its total income. Yet tropical colonies were not the only ones having difficulty in servicing such government loans; even a more established country like New Zealand was in a similar position.

A more considered British effort at development in the tropics arose as a result of two royal commissions following the 1914—18 war. The first, concluding in 1918, on the natural resources of the colonies, urged Britain to take a more scientific approach towards development.[7] The second, in 1924 on east Africa, pointed out the desirability of involving Africans more closely in development schemes;[8] local participation, financial as well as physical, was seen to be essential if a colony's economy was to take off in a truly dynamic fashion. Supplementing these reports was a growing emphasis upon research into tropical problems. This concerned mainly agriculture, investigating diseases of livestock and crop-pests, establishing a colonial agricultural service with training schemes to provide field officers who could go out to the tribal peasants and suggest how productivity might be increased and farming diversified. Research bodies, such as the Imperial Department of Agriculture, the Imperial College of Tropical Agriculture and the Botanical Gardens at Kew, were to be encouraged and facilities extended to the colonies.[9] Some industries, such as cotton, benefited considerably through this greater interest in research and planning; the Empire Cotton Growing Corporation (1921) assisted the expansion of production in places such as Nyasaland. At the same time, results were limited; only the surface of peasant agriculture in the tropics was being scratched.

New legislation in 1929 (the Colonial Development Act) aimed at formalizing and systematizing the rambling structure of colonial development that had grown up since the days of Chamberlain.[10] Instead of a separate parliamentary vote for each colonial grant, now all development projects were to be funded, after approval, out of an annual grant from the colonial development fund. The legislators claimed that their aim was to help both agriculture and industry in the colonies as well as commerce and industry in Britain, but in fact the latter concern received more emphasis. The aid was not given freely; among the stiff terms was the condition that orders for imports should be placed with Britain. The result was that the economies of most of the recipient colonies, reeling under the effect of the world depression, found that such aid could prove more burdensome than beneficial. In any case, the amount of money made available for development was not munificent: only £6,650,000 was paid out during the 1930s, over £2,000,000 short of the total recommended grants (which in themselves were not excessive). Unfortunately, priorities for development went somewhat askew, with projects for agriculture, fisheries, forestry, education and social development receiving less than favourable consideration. Of course, Britain at the time was in economic strife herself, but the problem was also compounded by confused thinking. Development was not seen primarily in terms of unrewarded benevolence; rather it was couched within the framework of returns flowing to the whole world (and especially the donor), as well as to the donee. Efficiency was the fashionable word; so the metropolitan power should develop the resources of the world as efficiently as possible for the benefit of all people; indeed, the donor expected a return for his charity.

The significant change in official thinking was the increasing acceptance of the principle that the state should be involved in planning. It was also now accepted that financial priming was needed from the government, because private enterprise alone could, or would, not arrange the economic take-off to prosperity that had occurred in white settlement areas. So the British and colonial governments involved themselves more in economic development, the former often providing finance, the latter generally attending to details of planning. Some results were achieved — especially in communications — and some economic growth was encouraged; there was a marked difference in the case of territories where British influence was light, such as in the high commission territories of southern Africa or the protected state of Zanzibar. In the latter cases, in the absence of official stimuli for change, stagnation and decline took over. Yet the overall results were limited: neither enough money nor enough long-term planning was provided, so only small projects were undertaken.

As to communications, the dependent territories had suffered from inadequate, or non-existent, communications in the 1880s. The major exception was Ceylon where in mid-century forced labour was called upon to upgrade the road between Kandy and Colombo to carry the valuable coffee crop from the British plantations in the hills to the port for export. At the end of the century Chamberlain perceived that one of the major obstacles to further economic progress in the tropics was this inadequate infrastructure. So he advocated cheap railway loans, financed by the British government at two per cent annual interest and repayable over fifty years; much money also came from the commercial market at ordinary rates for railway construction. Rail-lines were soon opening up new areas.[11] The British brought in Indian coolies to Mombasa in 1896 to push the rails inland through malarial swamps and over ranges, on the way combating lions, tsetse fly and bubonic plague, quelling mutiny and troublesome tribes, finally reaching Lake Victoria in 1901. Later, Northern Nigeria was linked to the coast and branch lines laid to the east, bringing to easy export groundnuts, coal and tin. The federated and unfederated states of Malaya received an iron backbone linking them to Siam. Even small territories such as Mauritius constructed rail-lines to help exports. By the beginning of the twentieth century the rail revolution had come to most of the tropical areas.

Road development was slower, most colonial roads until the 1920s being dignified with the title of bush tracks. A traveller might be able to make reasonable progress for a few miles from a government station; after that the condition of the track would deteriorate deplorably. Some colonial officials paid chiefs to keep the tracks open and clear of bushes — in the Gold Coast at 10s/0d per mile, with the loan of hatchets. An enquiry in 1907 deplored the whole situation; Southern Nigeria had only fifty-four miles of road open for wheeled traffic while the Gold Coast had thirty-two miles of metalled road, but this was not "metalled in the true meaning of the term".[12] Developments came more speedily in the 1920s and 1930s, to facilitate the use of lorries to carry crops to market. So in the Gold Coast, cocoa growing spread to new areas, with the government providing most of the transport services. Although high standards could not be achieved, most colonial governments accepted that they had a prime duty to increase rapidly the network of communications, because without these little economic growth could be hoped for. Advances in wireless and in air travel were looked to in eager anticipation as further ways of bridging the gap between colonies and the more developed world.[13] The British government also helped colonies of strategic significance, such as Gibraltar, Malta and Aden, by carrying out major public works on harbours and fortifications.

While the government did not directly involve itself in economic activities such as production and distribution, British individuals were trying to bring the tropical colonies into the western economic orbit. In the mid and late nineteenth century this role was restricted mainly to traders. For instance from the 1850s a handful of British traders in Fiji were dealing in copra, later sea-island cotton, and later still sugar; or in the Lake Nyasa-Zambezi river regions the African Lakes Company was seeking a fortune in the 1880s in ivory and general trade. In many areas British traders were the vanguard of British influence. The chartered companies in Nigeria, Rhodesia, east Africa and Borneo meant the introduction not only of an economic dominance but also of a degree of official British jurisdiction. Elsewhere, British traders went in regardless of British protection; in some cases they did not want interference from British officials as they engaged in activities of dubious legality.

The small individual trader, or barterer, could not be expected to play a major role in the economic development of the tropics. His main concern was to survive. With extraordinary luck he might make a fortune and retire; more likely he would be ravaged by drink, a hard life and angry indigenes; the less-than-scrupulous trader might make a temporary gain, only to be killed by a cheated chief. The historical function of these traders was to introduce the western trading system and he could feel he had succeeded if the indigenes acquired a taste for western material goods — something which was not too difficult to excite — and, provided there was some indigenous raw material desired in Europe, a trading pattern could be established. So began economic development at a rudimentary level. The chartered companies argued in more sophisticated terms. Goldie, in explaining the virtues of the Royal Niger Company, argued that the development of an area (the exploitation of its resources and the growth of more export crops) could not be adequately handled by small competing British traders and African growers. A single organization, with large amounts of capital, was needed to organize more efficiently the whole economic enterprise, with the Africans still as growers and his company handling distribution. The British South Africa Company adopted a different stance.[14] With the hope of wealth from gold, mineral concessions were obtained and mining was begun; but it never yielded a bonanza. The company, however, was also conceived in terms of white settlement and in the 1890s bands of pioneers moved into Matabeleland and Mashonaland, trying to exploit the pastoral and agricultural potential of the land. But they had difficulties. The two other chartered companies were less well conceived, obtaining general concessions (including trading), but having unclear prospects. The East African Company failed while in North Borneo the task of finding a suitable export was not easily solved; gold, tobacco, timber and rubber were tried at different stages, with varying success.

In most cases traders operated alone or in small groups. Sometimes, however, British trading establishments of considerable size emerged, coming to dominate the economic and political life of the colony. For example Hong Kong developed as an *entrepôt* for the China trade while Singapore developed as a trading centre in its own right, not only for the Malay Peninsula and the East Indies but also for Australasia and the east.[15] In both places a few British firms expanded into commercial and financial empires — Guthries in Singapore became trading, rubber and shipping magnates while Jardines in Hong Kong were not only general merchants but also insurers and transport agents. At the same time it should be noted that the emergence of these areas as independent trading centres was due to Chinese traders as well as to British initiatives.

Most British private investors ignored development in the tropics, the exception being the chartered companies and a few people searching for minerals. Colonies relying upon the export of agricultural and pastoral products generally found their economic future precarious; but the discovery of a mineral could provide that initial boost pushing the economy in the direction of growth and prosperity. The gold of the Gold Coast was always alluring, highlighted in the early twentieth century by Cade's Ashanti Goldfields Corporation.[16] Tin had been mined in Malaya and Nigeria before colonization but British rule brought more investment and more organization, so that in Malaya's case tin became a leading export. In the later nineteenth century phosphate deposits around the world were exploited, from uninhabited guano islands in the Pacific to Redonda in the West Indies; in the twentieth century the British Phosphate Commissioners ploughed into the deposits of Nauru and Ocean Island in the Pacific.[17] Asphalt from Trinidad was being worked by a British company after 1888.

The economic problems of the 1930s brought home to a number of colonies the value of minerals, providing economic survival at a time when no one wanted their agricultural exports. The diamonds and iron ore of Sierra Leone allowed it to weather out the depression. Southern Rhodesia's economy was helped along during the early twentieth century by minerals — gold, coal, asbestos and chrome — while Northern Rhodesia was lagging until the 1930s when copper deposits were brought into production. From early in the twentieth century British investors became increasingly interested in the search for petroleum. Most attention went to the middle east, following the success of the D'Arcy oil concession in Persia in 1901.[18] Thereafter British private capital went into Persia and Mesopotamia, accompanied by British government money and diplomatic influence. Here was an obvious case of the government, feeling on the defensive, now acting directly to assist and protect private British interests in the name of national interests. Apart from Persia, Mesopotamia, Kuwait and the Trucial States, British money was exploiting petroleum in Brunei and Trinidad.

Only a little British private investment found its way into agricultural pursuits in the tropics. The most notable case, and a very successful one, was in Malaya's rubber. From one tree in 1876 a boom was under way by the twentieth century.[19] In 1913 the Malay States were producing over one half of the world's rubber. British capital flowed in to set up flourishing plantations (in 1922 £38 million was invested) but it did not dominate the industry; Chinese and Malay growers soon realized the profits that could be made and by the 1920s were growing as many acres as British planters. In Ceylon also, British capital helped established tea plantations. But in other colonies a sparcity of capital in primary industries hindered development.

Understandably British investors were not very interested because prospects did not look good. Productivity in the tropics was low, primarily because agriculture still remained at a fairly basic subsistence level. Colonial governments had in most cases interfered very little with traditional systems of land holding and production. Agricultural extension services came only slowly, and peasants were hesitant to embrace newfangled ways. Only gradually were some peasants being convinced to go over to cash-cropping, especially if solely for export. Most governments in Africa insisted on indigenous land ownership, even if it meant inefficient and limited production.[20] So pressure was resisted from people like Lever Brothers, who claimed that the plantation system of palm oil production as used in central Africa and the East Indies would provide a better economic base for tropical development. But while there was much agricultural inertia some African peasants were responding to government inducements to better farming, higher production and crop diversification. Gold Coast cocoa farmers flourished, becoming capitalist farmers, accumulating and reinvesting capital, expanding their farms, moving into new operations such as transport and marketing, and becoming managers, until these developments were slowed down by the depression.[21] In Nigeria the production of palm products increased considerably, and although it lost its lead to the Netherlands East Indies as an exporter of palm oil it retained its position as the world's chief exporter of palm kernels.[22] Groundnut production also moved ahead in west Africa. By the 1920s some Kenyan and Ugandan farmers were responding readily to cash-cropping and market opportunities.[23] In east and central Africa considerable diversification was taking place, into crops such as cotton, tea, coffee and tobacco. In all cases there was some degree of white involvement but a growing number of Africans were showing themselves fully able and willing to participate in these agricultural developments; for example, Africans dominated cotton growing in Nyasaland.

Nevertheless, by the 1930s, even apart from the devastation caused by the world depression, the primary production base of tropical colonies was far from satisfactory. There were too many subsistence farmers; there was too much reliance upon one single export crop. Most of the islands in Oceania had little going for them; their copra was described as of the worst quality in the world while only limited fruit outlets existed. The monoculture of the West Indies had been a persistent problem; its sugar industry needed drastic reorganization and modernization.[24] Governments since the 1920s have been promoting changes, encouraging farmers to produce more efficiently, to use central sugar mills and join cooperatives. Diversification was encouraged, into cocoa and fruit. Cotton flourished in Montserrat while Dominica's bananas and limes replaced sugar as the leading export. Overall, however, sugar remained king and the total economy remained unsatisfactory.

So inefficient traditional production, combined with unreliable world markets, generally daunted the few steps towards higher growth that governments and more progressive local farmers were trying to take. Most success occurred mainly in those colonies where some white settlers resided, having been able either to acquire ownership of land or to establish a plantation system of cropping. Southern Rhodesia saw large-scale alienation of land to the chartered company and then to white settlers; even so, success came only slowly. The tsetse fly and diseases such as rinderpest played havoc with early farming; so grains, tobacco and cotton were tried as alternatives. White settlers in Kenya entrenched themselves with long (999 year) leases of land, and built up a flourishing economy. But the British government resisted their complete takeover. In Ceylon, British planters had set up a prosperous tea industry by the end of the nineteenth century, replacing earlier sources of supply (China and Assam). This development in Ceylon came fortuitously, for in the 1880s coffee, the former source of wealth, was almost completely wiped out by a fungus.[25] British planters, using Tamil labourers, were soon to find that they had to share the tea industry with wealthy Sinhalese. Villagers also began to grow tea, but on a less significant scale than the two groups of planters. In Malaya there was a similar pattern of development, rubber being produced not only by British planters but also by Chinese and Malay small holders. British copra planters functioned in the south Pacific alongside traditional harvesters; but neither group proved very efficient. In Fiji cotton growing was tried briefly but from the 1880s sugar took over. Since only Fijians could own land, Indian labourers were brought in, farming the crops on small plots under twenty-one year leases; Europeans participated only at the processing and distribution end. Overall the Pacific economies showed little development in this period.[26]

The dependent economies had no real industrial base of their own to provide diversity and growth. The thinking of the British government and British businessmen was that Britain's industrial might was sufficient to satisfy all the manufacturing needs of the colonies; they could supply the raw materials which Britain would process. Generally, however, the colonies suffered on the deal, the prices of primary products being more heavily buffeted than those for industrial goods. At the most, only very light processing was undertaken in the colonies, for example, sugar in the West Indies. Sometimes small factories producing simple consumer goods were set up. Lugard set the pattern, saying "a Government would not be wise to hasten the advent of the factory in Africa". Mineral exploitation, however, was accompanied by some degree of industrialization, as Northern Rhodesia experienced in the 1930s with its copper industry.[27]

Industrialization was a little more advanced in India than in any other part of the empire. After the destruction of the traditional handicraft home industries, small-scale textile factories were set up by a handful of Indian businessmen in the later nineteenth century. After the turn of the century a small steelworks was also established. The processing of commercial crops such as tea, cotton and jute (the latter mainly in Scottish hands) was also undertaken. Nevertheless the extent of industrialization was limited since Indian developments were held in a subsidiary relationship to British economic interests. Elsewhere in Asia, small moves towards industrialization were made in the twentieth century, mainly in the inter-war years, such as shipbuilding allied with the naval base at Singapore and textiles in Hong Kong.

By the end of the 1930s the economies of all Britain's tropical dependencies were still essentially conceived in colonial terms. They were pre-industrial, producing one or two export cash crops, short of capital, limited in development potential except for some infra-structure, basically still at a subsistence level. But in some cases seeds for some kind of economic take-off had been sown; those colonies giving the most signs of encouragement were Rhodesia, Kenya, Nigeria, the Gold Coast, Malaya, Ceylon, Hong Kong and Singapore.

The health and welfare of people in the empire became matters of government concern only slowly, especially in the tropics. The white settlement colonies continued to look after their own health problems quite adequately, closely following British trends. In the tropics, however, the notion of "white man's grave" persisted. The plight of the health of the indigenes received hardly any official attention in the nineteenth century. Saddled with little money and few staff the colonial governments had their time cut out in trying to provide rudimentary health services for the few white residents. But in the second half of the century a few improvements (mainly in drainage and sanitation) were being made in west Africa. Also a few small hospitals and dispensaries were constructed for a few indigenous communities, and the use of trained nurses began in 1895.

The problems were immense; there were so many diseases and so much ignorance about tropical medicine.[28] The colonies were riddled with disease — cholera, influenza, the plague, various fevers, blackwater, sleeping sickness, tuberculosis, venereal diseases, yaws, drug addiction in the east, and that perennial accompaniment of imperialism, alcoholism. The most healthy tropical areas were Ceylon, the Federated Malay States and some West Indies islands such as Grenada, but overall the tropical empire was unhealthy, for white and coloured alike. Some areas were physically devastated by the arrival of the whites. Pacific Islanders "died like flies" when they encountered European diseases, especially measles and tuberculosis. The Maoris went into a physical decline in the nineteenth century, not only because of warfare but because of disease, and this created psychological problems as well. Fiji provided a striking case where between 1859 and 1911 the population fell from an estimated 200,000 to 87,000. One year, 1875, was particularly disastrous when a measles epidemic wiped out about one quarter of the population. Mauritius was plagued by a variety of ailments — malaria, 1867–68, cholera, 1899–1909, influenza, 1918–19.

The attack on ignorance about tropical medicine was assisted by the encouragement Chamberlain gave to research in the 1890s. Private enterprise also participated, resulting in the establishment of schools of tropical medicine in Liverpool and London. The cause of tropical health was also aided by the discovery of Major Ronald Ross in the 1890s that malaria was carried by a mosquito rather than by bad air. Thereafter colonial governments began to undertake more serious campaigns concerning sanitation and drainage, to lift housing standards and even to segregate white and black dwellings in the fight against malaria. But colonial governments were still confounded by lack of funds and personnel. For example, Nigeria in the late 1930s spent only 6½d per head per annum on health. Non-official bodies, mainly missionaries, had to be relied upon. By the beginning of the twentieth century missionary health services had expanded considerably, as they built hospitals, provided trained staff and undertook the training of local people in elementary health matters.[29]

Take the case of east Africa.[30] The Church Missionary Society opened a hospital there in 1897, at first attending whites only. By the 1920s, however, considerable expansion was under way — treating indigenes, dispersing a dispensary system into new areas and using local trainees. By this latter stage the colonial government was also becoming involved, setting out policy and standards and assisting the missions with subsidies. This spread of western medicine brought new problems in its wake, especially when it created conflict with tradition in matters such as female circumcision. The government then had to initiate a public education campaign to counter local ignorance and magic. Meanwhile, research in London into problems of the tsetse fly and sleeping sickness were producing results which colonial governments could begin to put into practice.[31] So health standards were beginning to rise and health services were expanding (partly through the addition in 1922 of medicine to the curriculum of Makerere College). Yet the rate of progress was very slow. A solution in one area often created problems in another; for example, the building of new communications extended the area of tsetse fly infestation. By the 1930s, although groundwork had been laid, major problems of tropical health still existed. The Gold Coast was one of the more advanced African areas; yet it had only thirty-two hospitals for 3,787,000 Africans, while 3,000 whites had six hospitals.[32]

Education followed a similar pattern. The sons of wealthy white residents naturally chose to go to England. In India only slow progress was being made in English education. By the beginning of the century the literacy rate was about five per cent. In Africa and other parts of the empire the education of the indigenes received scant consideration, until the missionaries arrived, opening schools with the aim of conversion, discipline and "civilization". Colonial governments played only a minor role in education, opening very few state schools, more frequently giving subsidies to mission efforts. Lack of money was again the main problem; for example, in 1938—39 educational costs in Southern Nigeria were only 5d per head, and they were half that in Northern Nigeria. The missions sought to educate first the chiefs and their sons, and then spread out to other members of the community. They also trained African teachers who then scattered throughout the countryside setting up bush schools and independent schools.[33]

The curriculum was shaped for the needs of an academic, British way of life and had little or no local adaptation. This approach was chosen because this was what the locals wanted; they were pushed on by the fierce desire to emulate the whites, to show their worth, to establish their equality and ability. Indeed, some missionaries in the earlier nineteenth century had tried to offer practical and technical instruction to west

Africans but the latter rejected it as inferior. A western education seemed to offer indigenes new job opportunities, social mobility, wealth and power; they were conscious of becoming a new elite. A practical, agricultural training seemed to condemn them to a traditional, backward style of living. The Phelps-Stokes Commission of 1924, however, criticized this academic approach and recommended that a practical education be offered, more directly related to local life, its traditions, agriculture, industries; in the 1920s and 1930s however, only minor progress was made in this objective of indigenization, such as in the Jeanes training school.[34]

A multiplicity of schools existed. Apart from the missions and a few government schools, "independent" schools appeared, run by half-trained indigenes, anxious to break out at least partially from the western mould; here the seeds of nationalism were being sown. Religious and communal problems meant diversity in education; in many parts of Africa poor, backward Muslim schools operated; in Nigeria, native administration schools were set up with state assistance; Indians in east Africa had their own system; in Malaya there were Malay, Indian, Chinese and English schools; in Fiji Indian education was largely neglected; in central Africa white education was pushed ahead at the expense of black education. Higher education received minimal attention since so few people were highly educated. But there were a few developments in this respect. In 1876 Fourah Bay College affiliated with the University of Durham and began producing African teachers, clergy and physicians. Indeed west Africa in the nineteenth century produced a number of highly literate men who proved to the world that they were fully equal to their western brothers — people such as James A. B. Horton, Edward Blyden and James Casely-Hayford. In other parts of the empire similar moves were being made. Medical schools were set up in Ceylon in 1870 and Fiji in 1888. Various institutions were established in Africa in the early twentieth century — Achimota (the Gold Coast), Yaba (Nigeria), Makerere (Uganda), Fort Hare (South Africa). Codrington College continued in the West Indies and was joined by the Imperial College of Tropical Agriculture. Raffles College was opened in Singapore while Hong Kong acquired a university in 1911; Ceylon's college received similar status in 1942.[35] Except for Fort Hare these places of higher learning were not intended solely for indigenes, and whites did attend to obtain professional, teaching and administrative training. In the long term, however, these places, and especially those in west Africa, were to receive greater significance for fostering the development of a new educated indigenous elite, aware of the importance of nationalism and independence.

Education, like medicine, was a mirror image of the whole problem of development in the tropical empire. The problems were immense, the traditional background was a hindrance, and although British interest was rising, not enough capital and manpower was being injected to provide very positive results.

British power between the 1880s and the 1930s stood at its peak; yet it had now come under assault from various quarters and had been found lacking. In economic terms the pinnacle was reached probably by the 1890s, by which time both Germany and the United States could throw down successful challenges to various aspects of Britain's former industrial and economic supremacy. In political-military terms British power probably came to a peak about the time of the 1914-18 war, when its military hardware was assembled in a successful concerted effort, and the reserves of manpower in the empire were called upon. Thereafter Britain could no longer be so sure of the actual strength that the empire represented. Stirrings of discontent, thoughts of nationalism were beginning to weaken the fabric of British imperial power. Certainly it was premature to think of the dependent empire standing independently; yet, it could no longer be taken so much for granted as before.

British imperial power was beginning to close in upon itself. The free-ranging free trade imperialism of the mid-nineteenth century was yielding to a narrower protectionism. Britain was tightening her economic bonds with the other members of the empire, although the latter, for their part, were beginning to try to break out of such a strait-jacket. British traders and investors still operated outside the empire, but now found the former profitable hunting grounds more difficult to operate. Everywhere British economic relations came under competition from other industrially advanced nations; Britain no longer had the edge, and was often found wanting. It meant that the reality of British economic power was being severely tested — by the world community — and was looking weak. So, the British economic mind turned more towards thoughts of a closed, self-contained unit of Britain and empire. The great depression hastened this introspection for Britain, as it did for the international economy at large.

In one sense British imperial power had strengthened, at least in nominal terms. The white settlement colonies had stayed within the fold. Although they were pushing for a greater degree of economic nationalism their aspirations for political nationalism were satisfied with a legal formula — dominion status. The notion of political equality with Britain was acceptable to most white settlers, although the Boer descendants in South Africa and the French Canadians thought the new status more transparent than meaningful. Most of the white settlers, however, found it too comfortable and convenient to stay within the new commonwealth framework to want to break out in a fully independent manner.

The pity was that Britain dragged the chain with the idea of offering such a status to non-white territories. The Indians felt cheated of this prize; for many decades the word equality had been used — for even more decades Indians both in India and abroad in the empire had been treated like second class citizens. Not surprisingly Indian critics of British imperial power were now becoming more vociferous in their denunciation and were beginning to test just how effectively Britain's bureaucracy and even its military could govern unwilling, unhappy subjects. The reality of British power was coming under test, from within the empire.

With British citizens under assault from both within and without the empire, it was perhaps not unusual that they began to bask more in notions of imperial greatness. The psychological aspects of imperial power provided comfort and succour. Extremes of British nationalism and racism were seen during these fifty-odd years, but especially at the turn of the century; British behaviour in this respect was, however, probably no more marked than that of the other "racially aware" western nations. Increasingly the British (mainly in the home island but also in the settlement colonies) arrogated to themselves a sense of imperial rectitude; the notions of imperial mission provided a cloak of respectability to hide the more unsavoury aspects of imperial rule. The crude notion of the British as the nation most fit to govern was tossed around blithely, to the extent that it allowed the less scrupulous to camouflage crassly racist behaviour — unjust punishment, forced labour, petty discrimination. The earlier decades of the nineteenth century provided the grounds for the growth of this flagrant sense of superiority; Britain's undoubted greatness then was almost necessarily to spawn a fierce sense of cultural superiority. But the growing challenges and threats by the turn of the century provided a further reason for this sense of superiority; now, on the defensive, the British would choose such a cloak to mask possible weaknesses and flaws, to hide those feet of clay.

Yet the sense of superiority did not exist unalloyed: it was tempered by a sense of duty. The earlier strains of humanitarian endeavour for "lesser peoples" continued, and, indeed, became stronger as the twentieth century progressed. Some British thinkers grieved that the Indians, or the Maoris, had been unfairly treated; others, still harbouring notions of racial hierarchy, could not bring themselves to accept full racial equality, yet believed that Britain had a chosen role to help elevate the "lesser peoples" and extend to the utmost whatever talents they had. So ideas of imperial trust, of imperial responsibility were gathering support.

This rising notion, that the dependent empire should be developed, was seen to have benefit for both the local people and Britain. Indeed, the idea of tropical development seems to have been related to the whole problem of Britain's imperial power under challenge; since British agents could no longer operate so freely around the world, it was better to concentrate upon what Britain already possessed — the empire. Development was seen primarily in economic terms; advance the economic potential of the dependent territories, to help and sustain British economic power. British interests still came first, but some spin-off for the local economy was also expected. Official thinking was still laggard with respect to political development; the tropical empire was seen as too backward and immature for much political responsibility to be afforded to local inhabitants. And it seemed decades before positive steps would be made in that direction. Furthermore, even the economic aspects of development were showing only limited success in this period, mainly because such a late start was made and because more planning and more research, more finance and manpower, more assistance and direction was needed.

Whereas in the mid-nineteenth century British power seemed unbounded, it had become quite surely circumsribed during the early decades of the twentieth century. Furthermore, it was having to go increasingly onto the defensive. After the 1914—18 war the British government found itself engaged in a holding operation, trying to preserve and maintain whatever power she had built up over the previous centuries. Now, too, there was a growing gap between the appearance and the reality of British power. She still looked to be Great Britain and great empire; but beneath this surface lay stresses and tensions which would soon expose the frailty of the structure.

NOTES

1. Allan McPhee, *The Economic Revolution in British West Africa* (London: Cass, 1971)(1926), pp. 210—13; "Cost of Colonies, 1869—73", H. of C. No. 194, *Parl.Pap.* 51 (1875): 667; "Colonies (Advances by Imperial Government)", H. of C. No. 417, *Parl.Pap.* 64 (1881): 579.
2. Trevor Lloyd, "Africa and Hobson's 'Imperialism' ", *Past and Present* 55 (1972): 143.
3. Joseph Chamberlain, 22 August 1895, Great Britain, 4 Hansard *Parliamentary Debates* 36 (1895): 641—42.
4. See royal commission into sugar depression and general condition of West Indies, [C.8655], *Parl.Pap.* 50 (1898): 1.
5. Returns of revenue and expenditure in West Africa, 1885—1905, in [Cd.2564], *Parl.Pap.* 56 (1905): 411; Lugard's report on Nigeria, etc., [Cd.468], *Parl.Pap.* 36 (1919): 609; also re construction of railways in West Africa, [Cd.2325], *Parl.Pap.* 56 (1905): 361, especially pp. 365—85; also, McPhee, *Economic Revolution*.
6. George G. Abbott, "A Re-Examination of the 1929 Colonial Development Act", *Economic History Review* 24 (1971): 68—81. William K. Hancock, *Survey of British Commonwealth Affairs* (London: Oxford University Press, 1942) 2, part 2 covers many problems of the tropical development.
7. Reports of royal commission on natural resources, trade and legislation of certain colonies, [Cd.7210], *Parl.Pap.* 1914, 137 and [Cd.8462], *Parl.Pap.* 1917—18, X, 1; also, the committee into edible and oil-producing nuts and seeds, [Cd.8247], *Parl.Pap.* 1916, IV, 15.
8. "Report of the East Africa Commission", [Cd.2387], *Parl.Pap.* 9 (1924—25): 855.

9. G. B. Mansfield, *A History of the Colonial Agricultural Service* (London: Oxford University Press, 1972).
10. Abbott, above; David Meredith, "The British Government and Colonial Economic Policy, 1919—39", *Economic History Review* 28 (1975): 484—99; Neal R. Malmsten, "British Government Policy toward Colonial Development, 39", *Journal of Modern History* 49 (1977): 1—11.
11. J. S. Mills, *The Press and Communications of the Empire* (London: British Books, 1924); McPhee, *Economic Revolution*, pp. 108—10; also G. Paish, *The Statist*, supplement, 14 February 1914, p. iv, for railway table.
12. "Papers Relating to Mechanical Transport in the Colonies", [Cd.4589], *Parl.Pap.* 56 (1905): 361.
13. Wireless — "Report of the Imperial Wireless Telegraphy Committee, 1924", [Cd.2060], *Parl.Pap.* 12 (1924): 635; re cables, see 1914 royal commission on natural resources, note 7.
14. Re the chartered companies, see the previous chapter.
15. G. B. Endacott, *A History of Hong Kong* (London: Oxford University Press, 1974). Re Singapore — S. Cunyngham-Brown, *The Traders* (London: Newman Neame, 1973); C. M. Turnbull, *A History of Singapore, 1819—1975* (London: Oxford University Press, 1977).
16. Geoffrey Kay (ed.), *The Political Economy of Colonialism in Ghana* (Cambridge: University Press, 1970).
17. Nancy Viviani, *Nauru* (Canberra: Australian National University Press, 1970).
18. Marian Kent, *Oil and Empire* (London: Macmillan, 1975); C. Busch, *Britain and the Persian Gulf* (Berkeley: University of California Press, 1967); Rosa L. Greaves, *Persia and the Defence of India* (London: University of London Press, 1959); R. S. Zahlan, *The Origins of the United Arab Emirates* (London: Macmillan, 1978).
19. John H. Drabble, *Rubber in Malaya, 1876—1922* (Kuala Lumpur: Oxford University Press, 1973); Richard T. Stillson, "The Financing of Malayan Rubber, 1905—23", *Economic History Review* 24 (1971): 589—98.
20. On general economic response — A. G. Hopkins, *An Economic History of West Africa* (London: Longman, 1973).
21. Polly Hill, *The Migrant Cocoa Farmers of Southern Ghana* (Cambridge: University Press, 1963); R. Dummett, "The Rubber Trade of the Gold Coast and Asante in the Nineteenth Century", *Journal of African History* 12 (1971): 79—101.
22. R. O. Ekundare, *An Economic History of Nigeria, 1860—1960* (London: Methuen, 1973).
23. Richard Wolff, *The Economics of Colonialism* (New Haven: Yale University Press, 1974); E. A. Brett, *Colonialism and Underdevelopment in East Africa* (London: Heinemann, 1973); Roger van Zwenenberg, "The Development of Peasant Commodity Production in Kenya, 1920—40", *Economic History Review* 27 (1974): 442—54.
24. H. A. Hill, "Colonial Policy and Economic Development in the British West Indies, 1895—1903", *Economic History Review* 13 (1970): 129—47; royal commission re trade between Canada and West Indies, [Cd.5369], *Parl.Pap.* 11 (1910): 159.
25. N. Ramchandran, *Foreign Plantation Investment in Ceylon, 1889—1958* (Colombo: Central Bank of Ceylon, 1963); D. Forrest, *A Hundred Years of Ceylon Tea, 1867—1967* (London: Chatta & Windus, 1967).
26. Harold C. Brookfield, *Colonialism, Development and Independence* (Cambridge: University Press, 1972).
27. Sally Frankel, *Capital Investment in Africa* (London: Oxford University Press,

1938); Elena L. Berger, *Labour, Race and Colonial Rule* (Oxford: Clarendon, 1974) — the Copperbelt.
28. Andrew Balfour and H. H. Scott, *Health Problems of the Empire* (London: Collins, 1924); also Hancock, *Survey*.
29. William M. Hailey, *An African Survey* (London: Oxford University Press, 1938); McPhee, *Economic Revolution*, chap. viii; Hancock, *Survey*, II, 2, p. 264.
30. Ann Beck, *A History of the British Medical Administration of East Africa, 1900–50* (Cambridge, Mass.: Harvard University Press, 1970).
31. John Ford, *The Role of the Trypanosomiases in African Ecology* (Oxford: Clarendon, 1971).
32. *Colonial Office List*; Hancock, *Survey*.
33. Reports on education, including the training of native races, [Cd.2377], *Parl. Pap.* 25 (1905): 325, [Cd.2378], 26 (1905): 1, [Cd.2379], 26 (1905): 385; memorandum re native education in British tropical Africa, [Cmd.2374], *Parl. Pap.* 21 (1924–25): 27.
34. John Anderson, *The Struggle for the School* (London: Longman, 1970); K. J. King, *Pan-Africanism and Education* (Oxford: Clarendon, 1971); James Sheffield, *Education in Kenya* (New York: Teachers' College Press, 1972). Re West Africa, see Hancock, *Survey*, p. 263; McPhee, *Economic Revolution*, pp. 262–72; F. Hilliard, *A Short History of Education British West Africa* (London: Nelson, 1957).
35. For a review on higher education — "Report of the Commission on Higher Education in West Africa", [Cmd. 6655], *Parl.Pap.* 5 (1944–45): 593.

PART FOUR

Falling Away
1940s 1970s

16
Little Britain

Britain was slow in accepting after 1945 that her world power was dwindling.[1] The bull-doggedness of Churchill, refusing to contemplate any imperial dissolution, contributed partly to the long-lingering notion in British minds of their great power status. Churchill in the 1940s envisaged Britain emerging from the second world war as the great third force, Britain with the backing of the commonwealth-empire playing the role of vital *via media* between the super-powers, the United States and the USSR. The British people believed themselves entitled to that role, partly as a reward for their efforts in two global confrontations when they had doused the flames of totalitarianism and tyranny. And they still believed in the superiority of their civilization, and felt sure they had constructed the best of all possible empires. While Australians and New Zealanders might tend to agree other people were not so rapt in these British achievements. The Americans talked of decolonization and national freedom, the Soviets preached anti-imperialism and national liberation, and throughout the third world dependent peoples everywhere were beginning to arouse themselves from traditional torpor and tribalism, criticizing and despising their colonial masters and demanding control over their own destinies. Yet the British government and public alike were slow to understand this changing mood and continued to believe that British power had more substance and solidity than it really had. So Britain, with some Commonwealth help, fought to hold back the communists in Malaya in 1948 and in Korea in 1951.[2] Even more importantly, Britain cast herself, perhaps presumptuously, as an independent diplomatic arbiter — for example, trying to preside over summits between the United States and the USSR, and to negotiate a peace settlement in Vietnam. She followed the two super-powers into the nuclear arms age and tried to arrange defence treaties around the world, in the Atlantic and Europe, in the middle east and in the far east.

There was a deep ring of hollowness in this show of British arms, diplomacy and moral presence around the world. Although willing to combine with other powers (especially the United States or commonwealth members) or to use her good offices, she was much less inclined to act alone. She wisely calculated that her resources could not meet a sustained challenge from the rising nationalist forces in the empire. So she bowed to the Indian nationalists without armed struggle; she used only light force against the Mau Mau of Kenya;[3] in Cyprus her forces tried mainly to keep the fighting factions apart; she calculated that the armed intervention in Southern Rhodesia could only bring her high costs, much criticism and few positive results. Only in small places like Anguilla was she able to launch a sure-fire invasion with little cost. On the whole, she gave way to colonial nationalism without the anguish and disaster that hounded the French as they tried grimly to hang on to their empire in the 1950s. The British accepted their military weakness, and perhaps even moral weakness, against such a force, except for one fatal miscalculation. In 1956 Eden's government mistook the nationalism of Egypt for a recrudescence of tyranny and expansion.[4] So British forces, with French assistance, went in to protect British international rights in the Suez zone. The hostility of most of the world, including some commonwealth members, along with military mismanagement, brought a sudden halt to this incursion. Britain's ability to continue playing the great power role was seriously called into question. Yet over the next decade Britain still tried to keep up the facade of power, sometimes as America's special friend, sometimes as a moral force and world policeman, without any serious attempt being made to reconcile differences between those roles. Only by the end of the 1960s had the burden become too heavy and the irreconcilability too difficult. So Harold Wilson began the withdrawal from east of Suez;[5] so in Singapore and many other bases around the world was the British flag lowered for the last time, after having fluttered there for one hundred years or more. Finally by the 1970s Britain had reassessed her position in the world; she was just another European nation. Yet for one generation after the 1939—45 war she had squandered her limited resources in trying to maintain an illusion of great power. More is the pity, since the Britain government was much more realistic in its assessment of problems in the empire; while on the international scene Britain still tried to appear great, in the colonial setting she was ready to give in before it was too late.

The signs of Britain's declining position in the world were indicated only too clearly in the economic setting. As a world trader and financier Britain was slipping fast. In trade she was becoming increasingly dependent upon imports of food and raw materials. For a while in the 1940s the share of the dominions was increasing, but thereafter the newer independent members of the commonwealth were increasingly contributing to Britain's imports. An even more pronounced trend was the rising share of the foreign component in Britain's import figures from the end of the 1940s.[6] This was, of course, greatly heightened in the 1960s and 1970s, with Britain applying to join and eventually entering the EEC. There was also a strong swing towards obtaining imports from the middle east, quite evident even before the oil crisis of the 1970s.

The United States remained a constant supplier of British needs, often in the field of higher technology, while Japan, the USSR and eastern Europe became new sources of supply.[7] Among commonwealth members the newly independent states of Nigeria, Malaysia, Singapore, Zambia and the colony of Hong Kong contributed in various ways — oil from Nigeria, copper from Zambia, cheap manufactures from the east. South Africa proved to be an expanding source even after its departure from the commonwealth. Among the older dominions, Canada and New Zealand remained as significant, although declining, suppliers while Australia's share fell more sharply; so did India's.

As to British exports a similar pattern developed, with the foreign component dominating strongly, led by markets in the EEC and the United States. Canada, South Africa and the new commonwealth nations took a rising share of Britain's exports. New markets were being opened up in places like Japan while opportunities were being canvassed in the middle east. By the 1970s the economic links between Britain and commonwealth had dwindled to less than twenty per cent of Britain's total trade. Two of the former mainstays, Australia and India, were fading quite noticeably; but special arrangements were figured out to give most of the newer independent members some kind of link, either associate or special status, with the EEC. Nevertheless, it had become accepted in Britain that her trading future lay with Europe, north America and the middle east, and not with the commonwealth. Table 9 shows United Kingdom world trade in 1948, 1963 and 1972.

This erosion of economic ties was also quite noticeable from the viewpoint of the individual members of the commonwealth. The more established ones built upon the earlier vein of independence, although New Zealand was not so well-placed in this respect. Even among some of the newer members there was a falling reliance upon Britain, especially if they had a valuable export such as Nigeria's oil. For most countries there was diversification of production, increasing amounts of industrialization and the seeking of new trading outlets, especially looking to the United States. Japan and the United States made considerable inroads into the trade pattern of Pacific commonwealth countries. Regional trading links were also developed, for example, between Hong Kong and China, between India, the USSR and Japan. The poorest of the new commonwealth countries, however, were still limited in development and looked to Britain (and international bodies) for economic props. So in the mid-1970s, producers in Africa, the Caribbean and the Pacific were pleased when Britain arranged them trading access to the expanded EEC. New Zealand butter farmers also hoped for such assistance, but received only a temporizing agreement. For some states Britain was still a trading fulcrum, but their number was declining. Table 10 shows the trade of the commonwealth countries in 1948 and 1963, and table 11 shows the destination of trade of commonwealth countries in 1972.

Table 9. United Kingdom World Trade, 1948, 1963, 1972 (£m).

IMPORTS

1948		1963		1972	
Total	2,079	Total	4,280	Total	11,155
From Commonwealth	932	Commonwealth	368	Commonwealth	2,148
Canada	223	Canada	368	Canada	605
Australia	170	Australia	206	Australia	283
New Zealand	109	New Zealand	174	New Zealand	251
India	96	India	141	Hong Kong	185
Nigeria	54	Rhodesia/Nyasaland	98	Nigeria	156
S. Africa	32	Nigeria	79	India	112
Malaya	32	Hong Kong	68	Zambia	60
N. Rhodesia	20	Malaya/Singapore	42	Malaysia	47
S. Rhodesia	11	Malaya/Singapore	42	Singapore	40
Hong Kong	6				
Foreign	1,147	Foreign	3,283	Foreign	9,007
Europe	339	EEC	769	EEC	2,729
USA	183	USA	500	USA	1,180
Argentina	122	Middle East	392	Japan	314
Egypt	48	S. Africa	115	S. Africa	296
Iran	36			Bahrein/Persian Gulf	278
				S. Arabia	184
				Iran	124

EXPORTS

1948		1963		1972	
Total	1,642	Total	4,080	Total	9,746
To Commonwealth	757	Commonwealth	1,203	Commonwealth	1,838
Australia	145	Australia	236	Canada	380
S. Africa	121	Canada	173	Australia	318
India	97	India	137	Nigeria	154
Canada	74	New Zealand	115	New Zealand	148
New Zealand	53	Malaya/Singapore	79	India	141
Malaya	37	Nigeria	65	Hong Kong	101
Nigeria	25	Hong Kong	52	Singapore	77
Hong Kong	21	Rhodesia/Nyasaland	41	Malaysia	62
Kenya	17			Kenya	56
S. Rhodesia	16			Zambia	46
Foreign	885	Foreign	2,878	Foreign	7,908
Europe	388	EEC	826	EEC	2,230
USA	68	USA	344	USA	1,219
Argentina	53	S. Africa	196	S. Africa	308
Egypt	35	Middle East	78	Japan	172
Iran	25			Israel	135
				Iran	117
				Bahrein/Persian Gulf	95

Source: Adapted from: 1948, Great Britain, Board of Trade, *Statistical Abstract of the Commonwealth* 71 (1947-50); 1963, Great Britain, Board of Trade, *The Commonwealth and the Sterling Area, Statistical Abstract* 84 (1963) and *Board of Trade Journal*, 31 January 1964; 1972, Great Britain, Department of Trade and Industry, *Overseas Trade Statistics of the United Kingdom, 1972* and Statistical Office, *Annual Abstract of Statistics, 1973.*

Table 10. Trade of Commonwealth Countries, 1948, 1963.

	Imports (%) from								Exports (%) to					
	U.K.		Rest Commonwealth		Foreign		USA		U.K.		Rest Commonwealth		Foreign		USA	
	1948	1963	1948	1963	1948	1963	1948	1963	1948	1963	1948	1963	1948	1963	1948	1963
Australia	49	29	21	19	30	52	22	21	38	17	21	20	41	63	7	11
Canada	11	8	7	6	81	86	69	68	22	14	9	5	69	81	50	56
New Zealand	52	40	27	32	21	28	11	10	74	45	6	11	20	44	5	17
India	28	15	14	10	53	75	20	32	23	22	28	18	49	59	17	17
Pakistan	—	14	—	9	—	77	—	44	—	13	—	22	—	64	—	23
Nigeria	51	35	10	7	39	58	12	9	77	39	3	3	19	58	14	9
Ghana	60	34	7	7	33	59	7	6	28	19	10	5	62	76	34	17
Hong Kong	15	12	13	13	72	75	19	11	5	18	20	25	74	57	9	20
Malaya	19	24	19	15	62	61	12	4	13	8	18	10	69	82	26	19
Singapore	—	12	—	18	—	70	—	6	—	7	—	26	—	67	—	10
N. Rhodesia	31	—	44	—	25	—	13	—	68	—	18	—	14	—	7	—
S. Rhodesia	47	—	32	—	21	—	9	—	40	—	40	—	20	—	4	—
Central Africa	—	33	—	8	—	59	—	7	—	39	—	7	—	54	—	4

Source: Adapted from: 1948, Great Britain, Board of Trade, *Statistical Abstract of the Commonwealth* 71 (1947-50); 1963, *The Commonwealth and the Sterling Area, Statistical Abstract* 84 (1963).

Table 11. Destination of Trade of Commonwealth Countries, 1972 (%).

	Imports					Exports				
	UK	EEC	USA	Japan	Other		UK	EEC	USA	Japan	Other
Australia	21	14	22	16	—		9	10	13	28	—
Canada	5	6	70	5	Commonwealth 9		8	6	68	5	Commonwealth 12
New Zealand	29	9	12	10	Australia 21		34	11	17	9	Australia 9
India	7	11	27	5	Canada 7		11	6	13	13	USSR 13
					USSR 6						
Nigeria	31	16	15	6	—		28	37	12	1	—
Malaysia	15	10	7	20	Singapore 8		7	12	13	18	Singapore 22
Singapore	7	8	13	20	Malaya 17		6	7	12	7	Malaya 23
					Middle East 9						
Hong Kong	8	9	13	24	Commonwealth 19		12	9	35	7	Commonwealth 22
					China 16						
Zambia	24	13	8	6	S.A.F. 17		22	32	1	23	S.A.F. 1
Kenya	31	20	9	10	—		20	17	7	4	—

Source: Adapted from Great Britain Foreign and Commonwealth Office, *A Year Book of the Commonwealth, 1973*, (London: HMSO, 1973).

The outward flow of British capital from the 1940s presented a similar picture to that of trade — of Britain's reduced position in the world, and from the 1950s of an ebbing interest in the commonwealth.[8] The 1939–45 war brought financial havoc to a number of British investments, for example, in Japan and China, and interrupted returns from Malaya. Furthermore, the British ended up selling about forty-five per cent of their overseas assets to help finance the war: there was a big selling-out of foreign shares, especially in Argentinian rails and United States manufacturing and public utilities.[9] There was a general decline in dominion holdings, in fact, quite steeply for Canada and New Zealand government loans and Canadian rails; at the same time local capital was being generated so that often dominion interests were pleased with the British bailing-out.[10] India's move to independence, along with the Japanese war, was accompanied by a marked drop in British investment (in rail and government loans) in that sub-continent. Only in the developing colonies, in the middle east and in mineral interests was there constancy, or just a slight fall, in British investment during the 1940s. The overall result was that Britain's holdings in the dominions and the colonies came easily to dominate those in foreign countries;[11] and the industrialized and more developed countries of the world were taking a decreasing share of British capital — and paying a poorer return — while the developing colonies and middle east countries looked more interesting to the British investor. In terms of profit, Latin America, where British interests had built up so much during the nineteenth century, paid out very poorly. The returns from Australia, New Zealand and Canada were less than average. But South Africa and most of the African colonies were making good yields; so was the Asian empire. Best of all were places like Egypt and Iran, although the amount invested there was not large.

As to the type of shares attracting attention, between 1938 and 1948 petroleum shares averaged a yearly return of 11.6 per cent, tea and coffee 9.1 per cent, mining 7.9 per cent. Government and municipal loans were losing their popularity to private shares, but of the former commonwealth ones were preferred, partly because they paid out better. There was a rising interest in private investment in tropical areas, especially Malaya, British central Africa and British west Africa, and on most occasions the returns justified this confidence. United States shares remaining after the war were mostly in manufacturing and paid out well. But overall during the 1940s, the commonwealth yielded better results than most foreign investment; the average nominal return for 1938–48 on commonwealth investments was 5.4 per cent against the average on all investments of 4.4 per cent.

By the end of the 1940s Britain was poised for a new financial foray, based upon firmer foundations than before, in that the war had fortunately eliminated a number of unprofitable foreign investments. There was an increasing swing towards foreign investment, although the commonwealth, both new and old, did not miss out. Table 12 shows the destination of overseas investment of the United Kingdom in 1948 and 1972. The 1950s, redolent with a philosophy of growth and development, saw large sums flow out from Britain, especially to Australia, South Africa, Central Africa, and colonial territories. Most money was in private shares, with the proportion of government loans falling drastically except in the case of colonial territories. With respect to the latter there were some successful loan issues, but failures, such as the ground nut scheme in Tanganyika, helped to dampen interest in such public issues, while private interest was easily aroused in matters such as Jamaican bauxite, Trinidad oil and Aden refining. Mining in southern Africa continued to make huge capital demands although the United States was also beginning to participate in such projects. Indeed, American capital was overtaking British capital in many places around the world, such as in development-minded Australia.

In the 1960s the falling share of British investment in the commonwealth became more pronounced; by 1968 the amount invested in foreign countries had risen to almost being level with the commonwealth amount, and thereafter the former kept moving ahead. Also, from the mid-1960s Britain's flirtation with developing countries (which had been building up since the inter-war period) began to taper off. Increasingly Britain now looked to the developed, industrialized west, hoping to get its share of production in the EEC and trying to counter American financial strength by buying into American companies.

Among commonwealth members, however, there was in the 1960s no sense of rejection of United States capital — indeed, quite the opposite. Canada fell further prey to the financial domination of its neighbour; the annual flow of United States money to Australia exceeded that of Britain; American capital, in its world-wide sweep for resources, found itself at work in diverse ways such as exploiting the mineral wealth of central Africa or prospecting for minerals in New Guinea. The members of the commonwealth clamoured indiscriminately for the boon of foreign investment, whether it be American or British, and since the United States had more of the capital, so its share of the market was increasing. It was only as the 1970s progressed that the alarms began to sound, as many of the countries which one decade previously had so eagerly coaxed foreign investment for a spate of development projects began to have second thoughts as to the nature and extent of this capital inflow. So Canadians were lamenting bitterly their lack of control over their manufacturing and mineral industries; and although the Australians were not so sure about the issue, the majority of leaders in developing countries, whether of socialist leanings or military backgrounds, were taking a more definite stand.[12] They saw value and political mileage in stabbing out against the

Table 12. Destination of Overseas Investment of United Kingdom, 1948, 1972.

	1948			1948		1968	
	Amount (£m)	Av. rate of return % 1939-48			(£m)		(£m)
Commonwealth	1,111		Government & municipal loans			Australia	966
Australia	397	4.3	Commonwealth		554	Canada	687
Canada	162	4.3	Australia		345	New Zealand	140
S. Africa	127	10.4	New Zealand		57	Sterling area developing countries	1,156
India/Pakistan	69	7.7	Central Africa		42		
New Zealand	66	4.4	Canada		24	USA	600
Malaya	64		S. Africa		20	S. Africa	586
W. Africa	47	6.3	W. Africa		12	EEC – France	180
Ceylon	26	7.8	India		4	Germany	179
W. Indies	21	5.9	Foreign		254	Belgium/Luxembourg	112
E. Africa	15	4.8					
			UK companies operating abroad				
Foreign	749		Commonwealth		715		
Brazil	82	2.5	India		62		
USA	75		Malaya		61		
Argentina	51	3.2	Australia		36		
Persia	34	14.6	W. Africa		35		
			Cent. Africa		32		
			Foreign		303		
			Companies registered abroad				
			Commonwealth		243		
			Canada		126		
			S. Africa		83		
			Foreign		193		

Source: Adapted from: 1948, Bank of England, *United Kingdom Overseas Investments 1938 to 1948*; 1968, *Board of Trade Journal*, 23 September 1970, (Book values of direct investment).

"hoarders" of the rich, industrial west who had used their surplus profits to try to buy out the assets of the developing countries, thereby keeping an economic influence there even after the bonds of political colonialism had been destroyed. Those leaders accordingly were adopting various schemes of nationalization and industrialization and, obviously, this helped push the interest of British investors towards the more established and stable governments of the developed, industrialized world.

By the 1970s Britain had readjusted her sights, accepting her small power position in the world. The hardest and slowest scaling-down came in her defence role and in diplomacy where for too long she talked as though she were still a great power. As an imperial power, however, she took off the mantle of greatness more graciously and spontaneously. The imperial fabric in both its economic and political pattern was being loosened progressively in each year of the 1950s and 1960s. In most cases trading ties between Britain and individual commonwealth members were disintegrating with ease; only where Britain felt conscience-stricken — as to the economic condition of the developing commonwealth — was there some regard for keeping together some of the former economic binds, and even here the gesture by Britain was not wholly charitable. By the 1970s imperial preference was gone; Britain had to buy firstly where her new commitments lay, in Europe, and then wherever she could most cheaply. Whatever earlier emotional attachments may have existed in matters such as the purchase of "Kangaroo" brand butter had no place in the new economic order. Nevertheless, the commonwealth remained a large supplier in some products, especially sugar from tropical areas, sheep meat from New Zealand and various minerals. The commonwealth had dwindled in importance as a trading partner but it had not become negligible.

This latter point was even more apparent in financial matters; indeed, in the 1970s British financial ties were considerably stronger than trade ties. At the same time Britain's financial role in the commonwealth was in a sure and steady decline. Her own severe internal financial problem meant that she could hardly expect to retain her share of investment in the commonwealth. At the same time, she did rest upon a wide range of wise investments, made over the previous century in countries scattered around the globe and she could expect for years to come to be kept economically afloat partly by income received from those investments.

NOTES

1. As a general study, Colin Cross, *The Fall of the British Empire, 1918—68* (London: Hodder and Stoughton, 1968); for growing criticism — R. P. Dutt, *The Crisis of Britain and the British Empire* (London: Lawrence & Wishart, 1952); John Strachey, *The End of Empire* (London: Gollancz, 1959); Michael Barratt Brown, *After Imperialism* (London: Heinemann, 1963); J. Morris, *Farewell the Trumpets* (London: Faber and Faber, 1978).

2. Robert Clutterbuck, *Riot and Revolution in Singapore and Malaya, 1945–63* (London: Faber & Faber, 1973); Gene Hanrahan, *The Communist Struggle in Malaya* (New York: Institute of Pacific Relations, 1954).
3. Frank D. Corfield, *Historical Survey of the Origins and Growth of Mau Mau* (London: HMSO, 1960); Donald L. Barnett & K. Njama, *Mau Mau from Within* (London: McGibbon & Kee, 1966).
4. D. J. Goldsworthy, *Colonial Issues in British Politics, 1945–61* (Oxford: Clarendon, 1970).
5. Philip Darby, *British Defence Policy East of Suez, 1947–68* (London: Royal Institute of International Affairs, 1973).
6. For a review of the 1950s, John D. B. Miller, *Britain and the Old Dominions* (London: Chatto & Windus, 1966), pp. 225–29; "Report of the Commonwealth Trade and Economic Conference", [Cmd.539], *Parl.Pap.* 10 (1957–58): 305, at 309–12; "The Colonial Territories, 1958–59", [Cmd.780], *Parl.Pap.* 10 (1958–59): 475, at 562–67, 575, 666.
7. The following trade analyses come from the various statistical sources (see notes to chapter 11), especially the Statistical Office, *Annual Abstract of Statistics* and various yearbooks (of the Commonwealth, and of individual member countries).
8. Look at the Bank of England review, *United Kingdom Overseas Investments, 1938 to 1948* (London, 1950).
9. J. F. Rippy, *British Investments in Latin America* (Minneapolis: University of Minnesota Press, 1959), chap. xvi.
10. Miller, *Old Dominions*, pp. 230–32; also, A. R. Conan, *The Changing Pattern of International Investment in Selected Sterling Countries* (Princeton: University Press, 1956).
11. The analysis of investments comes from Bank of England review above (for 1948), *Board of Trade Journal*, 23 September 1970 (for 1968) and annual *Survey of Current Affairs*, for example (1972): 385, 544 (for 1970).
12. Brian Stock, "A Culture in Search of an Economy", *Times Literary Supplement* 26 October 1973.

17
Preparing an Independent New Commonwealth

The political disintegration of Britain's web of empire anticipated in many respects the direction and timing of the weakening of economic binds.[1] The growing sense of independence of the four established dominions by the end of the 1940s led Britain to switch attention to the stronger dependent colonies; but as they in turn moved to independence, in the 1950s and 1960s, so British interest swung elsewhere, to Europe in particular. The political and economic factors behind these weakening ties were inextricably linked. British investors and traders obviously became hesitant in a colony moving towards independence if a new political leadership was emerging talking stridently in nationalistic terms. Equivalently, as British economic interests swung increasingly to foreign countries so there seemed less need for Britain to maintain imperial commitments.

India set the model for political independence of the developing world, but whereas for the Indians the achievement of recognition as a nation came only after a protracted and arduous wrangle the like achievement for other British colonies came much more easily. The Indians had been frustrated in their claim to dominion status throughout the early twentieth century, but the Japanese eruption into south-east Asia brought many more political changes than British administrators had ever contemplated in the 1930s. The sudden and striking victory of the yellow man imposed a drastic rethinking as to the nature of imperial control in the area, and had reverberations around the whole of the colonial world, whether British, French or Dutch. The precipitous surrender of the British at Singapore in 1942 signalled to many colonial peoples the fragility of the British Raj. It drove home how hollow and shallow was the real imperial power of Britain, that a handful of administrators, often well-meaning, sometimes dictatorial, and a group of soldiers, not always of the highest calibre and often bumbling, were holding together the hugest of empires. But what a precarious hold — a sudden jolt at any point, such as the "Quit India" protests in 1942, could easily cause a loosening, and if the pressure was maintained the hold might collapse totally.

As the Japanese surrendered and the British returned to their Asian empire, it was realized by the British leadership, especially after Churchill's defeat, that India could easily slip from their grasp. The Indian naval mutiny in 1946 provided a foretaste. It was fully appreciated that India could not be held by force. Furthermore the Japanese had spread doctrines of nationalism throughout the conquered territories, so that the return of the former imperial masters to south-east Asia was being seriously hampered. Indian nationalist sentiments had been already inflamed before the Japanese came; so in 1945 the British began to plan for India's acceptance as an independent member of the commonwealth. The final solution was, however, partly bedevilled by serious religious differences between the two main communities of the sub-continent. With no chance of reconciling the two groups, as evident in the Muslim "direct action" day in 1946, the only answer seemed to be the division of the land mass into two separate states, which division unfortunately brought communal killings and large-scale migration. Out of these negotiations there emerged in 1947 two new dominoins, India and Pakistan.[2] At last the concept of the commonwealth as a white man's club had been broken. The way had been opened for the advance to nationhood of all the "coloured" colonies. But in the late 1940s and early 1950s no actual timetable had been figured out. Only at some vague time in the future would the dependent colonies reach nationhood.

India forced another change in the commonwealth structure in 1969. Queen Victoria may have been pleased to receive in 1875 the title of empress of India, and Indian princes may have been delighted to participate in George V's coronation durbar in 1911, but the new leaders of independent India were not prepared to acknowledge the British king as their emperor. Hitherto, a vital bond of the commonwealth-empire structure had been the notion of common allegiance to the British crown by all members. But that formula did not suit the Indians who wanted to have their own head of state — in fact, to be a republic with a President. With compromising skill the British were able to accommodate this desire and at a meeting of commonwealth prime ministers in 1949 it was agreed that India could be both a republic and still a member of the commonwealth; that India would not have to swear allegiance to the British crown but rather would merely acknowledge the British king as "head of the commonwealth". So the way was cleared for a multi-faceted commonwealth, where an independent state might claim the British king as its head (as in Australia), or where a republic might have a president as head (as in Tanzania), or even where a state might have its own monarch (as in Malaysia, Swaziland or Tonga). The common commonwealth link between such diverse political structures was the acknowledgment of the British monarch as the "head of the commonwealth". But this is to anticipate the rush of political developments in the 1950s and 1960s.

And rush it was. For many colonies in 1950 had still not even experimented with the elective principle, let alone taken on powers and duties involved in self-government and independence.[3] Yet by 1970 most had acquired full nationhood, although sometimes the elective principle was still lacking. The changes came fast, perhaps too fast. In the early 1950s British administrators planned a gradual and thorough preparation for independence. The principles of democracy, of fair and open elections, had to be instilled in the minds of the people. The Westminster system of government was considered to be the most suitable model, perhaps with a few local adaptations to suit chiefs and existing political leaders. So the emergence of parties was encouraged, to provide a government and a loyal opposition. The practice of cabinet government under a prime minister was introduced, with indigenes working their way into ministerial positions and cooperating under the one leader.[4] At the same time, programmes were being undertaken to familiarize the people with the idea of expressing their political wishes through voting and of participating in the local and national levels of political life. It was assumed that after such patient preparation the new nations would want to stay in the commonwealth, partly for emotional and historical reasons, partly because of economic and financial ties. So the empire would come to an end but the links would go on. Obviously, time was needed if all these objectives were to be properly taught and learned.

Time, however, would not wait, or at least new political elites springing up in the various colonies, especially in Africa, would not sit patiently by while British administrators waited to reach a sense of satisfaction that the people were fully mature in their appreciation of the task of nationhood. Very soon the British found themselves hastily revising political plans for the colonies, only to have to revise them again with a further speeding-up.[5] Fortunately most administrators were quick to appreciate that this growing sentiment of nationalism should be used constructively in creating the new nation rather than be thwarted. Gaoling and detention were used to try to slow down political ferment but in most cases the use of armed force and violence was avoided. The main exception was in Kenya where some of the excessive practices of the Mau Mau movement led Britain to doubt that political advances there were moving in the correct direction; of course, the presence of a vocal group of white settlers did complicate the issue for the British government. In the long run, however, the use of force there was only a temporary diversion from the final achievement of a black nation.

Some of the Asian colonies had a considerable political experience so that Britain was pleased enough for them to move speedily in India's path. Ceylon had already been undergoing a considerable political preparation throughout the twentieth century; by 1931 it had an almost wholly elective house with an almost full universal suffrage. Its independence came in 1948;[6] and the same year Burma became independent. In the Malay peninsular a federation was created in 1948 in an attempt to strengthen the whole political structure there. This move was accompanied by an extension of the elective principle, at both the federal and state level.

Political development moved along swiftly in the 1950s, partly because the area had long established its economic viability and partly as a counter to the communist insurgency. In 1957 independence was granted. Malaya expanded into Malaysia in 1963 when it was joined by Singapore (temporarily) and the Borneo states of Sarawak and North Borneo (which became Sabah).[7] As to the latter, they were products of a very hasty political education, having acquired only a rudimentary grasp of the principles and practice of democratic government.

It was in Africa that the most dramatic speeding-up of political developments took place.[8] The Gold Coast led the way but there had, in fact, been a groundwork of political interest growing up in all the colonies since the 1930s. The great depression provided an impetus for anti-colonialism amongst local communities, at a stage when the notions of nationalism and democracy were quite alien. The depression showed how colonial governments had mismanaged and misunderstood colonial economies. The attention which those governments in the 1920s had given to the production of cash-crops for export brought chaos in the 1930s when there was little demand (and low prices) for such products; in the meantime local food production had declined, making the spectre — and reality — of famine more familiar. Furthermore, contact with European manufacturing had led to the decline and even destruction of local traditional crafts and industries. The result was that in the 1930s many colonies lacked self-sufficiency, to an extent that had never been so fully experienced before, either in colonial or pre-colonial times. So the move towards modernizing tropical economies and binding them more fully into the international economy had only limited effects; benefits flowed while the times were good but when the world market turned topsy-turvy, local farmers were sorely hurt, becoming quite hesitant about dabbling in further economic innovation and developing a suspicion of colonial authorities. This provided a breeding ground for the new educated political elite that was arising; they saw that the western masters were not so invincible in their economic power, nor did they have any real answer to the economic problems that confronted everyone. This elite could play upon the fears and suspicions of the people and so arouse a more definite sense of anti-colonialism. At the same time, indigenous teachers and preachers were increasingly giving emphasis to ideas of nationalism, of African worthiness and even rejection of western ways. Defection set in amongst some of the main supporters of the colonial administration, the traditional authorities. Rising public consciousness about the nature of colonial rule, coupled with the pressure of a growing band of political leaders, meant that from the end of the 1940s political developments in Africa were going to proceed more quickly than the British had contemplated.

In 1946 the Gold Coast became the first legislative council in British

Africa to have a majority of African members.[9] Already the Gold Coast, Sierra Leone and Southern Nigeria hand been operating a partly elective system since the 1920s; and in 1947 the whole of Nigeria obtained a partly elective council. Kwame Nkrumah and his Convention People's Party generated a strong political appeal through the ballot box. The British administration soon realized that it had to come to terms with such a charismatic leader; holding him in jail could not extinguish the fire of nationalism.[10] Instead he was made prime minister in 1952; two years later an all-African cabinet was governing and in 1957 independence was granted. Then followed the rest of Africa — fourteen new nations between 1960 and 1968.[11] During those years it seemed that the union jack would never cease to set on the African empire. In places where British authority had operated only lightly, such as the three high commission territories (Bechuanaland, Basutoland, Swaziland), Zanzibar and Somaliland, there was virtually no political preparation for the indigenous inhabitants. It was hoped that traditional authorities there would be able both to retain the loyalty of their people and perhaps to lead them to a greater participation in a more modern, democratic society.

The political development of the West Indies, which had been so chequered during the nineteenth century, was resumed in the 1940s.[12] The elective principle was gradually returned to those colonies which had lost it in earlier years and it was widened in places such as Jamaica and Barbados where some degree of election had been allowed earlier. Jamaica took the lead; in 1944 it was given a lower house where all members were elected by universal suffrage and which exercised a measure of internal self-government. This was extended in the 1950s. Ideas of nationalism and independence had been taking root in the Indies certainly by the 1930s, under the inspiration of people such as the Jamaican Marcus Garvey. But no constructive moves were made until the end of the 1950s, partly because the British government felt the geographical problem of so many small and scattered islands, along with mainland territories, made the success of independence doubtful. A federal solution was thought of in 1958, but with little enthusiasm. Soon after, all hesitation about the viability of small independent island states was thrown to the wind, Jamaica, Trinidad and Tobago becoming independent in 1962. They were followed by British Guiana and Barbados in 1966, the Bahamas in 1973 and Grenada in 1974. Some of the very small islands, however, were not anxious to live alone and so, while during the 1950s and 1960s they progressed through various stages of operating democratic elections and internal self-government, they still chose to rely upon Britain for defence and external affairs. In 1967 these arrangements were clarified whereby Antigua, Dominica, St Christopher, Nevis, Anguilla, St Lucia and St Vincent assumed the status of association with Britain.

Political developments tended to pass by most of the Pacific territories during the twentieth century, except for Western Samoa.[13] New Zealand had acquired this as a League of Nations' mandate in 1920 and soon after there arose a growing nationalist movement among the Samoans. In 1947 the New Zealand government began to respond, creating an elected legislative assembly — quite an early constitutional move in the history of decolonization.[14] In 1962 independence was granted. Meanwhile New Zealand was also preparing the Cook Islands for as much local control as the people wanted. In 1965 this amounted to a grant of full internal self-government, with a continuing association with New Zealand; the islanders felt full independence was not appropriate for their situation. Nauru, another mandate, was given independence in 1968. This followed a campaign of criticism by the Nauruans who, since the 1950s, had been demanding full control of their only source of wealth, phosphate. Political developments in Fiji were slowed down by festering communal differences, in particular the numerical dominance of the Indians over the Fijians. A series of negotiations in the 1960s led to Britain hammering out a course of independence which was granted in 1970. The same year Tonga gave up its protected state relationship with Britain. In the largest of the Pacific territories, Papua New Guinea, political advance had been allowed to take a very leisurely course.[15] This was largely because the Australian government, which administered Papua as a colony and New Guinea as a mandate (later trust territory), tended to overlook the area. As late as the 1950s parts of the mountainous hinterland were still coming under white control for the first time; so Australian administrators settled down to policies of slow and paternalistic development. The blood-bath of the Belgian Congo in the early 1960s seemed to reinforce this point, that a patient and cautious level of action should be pursued. Although the elective principle was introduced in 1964, no withdrawal was planned before the next century. Suddenly, in the 1970s the international tide of nationalism swept over Papua New Guinea, causing the Australian government to reverse its policies. Independence was granted in 1975, even before the local leaders asked for it.

In the British territories of the Gilbert and Ellice islands and the Solomon Islands protectorate western political practices seemed quite irrelevant until the 1960s. Traditional authorities functioned fairly much in their usual roles, although a political movement in one of the Solomon Islands, Marching Rule, had shown that there was some resentment towards outside rule, even as light as it was in the Solomons. In the 1960s some western-style changes were introduced, along democratic lines, but it was also hoped to maintain traditional political patterns. Both the Solomons and the Gilbert group obtained independence under a speeded-up programme, in 1978 and 1979 respectively. A political solution for the New Hebrides was hampered by the joint rule that was imposed when, in 1887 and later in 1906, the British and French agreed to share administration. Indeed, an almost comical type of government developed under three different administrations, British, French and joint. This form of control angered some of the islanders but until the late 1970s, although elections were allowed at various levels of government, there was no clear sign that the French were prepared to hand over control to local hands.

As to the variety of small islands and bases which had helped to secure British influence around the world, the British pressures began to mount; in any case, with a declining world role there was a declining need for such bases.[16] So Cyprus became independent in 1960; indeed, there Britain was pleased to abandon a very sticky communal problem between Greek and Turkish residents. Malta had made some political progress inter-war, and in 1947 responsible government was restored. But in the 1950s Britain, still feeling a strong strategic interest in the Mediterranean, found it difficult to come to any satisfactory agreement with Maltese leaders as to future constitutional arrangements. The whole political structure broke down in 1959 and a state of emergency resulted. Finally it became clear that the only solution was independence, which was granted in 1964. Aden and its hinterland also held strategic interest for Britain. Plans were made in the 1950s and 1960s to transfer political power to a federation of local communities. The British government was also trying to secure the friendship of rulers in the hinterland by bringing peace and offering other assistance. Such an approach yielded few results in the face of a powerful nationalist movement. Finally, after some fighting and unsuccessful negotiations, independence was granted to the People's Republic of Southern Yemen in 1967.

Some bases, however, were not relinquished. Hong Kong stayed on as a crown colony; its eventual solution would have to wait on the wishes of the government of China. Gibraltar wanted to stay a British colony, and was not prepared to give in to the wishes of the Spanish government. The Falkland islands were caught in a claim of ownership between Argentina and Britain. There were other small island dependencies where only limited political advance made any sense — St Helena, the Pitcairn islands, the vast Antarctic wastes. The Seychelles, however, with a population just over fifty thousand, obtained independence in 1976. Some of the members of the commonwealth also had dependent territories — in particular, Australia and New Zealand — but in all such cases the status of dependency was likely to continue.

So, in less than three decades the map of red, of the British empire stretching around the world, was virtually ripped up and in its place a pink commonwealth emerged. Overall the transition occurred easily, but there were a number of hitches in individual cases. One of the most difficult problems in some territories was the communal situation, how to protect minority groups, such as the Asians in the three east African colonies, the Chinese in Malaya, the Indians in Fiji.[17] Many of the constitutional arrangements, both leading up to independence and in the constitution conferring independence, had to go through tortuous convolutions to try to protect and please the different communities. In both Malaya and Fiji the indigenes were determined to ensure that they retained a determining stake in the future of their countries. The interests of white settlers in colonies where there was a preponderate coloured population were also protected by special constitutional devices in the years before independence. The 1959 Northern Rhodesia constitution provided an elected majority in the legislative council, but via a complicated two-tier qualitative franchise for European and African voters. The 1955 Nyasaland constitution used a dual system of election and representation, African members being elected by African provincial councils while non-African members were elected directly by voters on a non-African electoral roll. But in most cases the ultimate aim was to have direct election from a common roll, based on universal adult suffrage, with no regard for race or religion. Unfortunately, it sometimes happened that after independence racial minorities found themselves greatly underprivileged in the new nations; the fire of nationalism burned so strongly that it was considered that only one national and cultural strand could be allowed.

Apart from communal problems there were also regional difficulties in some states. Nigeria was perhaps too much a creature of artifice. The British tried to weld it together to form a huge landmass out of a great variety of tribes and cultural influences. In the face of such diversity British administrators worked upon a basis of three regions linked in a federation. But the history of Nigeria since independence has shown how fragile this unity was; perhaps the British map-makers of the 1890s were too arbitrary and greedy in their slap-dash division of the world. Likewise, in Uganda, the spirited nationalism was for some people bifurcated by a sense of loyalty to the kingdom of Buganda existing within the Ugandan nation. A favourite device of the British was to resort to a federation whenever there were a number of different elements to try to weld together. It worked well in the nineteenth century — in Canada (1867), New Zealand, and Australia (1900) — but it seemed to fail elsewhere at other times. Federations were often created among the small West Indies islands between the eighteenth and twentieth centuries but none succeeded. In the 1950s an attempt was made to federate the two Rhodesias and Nyasaland, again ending in failure; similarly, south Arabia, in the 1950s and 1960s.[18] Today Nigeria, although still a federation, has yet to find its true medium, while even in Canada those of French descent are not so sure that federation fits their needs.

While in most cases the initiative for the transfer of government, as to both representation and powers of administration, lay superficially in British hands, mounting pressures from nationalist leaders in the 1950s and 1960s meant that in many cases Britain was not leading but being pushed. Sometimes British initiatives were deflected or thwarted by the nationalists' use of force, as in Aden. In Guyana, rioting, racial divisions and British fears of communist influence led to the use of British troops on two occasions, and the suspension of ministerial government for some years. The Chinese communists in Malaya hastened the course of independence; the Mau Mau rebellion in Kenya probably slowed political developments. Terrorism and virtual civil war in Cyprus made an easy solution impossible, yet Britain shrank back from the partition of the island between the Greeks and the Turks. Even in the case of peaceful transition to independence, British administrators at various stages tried to keep the initiative and quieten the pace of nationalism by resorting to arrest and detention; but this generally was counter-productive, giving the incarcerated leader a halo of martyrdom in the cause. So he would be released, and negotiations resumed.

Overall, the emergence of the "new commonwealth" was a peaceful operation, but not all former colonies wanted to continue ties with Britain. There was the precedent of the thirteen north American colonies which forcibly took their independence between 1776 and 1783. In the twentieth century, however, the withdrawals were agreed to more amicably. Sometime during the 1930s the Irish, or at least the southern Irish, extracted themselves from the British connection although the independence of Eire was not formally recognized until 1949. Egypt had never formally been a part of the empire, although a protectorate was established there between 1914 and 1922 and various degrees of British military occupation had been imposed between 1886 and 1956. The Anglo-Egyptian Sudan, which had been run as a condominium by Britain and Egypt since 1899, was granted its independence in 1956; and it withdrew from the commonwealth. Britain's rule over League of Nations' mandates in the middle east was exercised fairly lightly, with independence being granted to Iraq in 1932 and the Trans-Jordan in 1946. The violence of the two communities in Palestine led Britain to relinquish quickly its charge there and the independent state of Israel emerged. Burma, on receiving its independence in 1947, immediately left the commonwealth. In 1960 British Somaliland joined up with Italian Somalia to become an independent state outside the commonwealth; in similar fashion the Southern Cameroons joined the French Cameroons in 1961 and left the commonwealth. The People's Republic of South Yemen pulled out in 1967, while Pakistan left in 1972 after failing to receive support in its civil war. East Pakistan, however, stayed within the commonwealth, as the new state of Bangladesh. In 1961 South Africa voluntarily withdrew from the commonwealth, probably just before being pushed out because of its racial policies. The white settlers of Southern Rhodesia in 1965 unilaterally declared their independence of Britain; this followed unsuccessful attempts by the British government and black pressure groups to coax or coerce the whites into granting adequate political rights to the black majority population.

The new commonwealth reflected the basic changes in power that were occurring in the United Nations and the world at large.[19] The hold of the British and of the white dominions was broken and in their place rose the newly independent and economically fragile nations of the third world. They denounced the evils of colonialism and neo-colonialism, they emphasized the needs of development and of aid, they claimed that retribution and compensation was due to them from the rich, industrial nations of the west. No longer was the British lead or the British example needed, or respected. It was even contemplated at one of the commonwealth conferences — Singapore, 1971 — that there might be a commonwealth without Britain. Through the 1970s the question of Southern Rhodesia-Zimbabwe proved an almost insoluble problem, even likely to cause the disintegration of the commonwealth. It had been supposed in the early, heady days of the new commonwealth that one of the vital bonds between all the members would be their common political heritage, in particular that at independence the British had transferred to them a constitution based upon the essential virtues of the Westminster system. But it did not take long for this common link to fray and break. The constitutions which Britain moulded tried to emphasize the principle of two-party government and widespread popular representation, but these elements were soon altered after independence. In most of the colonies the time of political preparation had been so short that the workings of a western democracy were not clearly understood or appreciated. In any case, the constitutions had often tried to work in harmony with aspects of the traditional polity, but upon independence this could lead to grave difficulties. Many of the African states found themselves plagued by tribal rivalries so that the very existence of two parties and rival leaders seemed a political luxury, pointing to disintegration rather than unity. A strong single leadership seemed more desirable if the nation was to survive, so the regular trend was for a one-party state to emerge or for a military takeover to be staged. The British political system did not transplant very well to non-British communities. For example, in Africa by 1976 there were only three working democracies in the British sense of free and open elections — the Gambia, Mauritius and Botswana.

The commonwealth failed in the sense of showing how imperial stewardship could create mature western-devised democracies out of previously small, traditional communities. The strength of former governmental patterns, along with the brief period of imperial tutelage, meant it was impossible to achieve any uniformity in political development. Only where white settlers went out with the British political system firmly established in their minds could a fairly uniform development occur, lying within the framework of the western democratic tradition.

In the tropical colonies, however, political developments came late and rapidly, frequently within one generation. Needless to say the majority of the coloured population responded more clearly to their own traditional institutions than to the Westminster implant. The British imperialists did, however, leave one significant political heritage: they fashioned nation-states where none existed before. They pushed together various groups, trying to make them think in larger regional terms than had traditionally been the case. Although the results were in a number of cases artificial, although sometimes the boundaries were unreal, although fragility is a political hallmark of some of the new nations, with few exceptions they all have survived in unaltered form. The independence leaders were determined to preserve the national boundaries, almost regardless of cost. So Nigeria was not allowed to break into smaller units, even though this meant civil war.

Paradoxically the survival of the commonwealth is linked with the looseness of the links between the various members. In 1979 there were forty members (and two special members, Nauru and Tuvalu); these are independent states freely associating, with the one common bond of having been part of the British empire. Yet this common heritage has had different effects and significance for the different members. For a while, in the late 1950s, the commonwealth was described in admiring terms as an example of multi-racial cooperation. The former all-white club was now happily mixing with black and brown and yellow members. But the difficulty that Britain and the commonwealth experienced in the 1970s trying to find a solution for the quarter million white and five million black Southern Rhodesians, the restrictions that Britain and other commonwealth members put on the immigration of other peoples from the commonwealth, and the problem of racial tensions in various countries illustrated that in many respects the racial harmony of the commonwealth was only skin-deep, or perhaps not even that deep. So the virtue of the commonwealth has been its casualness, almost a lack of purpose and direction. The members have continued their association because the burdens created by the commonwealth are practically non-existent, and there are a few benefits. It operates as a useful medium of communication — prime ministers' meetings, finance meetings, conferences on education, health, transport, development and so on. Grievances can be aired, common problems discussed. It is smaller and more manageable than the United Nations, and not so costly. In 1965 a small degree of formalization was introduced in the creation of a secretariat but this was valuable mainly in organizing and coordinating the multifarious activities of commonwealth agencies and bodies. The great empire which once stood for power and wealth is now represented by a commonwealth of conferences and cooperation.

NOTES

1. General — Rupert Emerson, *From Empire to Nation* (Cambridge, Mass.: Harvard University Press, 1960); and good, synoptic study, Frank H. Underhill, *The British Commonwealth* (Durham, N.C.: Duke University Press, 1956); William D. McIntyre, *Colonies into Commonwealth* (New York: Walker, 1967).
2. Vapal P. Menon, *The Transfer of Power in India* (Bombay: Longmans, 1957); C. H. Philips & M. D. Wainwright (eds.), *The Partition of India* (Cambridge, Mass.: Harvard University Press, 1970); B. N. Pandy, *The Break-up of British India* (London: Macmillan, 1969); P. Moon, *Gandhi and Modern India* (London: English Universities Press, 1968); S. Gopal, *Jawaharlal Nehru* (Cambridge, Mass.: Harvard University Press, 1976); P. J. Marshall, "The Transfer of Power in India", *Journal of Imperial and Commonwealth History* 5 (1976–77): 330–34.
3. Nicholas Mansergh, *Documents and Speeches on British Commonwealth Affairs, 1952–62* (London: Oxford University Press, 1963); William A. Hamilton (ed.), *A Decade of Commonwealth, 1955–64* (Durham, NC: Duke University Press, 1966); John D. B. Miller, *Survey of Commonwealth Affairs, 1953–69* (London: Oxford University Press, 1974).
4. Herbert V. Wiseman, *The Cabinet in the Commonwealth* (London: Stevens, 1958).
5. M. Wight, *British Colonial Constitutions, 1947* (Oxford: Clarendon, 1952); S. A. de Smith, *The New Commonwealth and its Constitutions* (London: Stevens, 1964); Kenneth C. Wheare, *The Constitutional Structure of the Commonwealth* (Oxford: Clarendon, 1960).
6. E. F. C. Ludowyk, *The Modern History of Ceylon* (London: Weidenfeld & Nicolson, 1966).
7. L. A. Mills, *British Rule in Eastern Asia* (London: Oxford University Press, 1942) and Rupert Emerson, *Malaysia* (New York: Macmillan, 1937) for earlier political developments; K. G. Tregonning, *A History of Modern Malaya* (London: University Press, 1964) and *A History of Modern Sabah, 1881–1963* 2nd ed. (Singapore: University of Malaya Press, 1965).
8. General African nationalism — T. Hodgkin, *Nationalism in Colonial Africa* (New York: University Press, 1956); Robert Rotberg and Ali Mazrui, *Protest and Power in Black Africa* (New York: Oxford University Press, 1971); John Lonsdale, "The Emergence of African Nations", *African Affairs* 67 (1968): 12–28; T. O. Ranger, "Connexions between 'Primary Resistance' Movements and Modern Mass Nationalism in East and Central Africa", *Journal of African History* 9 (1968): 437–53, 631–41.
9. M. Wight, *Gold Coast Legislative Council* (London: Faber, 1947); David Kimble, *A Political History of Ghana* (Oxford: Clarendon, 1963); Dennis Austin, *Politics in Ghana, 1946–60* (London: Oxford University Press, 1970).
10. Kwame Nkrumah, *Towards Colonial Freedom* (London: Heinemann, 1962); other nationalist leader-writers — Julius Nyerere, *Freedom and Unity* (London: Oxford University Press, 1967); Kenneth Kaunda, *Zambia Shall Be Free* (London: Heinemann, 1962).
11. James S. Coleman, *Nigeria* (Berkeley: University of California Press, 1958); Robert I. Rotberg, *The Rise of Nationalism in Central Africa* (Cambridge, Mass.: Harvard University Press, 1966).
12. H. A. Will, *Constitutional Change in the British West Indies, 1880–1903* (Oxford: Clarendon, 1971); Harold Mitchell, *Europe in the Caribbean* (Edinburgh: Chambers, 1963); Elisabeth Wallace, *The British Caribbean* (Toronto: University Press, 1977).
13. A. Haas, "Independence Movements in South Pacific", *Pacific Viewpoint* 11

(1970): 97–119; Harold Brookfield, *Colonialism, Development and Independence* (Cambridge: University Press, 1972).
14. J. W. Davidson, *Samoa mo Samoa* (Oxford: University Press, 1967).
15. Don Woolford, *Papua New Guinea* (Brisbane: University of Queensland Press, 1976). The New Hebrides became independent in 1980.
16. As to the constitutional development of the many smaller territories, see the annual *Commonwealth Yearbook* and the earlier *Colonial Office List*.
17. As an example of communal problems, Robert Norton, *Race and Politics in Fiji* (Brisbane: University of Queensland Press, 1978); R. Vasil, "Communalism and Constitution-Making in Fiji", *Pacific Affairs* 45 (1972): 21–41; in Malaya, see P. L. F. Seng, *Seeds of Separatism* (Kuala Lumpur: Oxford University Press, 1975).
18. A. H. M. Kirk-Grene, *Crisis and Conflict in Nigeria* (London: Oxford University Press, 1971); S. K. Panter-Brick (ed.), *Nigerian Politics and Military Rule* (London: University Press, 1974).
19. On general interpretations of the commonwealth — Derek Ingram, *Commonwealth for a Colour Blind World* (London: Allen & Unwin, 1965); Nicholas Mansergh, *The Commonwealth Experience* (London: Oxford University Press, 1969); M. M. Ball, *The "Open" Commonwealth* (Durham, NC: Duke University Press, 1971). A final solution for Southern Rhodesia/Zimbabwe was figured out in 1979–80.

18
Developing Economic Independence

The new members have seen value in maintaining the commonwealth connection from the angle of economic development. After the 1939—45 war the British government (and people) developed a conscience of increasingly guilty proportions. As the venom of writers from the left spurted out with utter condemnation for the way the imperialist powers had raped and pillaged the underdeveloped countries, for the way imperialists had expropriated the wealth of the colonies for their own benefits thereby leaving colonial peoples wretched and destitute, for the way the industrialized west had deflected the economies of the third world from their previous supposedly natural, prosperous and balanced path, so the former imperial powers began to think more positively of helping the new nations achieve greater economic viability. These denunciations by writers on the left were taken up by the nationalist heroes and liberators in the third world. Their anger increased year after year so that western governments, at least for public show and probably with some ring of sincerity, found it wise to undertake policies of economic aid for poorer countries, partly as compensation and retribution for the past. But the policies of aid were also based upon shrewd economic considerations, and probably this carried more weight in the making of government policy than the arousal of feelings of guilt.

A turning point in British government policy on the economic development of the colonies came in 1940, with a white paper and the subsequent Colonial Development and Welfare Act.[1] The financial plight and indebtedness of the West Indies (and other colonies) during the 1930s prompted the British government to make a reassessment of the economic future of the empire.[2] Declaring, probably more genuinely than before, that she was trustee for the well-being of colonial peoples and that she had a duty to protect and advance their interests, the government of Britain determined to give greater financial assistance to colonies with budget problems and to bring more planning assistance into the whole field of development. A new fund was set up to encourage and assist development; now money would be allowed to go towards recurrent expenditure and not only to capital expenditure; now more attention would be given to agriculture, education, health, housing and other such social capital. Now it was announced that the dual objective of helping both the colonies and Britain was dropped;

instead the legislation was aimed at the single task of improving the economic position of the colonies so that they could stand alone in the future. Nevertheless, it is only reasonable to assume that the British government considered that through giving financial aid to the colonies Britain would receive some trading and financial return.

The original scheme was extended, both in time and in capital allocations. After the 1939—45 war the giving of aid became an accepted practice on the part of the more developed nations, at first for war reconstruction and later for boosting the economies of colonial countries moving towards independence. In fact, aid became part of international diplomacy, hoping to win support from newly independent countries as the forces of capitalism and communism confronted one another in the cold war. British aid policies were partly geared to this need, since she saw herself as one of the bulwarks of the capitalist free world. But they were probably more closely aligned to the economic needs of Britain, trying to continue trading and financial ties with the empire rather than allowing other western countries to move in. There were also the moral reasons given above. Until 1970 total British aid under the legislation amounted to £490 million, with the largest sum going to communications, education and agricultural development (£78 million, £72 million, £66 million respectively).[3] A wide range of tasks was assisted, such as road building in Nigeria, land settlement in Kenya, airport construction in the West Indies, the building of a new capital in British Honduras.

In the first phase Britain paid most attention to reviving, yet again, the economy of the West Indies; war-ravaged areas also received aid, such as £10 million going each to Malta and Malaya. Then aid schemes underwent considerable expansion: by the mid-1950s Britain's total financial investment (public and private) in the commonwealth and colonies was about £200 million per annum, equal to 1¼ per cent of her gross national product.[4] Practical, technical and educational schemes received consideration, Britain supplying about 350 advisors at that stage. Also, various advisory and research agencies were at work, looking into problems ranging from pesticides to the Falkland Islands dependency. Nearly ten thousand students were taken to British universities, technical institutions and nursing hospitals to train them for the benefit of their homelands. This wide-ranging approach, revolving around financial assistance, practical guidance and training, was continued through the 1960s and 1970s with various refinements.[5] Conditions of aid were improved, to the benefit of the recipients. Britain increased to over one half of the total financial aid bill, the amount she gave as outright grants, mainly to areas still of colonial status. At the same time, loan terms were softened so that most loans were for long periods, twenty years or more, with a low (or after 1965 nil) rate of interest, plus a small management charge. Furthermore, the amount of tied aid was reduced so that donees could shop around for imports rather than be constrained to send the aid money back through the purchase of British goods.

Apart from development assistance to colonies trying to build up an economic base before being granted independence, considerable British funds continued to flow to those countries that had just recently acquired nationhood. India, Kenya and Nigeria were the biggest recipients, the money coming mainly as loans rather than grants. Some British aid went for specific purposes, such as the Volta hydro-electric scheme in Ghana, or the Indus basin development fund. Sometimes the giving of aid retained a strong British connection; for example, a large sum was given to the east African states to be used for compensation of expatriate officials and for the commutation of their pensions; elsewhere, aid was set aside for paying salary differentials due to British workers in the poorer countries.

The vast bulk of British aid was allocated bilaterally but Britain did also make contributions at a multi-lateral level, through the United Nations, the World Bank and such bodies. Most British aid went to countries that had been, or still were, part of the empire; of the small proportion that went to foreign countries, the major recipients were in the middle east — oil states of the Persian gulf, Jordan and, for a while, Libya.

The Colombo Plan was one special aspect of British development assistance. Although started on the initiative of Spender, the Australian repres-- representative, at a meeting of British commonwealth foreign ministers in 1950, it was not restricted to commonwealth countries and from the start foreign states, especially the United States and Japan, participated. The aim was to improve the standard of life for people mainly in south and south-east Asia. Emphasis was given to technical assistance and education, so that Britain acted as a training centre for Indians and other Asians in fields such as engineering, industry, administration and health. Britain also provided experts and consultancy services, and other commonwealth countries, Canada, Australia, New Zealand and Malaysia, also joined in offering assistance.[6]

Overall, British aid policies have probably had most effect at the educational and technical level. Access to British education by thousands of students from the colonies and the new commonwealth, at a time when local educational institutions were either non-existent or of a low standard, provided an inestimable boost to the development of those countries once the students returned; it meant that the initiative for development in those countries lay with the local people, and these people were possessed of the requisite educational skills to be able to understand the problems of development. In addition, Britain was providing an army of expert advisers; in 1970 about fourteen thousand people were engaged in the Overseas Service Aid Scheme and similar projects, acting as teachers, engineers, doctors and so on, with the British government supplementing the local salaries.[7]

The British government promoted commercial and industrial projects in poor countries through the Commonwealth Development Corporation. Created in 1948 (as the Colonial Development Corporation) its aim was to encourage projects developing colonial resources so that commercially saleable products or services would be produced, to the benefit of the country's social situation. Schemes have been promoted such as the spread of African small-farmer ownership of the tea industry in Kenya, the establishment of a farm management training centre in Swaziland, a housing project in Nairobi; and tourist schemes have also been undertaken, such as Serengeti Park in Tanzania.

British public assistance in the 1970s was going into a steady decline. This arose partly from the economic problems that beset Britain, at first internally and then internationally. In times of recession aid plans were easy targets for cuts. But the intellectual climate of the 1970s also threw into doubt the wisdom and efficiency of aid. Critics on the left pointed the finger of scorn at donor countries, on the grounds that the supposed charity was in reality self-seeking. The donor, not unnaturally, tended to expect some return, either financial or moral. Questions were asked as to what benefits twenty-odd years of aid had bought.[8] In some cases it had seemed to increase the economic dependence rather than independence of underdeveloped countries. Examples could readily be given of inappropriate aid projects: tractors rusting in the fields with no one to maintain them and no spare-parts; the ornate grandstands and public monuments for a country with a totally inadequate infrastructure. At the same time tax-payers and politicians in the donor countries began increasingly to wonder and grumble about where the aid was going, with no thanks and seemingly few results. In fact, the total amount that the rich, developed countries of the west donated was very small — much less than the new leaders hoped for — so that it was not surprising that startling results were not to be seen.

Private aid, or investment, has continued its role in the development of third world economies, obviously with fluctuations but at a greater rate than public aid, until a peak was reached in the mid-1960s. After that, with the British economy performing under difficulty, private confidence began to erode, with an effect upon overseas investment in developing countries. Instability and insecurity in those countries also played a role. To try to revive such private investment, the British government offered various inducements: an investment insurance scheme, official representation for compensation when expropriation occurred. The government also tried to provide assurances for trade between Britain and developing countries by providing guaranteed export credits. The private investor was, of course, pushed on by the lure of profit rather than the spirit of development, with one major exception, the Commonwealth Development Finance Company, established in 1953. By providing finance in the form of share capital and loans it aimed at supporting overseas commercial enterprises, to the advantage of local economies. It was not restricted to the developing commonwealth and operated in various ways, such as hotels and building. The bulk of private interest, however, centred on minerals. For example, bauxite deposits in the Gold Coast were brought into production by a combination of private and public capital; this was a huge project requiring not only the mining works and smelter, but also roads, a rail system, port developments and the damming of the Volta River to provide hydro-electric power. Similarly, bauxite deposits in Jamaica and Guyana and copper deposits in Papua New Guinea were opened up, mainly through private capital.[9]

Nearly all the colonial governments moving towards independence speeded up plans for industrialization. A number of countries, following the example of India, devised five-year development plans, and often these plans gave emphasis to secondary industry too much over the primary sector. Factories undertaking simple processing of food and raw materials, or supplying the building industry, or refining raw materials sprang up in most colonies, with the aim of cutting down reliance upon imports from Britain and other foreign countries. After independence Kenya probably set the pattern, with the government putting prime emphasis upon the establishment of an industrial base which could supply the whole of east Africa and cut down on imports. By the end of the 1960s Kenya boasted factories producing food, beer, cigarettes, textiles, footwear, cement, wood pulp and oil.[10] In Hong Kong and Singapore more advanced industrialization got under way — ship building, electronics, a highly developed textile industry. Most other areas, however, were making only small industrial progress, unless some valuable mineral deposit was opened up, bringing with it a host of subsidiary industries. In Nigeria the discovery of oil led to a rapid expansion of its industrial base, of the construction industry as well as the refining of oil.[11] Oil rich areas, such as Brunei and the middle east, where Britain had maintained protectorate or friendship agreements, saw only slow industrial development at first but by the 1970s these countries, flush with funds, began a more serious drive to expand their economic base. In most other cases industrialization only made faltering steps, mainly at an elementary level; and in a large number of cases, control lay in British hands, through the use of British capital or through the ownership and management by British residents.

The factor of outside economic control at a time when nationalism rode high, the thought of income flowing to non-indigenes and even out of the country, often rankled the new nationalist leaders so that they took up schemes of nationalization. An early attempt was set by the nationalization of the oil industry in Iran in 1951; later (by the 1970s), other oil producers, such as Iraq, Libya, the Persian Gulf states and Nigeria, were following suit, taking major or complete control of their oil industries.

Nor was nationalization reserved for the oil industries; the Nauruans considered that their only source of wealth (phosphate) had been for too long exploited to the economic advantage of farmers in Australia, New Zealand and Britain: in 1968 the island's phosphate was transferred to Nauruan hands. In Zambia the government took over a major holding in the copper industry.[12] In most of the states of Africa indigenization became a major plank of the nationalist programme after independence. Nigeria and Ghana laid out a scale of indigenization for different kinds of industry, the most simple tasks requiring complete local control. In some countries, not only were factories and businesses taken over from white control but also farm-lands, such as tea estates in Tanzania. Economic nationalism became the catch-cry of the new political elite during the first decade of independence. In most cases some compensation was calculated for the expropriation. The newer commonwealth countries looked more to the state than did the older commonwealth to bring about economic development. The socialist model of five year plans was adopted in most new countries, with the state participating at a variety of economic levels — planning bodies, marketing boards, even the ownership and management of industrial plants.

Most new countries still felt a need for foreign capital. Only a few places, notably Tanzania, set themselves against the pattern of development based upon firstly industrialization and secondly agriculture.[13] After 1967 resources-poor Tanzania reversed the usual pattern, putting industrialization and foreign capital into a subsidiary position. It was felt that its needs could best be satisfied by trying to achieve basic economic subsistence — to expand food production, so that food imports would not be necessary, and at the same time to limit the need for manufactured imports. Tanzania's President Nyerere stressed the utmost importance of economic control resting with the local government and its people; he insisted that only limited, and attainable, objectives for development should be set. By contrast most of the new leaders, and especially Nyerere's neighbour, Kenyatta of Kenya, welcomed foreign aid and investment; and most also assumed that economic progress would easily follow upon the achievement of independence. By the mid-1970s, with the industrialized world racked by economic disorder, the economies of the newer developing countries found themselves even more in peril and it became strikingly clear that economic progress, especially along the path of industrial development that the older commonwealth or Britain herself had taken, could not be easily achieved.

So attention swung back to the agricultural sector, which had been allowed to drag along in the 1950s and 1960s. Plans were prepared to educate rural peasants, to encourage the use of more machinery and fertilizers, and schemes of land allocation and land resettlement were considered. Indigenization was also a plank of rural policy in areas where expatriates had obtained land ownership. Already some successful examples of indigenous rural enterprise could be pointed to, such as coffee-growers in the New Guinea highlands. But there were many cases of poor and inefficient farming, of agricultural economies still geared to one or two export crops to the neglect of local food production. Some of the Pacific islands had seen little agricultural development in a century, and even imported canned fish. Fishing was one of the possible growth industries, but the initiative had been lost to foreigners, Japanese and Americans. Some Pacific islands, accepting the burdens of a stagnant agricultural economy, looked to tourism as an answer; but the results were similar, foreigners having considerable control and taking most of the profit, both in tourism and ancillary industries. The idea of local participation in industry reached the Pacific later than most of the African countries. But the poverty of agriculture and the limitations of development were problems known not only in the Pacific.[14] The grasslands of Lesotho were devastated, decade after decade, by overstocking and erosion, relieved only by drought. Only slowly and late were attempts made to grapple with these problems and to widen the economy. Even those states with a more balanced and efficient rural sector have had difficulty in functioning prosperously in the world market. Traditionally primary product prices have fluctuated widely; the growth of the nineteenth century self-governing colonies probably rode as many booms and crashes as third world countries in the twentieth century; in either case survival was most assured if gold or some valuable mineral was discovered. Since 1945, while the prices of primary products have had some booms, there have also been quick crashes. In view of the ability of the industrial countries to arrange market prices, primary producers have had most success when they have operated as one unit, bargaining with the industrial producers. But often the poorest countries are also producing materials which are not in high demand and so their negotiating power is limited.

Britain's willingness to give up political control of her dependencies was not matched by an equal abandonment of economic influence. She graciously created the new commonwealth, in the hope that she would thereby maintain her trading and financial role in the former colonies. In this respect she has partially succeeded, although it is subject to a slow and continuing erosion. Since obtaining political independence, the new nations have come to realize that they must also achieve economic independence, and as a result of this struggle British economic influence must necessarily dwindle.

NOTES

1. "Statement of Policy on Colonial Development and Welfare", [Cd.6175], *Parl.Pap.* 10 (1939—40): 25 at 28—32; J. M. Lee, " 'Forward Thinking' and War", *Journal of Imperial and Commonwealth History* 6 (1977—78): 64—79.

2. "Report of the West India Royal Commission", [Cd.6607], *Parl. Pap.* 6 (1944–45): 245 at 422–32.
3. "An Account of the British Aid Programme", [Cd.5545], *Parl.Pap.* 27 (1972–73): 1; also the annual *Survey of Current Affairs*, for example 2 (1972): 397, and 9 (1979): 8; an earlier review, "Select Committee on Overseas Aid", H. of C. No. 285, *Parl.Pap.* 23 (1969–70): 173; Ministry of Overseas Development, *British Aid Statistics* (London: HMSO, 1973): *The Times*, 29 January 1975.
4. See "The United Kingdom's Role in Commonealth Development", [Cd.237], *Parl.Pap.* 26 (1956–57): 429, at 447. The proportion has dropped back since the mid-1950s.
5. "Aid to Developing Countries", [Cd.2147], *Parl.Pap.* 31 (1962–63): 163, at 171 ff.; "Second Special Report from the Select Committee on Overseas Aid, 1968–69", H. of C. No. 394, *Parl.Pap.* 17 (1968–69): 33.
6. See the 1968–69 and 1972–73 parliamentary reports in notes 5 and 3; also, *Survey of Current Affairs*, for example 2 (1972): 43–45.
7. See 1972–73 parliamentary paper in note 3.
8. As an example of the criticism, T. Hayter, *Aid as Imperialism* (Harmondsworth: Penguin, 1971); Samir Amin, *Neo-Colonialism in West Africa* (Harmondsworth: Penguin, 1974).
9. As to the activities of the Commonwealth Development Corporation and the private fund, see annual *Survey of Current Affairs*; also, *The Times*, 6 June 1973.
10. Colin Leys, *Underdevelopment in Kenya* (London: Heinemann, 1975).
11. Carl Eicher and C. Liedholm, *Growth and Development of the Nigerian Economy* (East Lansing: Michigan State University Press, 1970); R. O. Ekundare, "The Political Economy of Private Investment in Nigeria", *Journal of Modern African Studies* 10 (1972): 37–56; P. C. Garlick, *African Traders and Economic Development in Ghana* (London: Oxford University Press, 1971).
12. M. L. O. Faber, *Towards Economic Independence* (London: Cambridge University Press, 1971) – Zambia; P. C. W. Guttkind & I. Wallerstein. *The Political Economy of Contemporary Africa* (London: Sage, 1977) – general.
13. Justinian Rweyemamu, *Underdevelopment and Industrialization in Tanzania* (Nairobi: Oxford University Press, 1973); see Nyerere's Arusha declaration.
14. I. J. Fairbairn, "Pacific Island Economies", *Journal of Polynesian Society* 80 (1971): 74–118; Fiji example – R. F. Watters, *Koro* (Oxford: Clarendon, 1969).

19
Imperial Conscience and Culture

The older dominions — Canada, Australia, New Zealand, and South Africa until 1961 — increasingly went their own way as a result of the 1939—45 war. Already in the 1930s Canada and South Africa had shown an impatience with the notion that they were still subject in any way to British control. The fall of Singapore in 1942 rattled the antipodeans, and with an inbuilt sense of insecurity the Australians and New Zealanders wasted no time in finding another friend with a protective umbrella. From the 1940s these two countries were to swing increasingly into the American Pacific orbit. Already Canada was under the military and financial wing of the United States; and soon Australia was canvassing for American financial props (and later still for Japanese capital). New Zealand, however, was slower in shedding trading and financial links with Britain.

Just how completely these countries were breaking with Britain was indicated in migration policies. The halt in migration brought about by the depression was reversed after 1945. The governments of Canada, Australia, New Zealand and South Africa were again anxious for a rapid build-up of population to boost manpower for their economic expansion. Canada and Australia were the most popular choice for British migrants, and between 1945 and 1970 almost one million went out, many on assisted passages with the host country paying most of the bill. For a while South Africa, Rhodesia and Kenya also proved attractive; between 1946 and 1953 twelve per cent of the British total went there. But the governments of these countries were no longer recruiting only British labour so as to build "another England across the seas".[1] The Australian government canvassed throughout Europe, and even beyond; gradually, even non-white migrants were accepted, partly for humanitarian reasons and also in accordance with the changing dictates of international morality as to racial discrimination. Only in New Zealand was the flow from Britain more than fifty per cent of the total; for Canada, Australia and South Africa the non-British flow increasingly replaced that from Britain, with a consequent reduction of pro-British sentiment.

The more established members of the commonwealth were also undergoing a degree of cultural transformation, since British cultural supremacy was no longer a self-evident fact. Indeed, in South Africa and Canada the basically British culture came under serious assault from other European groups. The Afrikaners of South Africa were not to be swamped by the British, and while for the first three decades of the Union some sort of balance was achieved between the two European communities, from the end of the 1930s the Afrikaners began to assert greater political power, and have continued to do so with increasing intensity since.[2] A similar situation was occurring in Canada. While for one hundred years it seemed that Lord Durham's hope of submerging the French spirit of Quebec might be achieved, after the 1940s the French could no longer be contained and increasingly concessions had to be made diluting the British cultural hold and attempting to create a bilingual and bicultural society. In any case the Britishness of Canada had already been bastardized by strong influences from the southern neighbour. For Australia there was no problem of relations between two European groups but it also has been faced with a major problem of cultural indentity. Indeed, certainly with respect to the settlement colonies, it was probably in this matter of cultural identity, rather than in political or economic development, that the British failed most to prepare these colonial wards for nationhood. The Australian's culture or cultural identity seemed either an elusive or perhaps unimportant commodity; they could always fall back on a British heritage although the American versions seemed easier to buy; as for a peculiarly Australian one, no one could agree, and most were not interested. Meanwhile their New Zealand friends seemed to persist in being "little Englanders" in the antipodes.

By contrast, those new countries of the commonwealth, where British contact had not existed for long and where British settlement had been limited, were lucky to have their own established traditional culture to live by and for it to survive somewhat unscathed by British colonialism. British cultural imperialism had not made an ineradicable imprint and although the traditional cultures had been modified through colonial contact there still existed a strong body of traditional culture that the leaders could work with and build upon in controlling the destiny of their people. In some tropical areas, however, traditional culture did suffer, to be replaced by a very mixed cultural pattern. In the West Indies in particular there was a variety of cultural influences — Spanish, French, Dutch, British, African, as well as local Carib. Other European influences persisted in a number of colonies, such as the Dutch language, legal and political practices in the Cape, Ceylon and Guyana; Spanish influence in Jamaica; French culture in Canada, some of the West Indies and Mauritius.

Questions of race became a sensitive commonwealth issue in the 1950s. The admission of non-whites into the commonwealth meant that the white settlement areas had to do some serious rethinking, especially about the indigenous people within their own borders. The urgency of this rethinking was reinforced by the rising condemnation of racism that had become an essential part of the anti-imperial ideology of the time. So indigenous peoples, who had earlier been treated as outcastes in their own land, began to find themselves being dragged back into the mainstream of life in those countries. For example, starting in 1966 census-takers made a serious effort to count Aborigines, nomadic as well as settled. By the 1970s full political rights, economic assistance and anti-discriminatory legislation had become the new public values of the government. Similar changes occurred earlier for the Canadian Indian; luckily for the Eskimo, since he did not encroach very much on white preserves, he had been able to continue his life with not so much adverse effect from white civilization. The most success in combining races had been achieved by the New Zealanders where through the twentieth century Maori and *Pakehas* had shown an ability to live, work and play together.[3] The government gave positive assistance in welfare and education; by 1960 official policy was set on a course of integration, with the two cultures functioning alongside one another; the basically white population seemed to be able to accept the Maori in terms of racial equality, as indicated by figures for inter-racial marriage. Yet there were flaws in this appearance of inter-racial harmony. Significant economic, employment, land, educational and health disparities existed between the two races. New Zealand remains basically a white culture, with Polynesian influences mainly as frippery.

The abatement of the rather blatant racism of the white settlers of New Zealand, Canada and Australia came late and slowly. But it never came at all in South Africa where, outnumbered by the blacks by more than four to one, the whites felt they could not relax their hold, especially since they possessed eighty-three per cent of the land (generally the most fertile parts). The rise of the Afrikaners brought a more entrenched nation of white supremacy and black separation. The government of 1948 enshrined the earlier reserves policy into a system of apartheid, or separate development.[4] The black Bantustans or homelands were to develop, slowly, on their own, towards nationhood, although in economic terms they would have to continue as dependent states. In the white homeland, blacks would be allowed as temporary sojourners — in fact, essential cheap labour for the mines, factories and farms. To control the whole structure an elaborate state operation was set up, checking subversion, treason and the possibility of communist inroads, prosecuting "immorality" between the races, extending censorship, equipping police with wide powers of arrest, banishment and detention. So the state aimed to contain and control black power, but could not fully succeed. Black workers were prepared to defy the state and push for better conditions and wages. Slowly the latter were improved. The state also found that in spite of its relentless watching, black-consciousness could not be stifled. Increasingly the South African government hoped for the success of its Bantustan policy but increasingly international pressures bore upon South Africa's racist stance, bringing into question the whole survival of the nation.

Under much pressure South Africa withdrew from the commonwealth in 1961 but the pressure has continued. In a similar situation Southern Rhodesia unilaterally left the British fold in 1965 when it resisted pressure aimed at weakening the control of the government and the possession of half of the land by a tiny white minority.[5]

Such racism, however, has not been the sole prerogative of the white settlers. Arabs and Asians have found themselves objects of discrimination in a number of the newer independent members of the commonwealth; the Asians of east Africa were made to realize soon after independence that they were not living in their homeland. In some places, notably Malaya and Fiji, racial equality is denied in one sense by the concern of the indigenous population that their position be entrenched. Britain herself was caught out in a racial furore as groups of coloured people flocked there, some as dispossessed Asians from Africa, others just leaving their tropical homelands in the hope of greater opportunities in Britain.

From the 1940s the policy of the British government increasingly stressed full acceptance of racial equality in tropical countries.[6] By that stage the failings of indirect rule and paternalism were acknowledged and instead emphasis was put upon the rapid development of the colonies in the interests of the local people. The 1930s showed that paternalism retarded the development of tropical areas. The thorough and gradual approach of indirect rule had produced only minimal change. While Britain could benefit by exploitation of colonial resources, insufficient returns were going to the colonies. Education was lagging, health services were curtailed by lack of money and personnel, economic development and communications had generally been governed by the needs of western entrepreneurs rather than of the local people.

From the 1940s British policy increasingly accepted the equality of the different cultures of the empire with that of the British. At the same time Britain was not prepared to allow the different communities to bask in a stagnating, traditional, insular culture. The British government took upon itself the task of trying to figure out a balance between allowing the communities to control their way of life while also modernizing sufficiently to be able to compete in the world scene. The problem of balancing modernization with local cultures was most clearly evidenced in the field of education. This was one matter where the British conscience of the 1940s was sorely distressed. Progress had been very slow, illiteracy was pervasive, secondary and higher education had largely been overlooked. In 1942 British west Africa, with a total population of about twenty-seven million, had only forty-three recognized secondary schools teaching eleven thousand students, most in Nigeria.[7] The standard of education was not high, based on rote learning; emphasis was placed upon passing exams which had a British bias; the standard of spoken English was poor. The Gold Coast, which had the most extensive school system of all black

Africa, had a functional literacy rate well below twenty per cent. In 1948 only four per cent of its population had been educated for six years or more; and in 1951 less than one per cent of its pupils were taking technical and agricultural courses. A similar (or worse) situation existed in the other tropical colonies. Of course there was considerable variation: Barbados, with a long British contact, had eighty-eight per cent of its children at primary school but nearby St Vincent had less than fifty per cent.[8] Among the more advanced West Indies islands — Barbados, the Bahamas, Bermuda and Trinidad — free, and in some cases compulsory, education had been introduced. Even so, standards were low, with poorly trained teachers and inadequate facilities.

By the 1950s and 1960s educational advance was seen as one of the prime tasks of development, with great emphasis being placed on the provision of a primary education for all children, the extension of a secondary school network and the improvement of teacher training and industrial training.[9] But progress was hampered by the serious backlog that had built up in previous years; there was a serious teacher shortage, especially at the secondary school level; colonial populations kept expanding at a rapid rate so that expansion of education services sometimes found any gains eaten up by the bigger population; and funds from the colonial and British governments, although always expanding, were never quite enough. Initially the expansion seemed to help the local white residents more than the indigenous population but soon that aspect was reversed. At first the curriculum was too British-inspired but in time education became more localized and geared to the needs of the developing country. Increasingly education became a matter of state control, and progressively the old-established role of the missions as educators was whittled away. The British government, apart from providing financial aid, also supplied teachers to help overcome the local shortage and sent equipment and technical assistance. For example in 1970—71 the British Council was recruiting over eight hundred British teachers to serve abroad, partly with the hope of promoting and improving the teaching of the English language. A continuing series of commonwealth education conferences was called where problems of education in developing countries could be aired, and advice and assistance given by the more developed ones. Again, in education, it became accepted — although fairly late — that the British system was not very suitable for tropical, undeveloped countries, and so, in time, the shaping of education in these countries was passed over to local hands to be moulded more to suit their own way of life.

Higher education also received a sharp boost in the 1950s and 1960s, as it was realized that an educated elite was needed to handle the government, administration, the economy and professions of countries moving towards independence.[10] This was tackled in two ways: by taking colonial students to London to be trained for service back in their homelands, and by developing colonial institutions. As to the former, commonwealth scholarship and fellowship plans were devised (after 1959) to help students and staff in developing countries where academic facilities were limited or non-existent to go to more advanced countries. Britain at first offered five hundred places; this was later extended, while other commonwealth countries also provided similar schemes. Most of the students followed post-graduate courses in engineering, technology and health. In addition Britain provided basic training for a great number of students from developing countries. For example, in 1970 there were almost forty-three thousand students there, seventeen thousand doing nursing, ten thousand in technical colleges and nine thousand in universities.[11]

At the same time the British government was providing money for capital works, teachers (and salary supplements) and equipment to help expand the institutions of higher learning in the developing commonwealth. In the 1940s the colonial empire (excluding the dominions and India, which had well-established universities) boasted four universities — Malta, Hong Kong, Ceylon and the Hebrew University in Jerusalem — and twelve institutions of higher learning, meaning places of post-secondary level but not fully of university status.[12] In this group were places such as Fourah Bay College (in Sierra Leone), Achimoto College (in the Gold Coast) and Makerere College (in Uganda). These institutions trained teachers, prepared students in arts, science and education, and sometimes offered professional training. Frequently they were used as stepping-stones to British universities. After 1945 the British government pushed ahead with a crash programme to grant these bodies full university status. To ensure quality, British standards were set and they entered into a special relationship with the University of London, before being granted full autonomy. The ultimate aim was that these bodies should prepare local students fully in arts, science, teaching and professional subjects, even in law, although colonial students seemed to maintain a marked preference for training at the bar in Britain.[13] The curricula of these institutions remained a problem until autonomy was granted, because the British bias meant that in a number of respects a less than suitable tertiary education was being provided for these developing countries. The finding of a balance between standards and local needs was not easy. After independence indigenization of education (both as to curriculum and as to staff) proceeded more rapidly.

The British record on education in the developing colonies was not good in 1945. Previous neglect had been cloaked in the supposed virtues of local control and indirect rule. After 1945, the British government rushed through with schemes of educational development. At first the British example was emphasized, probably too strongly, but slowly the indigenization of education crept in and cultural equality was accepted.